Social Mobility

Anthony Heath has been university lecturer in sociology and fellow of Jesus College, Oxford, since 1970. He read classics then economics at Trinity College, Cambridge, achieving first-class honours in both. He gained his Ph.D. in sociology from Cambridge University where in 1967 he became a fellow of Churchill College and, in 1968, an assistant lecturer in the faculty of economics.

His articles have been published in *Sociology, European Journal of Sociology, British Journal of Political Science* and *Oxford Review of Education*; and he is the author of *Rational Choice and Social Exchange* (1976) and, with A. H. Halsey and J. M. Ridge, *Origins and Destinations* (1980).

D0813167

Fontana New Sociology

Editor: Gavin Mackenzie, lecturer in sociology at the University of Cambridge and fellow of Jesus College, Cambridge

Published

Social Mobility Anthony Heath

Class and the Corporation Graeme Salaman

Culture Raymond Williams

Forthcoming

Education and the Reproduction of Inequality Paul Corrigan

The Sociology of Trade Unionism Colin Crouch

Corporatism and Modern Capitalism Leo Panitch

Race John Stone

Social Mobility

Anthony Heath

Fontana Paperbacks

to **John Ridge**

First published by Fontana Paperbacks 1981
Copyright © Anthony Heath 1981
Set in 10/12pt Monophoto Plantin
Made and printed in Great Britain by
William Collins Sons & Co. Ltd, Glasgow

Conditions of sale: This book is sold subject to
the condition that it shall not, by way of trade or
otherwise, be lent, re-sold, hired out or otherwise
circulated without the publisher's prior consent in
any form of binding or cover other than that in
which it is published and without a similar
condition including this condition being imposed
on the subsequent purchaser

Contents

Tables in the Text

Editor's Preface

This series is designed to provide comprehensive and authoritative analyses of issues at the centre of contemporary sociological discussion. Each volume will therefore present and evaluate both the major theoretical standpoints and the empirical findings relevant to specific problems within sociology; but, in addition, each volume will itself be an original contribution to our understanding of that topic. So the series will be of value to laymen and professional sociologists alike.

The focus will be on contemporary Britain, although comparison with the institutional orders of other advanced societies and, indeed, with pre-capitalist social formations, will form an integral part of each book. Analyses of the division of labour, its structure and consequences, of social class and other forms of inequality, and of the institutions and the distribution of power in politics and in industry, will dominate the collection. Yet this emphasis will not preclude discussion of other aspects of contemporary British society, such as the family, urbanism or law-breaking.

The series is based on three premises. First, the primary concern of sociology as an academic discipline is the analysis of *social structure* – of the institutions and social processes characteristic of advanced industrial societies. Second, the distinction between 'sociological theory' and 'empirical sociology', found so often within the subject, is false. Finally, sociological explanation incorporates historical explanation; and 'social' institutions cannot be examined in isolation from 'economic' or 'political' ones.

Indeed, one of the most important changes now taking place in the social sciences is the recognition that the boundaries which hitherto have separated one discipline from another are artificial. On these premises, the series determines to help us understand the functioning of the society in which we live.

Gavin Mackenzie
Jesus College, Cambridge

Acknowledgements

I have received an enormous amount of practical help, encouragement, and ideas from the members of the Oxford Social Mobility Group over the decade that I have been at Oxford. I owe so much to, among others, John Goldthorpe, A. H. Halsey, Keith Hope and John Ridge that it is hard to know where to begin. Certainly I could never have written this book without their help. I have been extremely fortunate to have had access to the data collected in 1972; I have had the benefits of years of discussion and circulated papers; and John Ridge has devoted uncounted hours of his time to my statistical problems. It would be a much fairer reflection of reality if this were a multi-authored book. I suspect that most of the ideas in it can be traced to other members of the Group. The influence on my work of John Goldthorpe's *Social Mobility and Class Structure in Modern Britain* is evident, but there must be many half-remembered conversations that have been almost equally influential. Inevitably, I have not always developed ideas in the ways that my colleagues might have wished. They cannot be blamed for the errors and omissions.

I must also acknowledge the help I have received from many other people, particularly from my students who criticized early drafts and tried to persuade me to make them more readable. I would also like to mention specifically Bob Blackburn, Peter Clifford, Lawrence Hazelrigg, Jacqueline Hincklcy, Alan Kerckhoff, Gavin Mackenzie, Nicholas Mascie-Taylor, and George Psacharopoulos. I am very grateful to them all.

My thanks are also due to the publishers and authors who have given me permission to reproduce copyright material.

1 Landmarks

Wherever there are unequal societies, the question will sooner or later be asked: how are men to be recruited to positions of power and privilege? Many different answers have been suggested and tried out, from the principle of hereditary monarchy to the experiment, tried briefly in fifth-century Athens, of selecting the 'archons' (the rulers) by lot from the citizens of the society. The question was at first an issue in political theory, a distinctively socio-logical treatment of recruitment and mobility emerging only in the twentieth century. But even today the questions asked about social mobility, and even some of the answers, are not so very different from those of the early political theorists. Plato, for example, in his *Republic*, advanced a theory of social selection and recruitment that would have found favour with, and even may have influenced, the architects of the tripartite system of education that flourished in mid-twentieth-century Britain. In Plato's ideal republic there were to be three classes of citizen: the guardians or rulers, the auxiliaries or soldiers, and the rest of the citizen body – the farmers, builders, weavers and the like. Recruitment to the three classes was to be on merit, which meant, since Plato was a strong believer in heredity, that there was to be substantial self-recruitment to the three classes. However, where children from the lower classes possessed the qualities appropriate for a higher one, they were to receive the education which fitted them for upward mobility.

Plato put these ideas in a myth which the citizens of his ideal society were to be taught: 'You are all brothers, fellow citizens, but when God made you he mixed gold in the nature of those who are fitted to be rulers – and that is why they are held in the highest esteem. He put silver in those who were to be their assistants, and iron and bronze in the farmers and workers. Children will usually have the same nature as their parents, but since you all come from the same stock there will sometimes be "golden" parents with a "silver" child, "silver" parents with a "gold" child, and so on. God's first and most important commandment to the rulers, therefore, is that they must scrutinize the mixture of metals in their children's characters. If one of their own children has iron or bronze in its make-up, they must harden themselves and assign him to his appropriate level among farming or working people. Conversely, a child from the latter origins with gold or silver in his nature must be promoted accordingly to become a ruler or an assistant. For the oracle has prophesied that the State will be destroyed if it ever comes to have rulers of iron or bronze.' (*Republic*: 415a; my translation.) The language may be archaic but the ideas are those behind the 'eleven plus', the tripartite system of grammar, technical and modern schools, and the 'sponsored mode of ascent through education' devised for post-war Britain by former classical scholars such as Cyril Burt.[1] And Marxist critics of modern education would argue that Burt and his disciples' writing themselves constituted a contemporary myth, not unlike Plato's, devised by the rulers to justify and legitimate the social order.[2]

But whatever may have been its actual influence on

twentieth-century thought, Plato's theory illustrates two of the concerns that have dominated the study of social mobility – efficiency and order. How much, and what kinds of mobility are required for a stable social order and the efficient operation of an advanced industrial society?

Karl Marx and class formation

The assertion that too little mobility may lead to social upheaval became one of the commonplaces of political theory, running through Western political thought from Plato onwards. The same idea surfaces in Marxism, although reversed. For Marx, upward mobility will strengthen the hold of the ruling class and thus serve as a stabilizing, anti-revolutionary process.[3] In a famous passage he wrote: 'The circumstance that a man without fortune, but possessing energy, solidity, ability and business acumen may become a capitalist ... is greatly admired by apologists of the capitalist system. Although this circumstance continually brings an unwelcome number of new soldiers of fortune into the field and into competition with the already existing individual capitalists, it also reinforces the supremacy of capital itself, expands its base and enables it to recruit ever new forces for itself out of the substratum of society. In a similar way, the circumstance that the Catholic Church in the Middle Ages formed its hierarchy out of the best brains in the land, regardless of their estate, birth or fortune, was one of the principal means of consolidating ecclesiastical rule and suppressing the laity. *The more a ruling class is able to assimilate the foremost minds of a ruled class, the more stable and dangerous becomes its rule.*' (Marx, 1894 : 587; my emphasis.)

It is true, however, that social mobility was not a central concern in Marx's work or in contemporary Marxism. Indeed, Poulantzas has asserted that social mobility is merely *'une problematique bourgeoise'* (Poulantzas, 1974: 37), but that is to go too far. A more conventional Marxist view is that while questions about social mobility are secondary, they are by no means unimportant: 'they concern the recruitment of people to classes; not the brute fact of the existence of class. It is that which is primary.' (Westergaard and Resler, 1975: 280.) The central point of the Marxist position is that society is still divided into wage labourers and owners of property, with all the conflicts of interest that that implies, whatever the social origins of those labourers and men of property. Schumpeter captured the point neatly with his analogy between a social class and a hotel or bus. 'For the duration of its collective life, or the time during which its identity may be assumed, each class resembles a hotel or an omnibus, always full, but always of different people.' (Schumpeter, 1943: 129.)

However, while high rates of social mobility cannot in themselves undermine 'the brute fact of the existence of class', they may nonetheless have important implications for class consciousness and class formation. The distinction is simply that between a 'class in itself' and 'class for itself'; between men's relation to the means of production and their social organization along class lines.

Marx himself had made the point that the high rates of mobility which he believed to characterize America were partly responsible for the lack of an organized labour movement there. He contrasted America with the older European societies where class formation had proceeded further. In the United States, although classes existed in the sense of 'class in itself' – there were property-owners, wage labourers and their associated conflicts of interest – these had not yet become settled formations with a consciousness of shared interest and a collective political organization: '. . . in the United States of North America . . . though classes already exist, they have not yet become fixed, but continually change and interchange their elements in constant flux.' (Marx, 1852 : 255.)

Marx has thus rephrased the old hypothesis. A class that is self-recruiting will more readily develop class consciousness and class organization. The transformation from a 'class in itself' to a 'class for itself' will be more easily achieved. Class struggle will therefore be accentuated, and the overthrow of capitalism brought nearer. Conversely, high rates of interchange between the classes will act as a safety valve (from the capitalists' point of view), serving to keep the pressures of discontent low. Marx does not expand on the social processes lying behind this, but it is easy to suggest some. When there is a possibility of upward mobility, the hopes of the underprivileged will focus more on individual achievement, either for themselves or for their children, rather than on collective resistance.

Furthermore, as Westergaard and Resler suggest, 'Anxieties may be focused on the risks of individual failure; and failure itself may be ascribed by those who experience it to adversity, shortcomings or "bad luck" peculiar to themselves, rather than to "the system". The sense of shared experience and common prospects among the victims of inequality could thus be weakened, and a precondition for radical mass dissent undermined. Internal fragmentation of labour as a political force could be accentuated further in so far as social circulation makes for ties of kinship, personal acquaintance, cultural emulation and social sympathy across the lines of class division.' (Westergaard and Resler, 1975 : 285.)

In short, the mobile society individualizes success and failure, and weakens the bonds of class solidarity.

Vilfredo Pareto and the circulation of elites

Marx's scattered remarks about mobility hardly constitute a systematic theory, or even a large-scale assault on the topic. Nor does mobility figure prominently in the work of the other masters, Durkheim and Weber. The only one of the 'founding fathers' to concentrate on mobility was the now neglected Vilfredo Pareto, whose work, though scarcely systematic, certainly had the attribute of scale. His *Trattato di Sociologia Generale* (1916) contains over a million words (and is correspondingly difficult to summarize succinctly).

Pareto was born in 1848, the son of an Italian nobleman, the Marchese Rafaelle Pareto, who had become a civil engineer. Vilfredo too studied engineering; then he became a businessman. In this role he began as a passionate advocate of the free market and of free trade, becoming increasingly irritated and frustrated by the need to negotiate and make deals with influential civil servants and parliamentary deputies. Consequently, he spent more and more of his time in political campaigning, attacking the interventionist and protectionist policies of the left-wing governments of his day. He came to work closely with the leading economists who were making important developments in the pure theory of free markets and market equilibria, and from there moved to a new career as an academic economist, in which he had some major achievements: the Pareto optimum and the Pareto curve of income distribution are basic concepts still found in economics textbooks. But as his disillusion with practical politics deepened, Pareto gave up economics too, instead engaging more and more in what we would now call the political sociology of the state. His cynicism and disillusion led him to believe that the extension of the suffrage had merely led to bourgeois privileges being replaced with working-class privileges and the replacement of one group of rulers by another. The new rulers might espouse socialist ideals, but he now saw ideals as a superficial veneer or rationalization of more basic impulses. Marxism, for example, he held to be demonstrably false; its popularity therefore had to be explained in terms of the psychological needs which it met. Sociologically, then, the content of a particular ideology or belief was less significant than the more basic psychological attributes of which it was a manifestation.[4]

The kernel of Pareto's theory is that elites are inevitable and that history demonstrates a continual succession or circulation of these elites. In a famous passage he wrote, 'History is a graveyard of aristocracies.' He went on: 'Aristocracies decay not only in number but also in quality, in the sense that their energy diminishes and there is a debilitating alteration in the proportion of the residues [the psychological attributes] which originally favoured their capture and retention of power.... The governing class is renovated not only in number but also – and this is more important – in quality, by recruiting to it families rising from the lower classes, bringing with them the energy and proportions of the residues necessary for maintaining them in power. It is renovated also by the loss of its more degenerate elements. If one of these essential components decays or – worse still – if energy and residues peter out, then the governing class topples into ruin, often dragging the whole nation with it. The accumulation of superior elements in the lower classes and, conversely, of inferior elements in the upper classes, is a potent cause of disturbance in the social equilibrium.' (Pareto, 1916: §2054, 2055.)

The broad outline of Pareto's theory, then – that governing elites must allow recruitment from below, otherwise they will decay and be supplanted – is very simple and is really only a restatement of Plato's ideas from over two millennia before. It echoes, too, Marx's point that 'the more a ruling class is able to assimilate the foremost minds of a ruled class, the more stable becomes its rule.' Pareto does not, of course, accept the rest of the Marxian analysis. Socialism may replace bourgeois government, but socialism is itself a chimera. There will simply be a new socialist elite. This is not quite to say that nothing really changes. The important elements are the underlying personalities (the 'residues') not the beliefs and ideals which form their surface manifestations (the 'derivations'), but since the new elite will contain a different mix of person-alities, its character too will alter.

Pareto's analysis of the residues is perhaps the least satis-factory part of his work. The concepts are vaguely defined and almost impossible to measure. But it contains a few memorable ideas (albeit ones borrowed from Machiavelli), notably the distinction between the lions and the foxes. The foxes are those 'who are most adept in the art of undermining opponents by bribery and corruption and of regaining by fraud and deception what appeared to have been conceded under the threat of force', whereas the lions are those 'whose impulse is to resist and are incapable of giving way as time and occasion require' (Pareto, 1916: §2178). The character of the elite, and thus of the society, will therefore depend on which of the two pre-dominates within the governing elite, foxes, for example, dominating within modern commercial democracies and lions in militaristic regimes such as ancient Sparta or crusading ones such as Islam.

There is, moreover, a tension between the lions and the foxes. A regime established by lions is liable to be subverted as the foxes manipulate and infiltrate their way in, but in turn a regime dominated by foxes is liable to be overthrown by the energy of less civilized groups or nations, as for example 'the subtle diplomatic skill of the Christian lords of Constantinople could not save them from ruin under the onslaught of Turkish fanaticism and power' (Pareto, 1916 : §2180). In his own time, too, Pareto saw the foxes threatened by the lions and making unavailing efforts to placate them. His greatest scorn was reserved for the humanitarians, for 'the great error of the present age is of believing that men can be governed by pure reasoning, without resort to force' (Pareto, 1909 : §107). One of his favourite sayings is the Italian adage, 'He who plays the sheep will meet the butcher', and slaughter was the fate that he expected to befall the humanitarians of his time. It is not perhaps surprising, then, that the apparently lion-like qualities of Mussolini appealed to Pareto, and that he was eventually hailed as a proto-Fascist and made an Italian Senator.

Pareto is one of the least satisfactory of the 'founding fathers' of modern sociology. His anti-humanitarianism makes us antipathetic to him; his concepts and theories are developed unsystematically and at excessive length, their formulation not remotely lending itself to rigorous test; his own incursions into empirical evidence are cursory and anecdotal in the extreme. He lacks the proselytizing vision of Marx; Weber's attempt at historical scholarship, although flawed, is far more serious; even Durkheim's severest critics must agree that he makes a better attempt to be scientific than does the scientifically trained Pareto.

But many of Pareto's ideas are the stock-in-trade of later thought. His distinction beween residues and derivations, his emphasis on the inevitability of elites, and his analysis of the relation between mobility and social equilibrium have had considerable popularity in one form or another.

There is, however, an interesting and important way in which Pareto's thought differed from the mainstream of twentieth-century writing. Pareto was a cynic, dis-illusioned by the society of his day and pessimistic about the future. He did not believe that there could in the long term be a stable balance between lions and foxes in the governing elite. He saw an inevitable tension between them. At best there would be an unstable equilibrium. Social mobility could lengthen the life of a regime, but not sustain it indefinitely. Instead of stability and social progress, there would be an oscillation, an alternation of elites, possibly over very long time-periods (Pareto himself takes as his time-span the last two thousand years): 'By the circulation of elites, the governing elite is in a state of continuous and slow transformation. It flows like a river, and what it is today is different from what it was yesterday. Every so often, there are sudden and violent disturbances. The river floods and breaks its banks. Then, afterwards, the new governing elite resumes again the slow process of self-transformation.' (Pareto, 1916:§2056.) In contrast, modern writers are more often optimists who believe in social progress and the possibility of achieving a lasting equilibrium.

Pitirim Sorokin's functional theory

Sorokin's *Social Mobility* (1927) represents the coming-of-age of the sociological study of mobility. Pareto's work has a curiously archaic quality, with its overt invective, its strange language of residues and derivations, its wide anecdotal evidence drawn from a vast period of European history. We do not accept it as a modern work of scientific sociology. But Sorokin's work, though published only eleven years after the *Trattato*, with which it has many affinities, is nevertheless recognizably that of a modern sociologist. Sorokin was certainly influenced by Pareto: his work contains many references to him; he covers the same huge time-span; he shares his contempt for complacent theories of social progress. But Sorokin's methods of treating the subject, his way of posing the questions, and his recourse to data are not so very different from those of writers of the 1950s and 1960s.

Sorokin himself was self-assured and well aware of his achievement. In his foreword to the 1959 reprint of his book, he boldly wrote: 'As a pioneer work that opened the vast domain of social mobility for subsequent explorations, *Social Mobility* (published in 1927) is still, according to Dr Glass, editor of *Social Mobility in Great Britain*, "The only comprehensive work" in this field. I am naturally gratified that *Social Mobility* has initiated numerous and ever increasing studies in this realm, that my main concepts and terminology have become commonly accepted by other investigators (even by those who use them without any reference to my volume), and that practically all my main generalized conclusions have been confirmed by the subsequent important studies of these phenomena.' (Sorokin, 1959:i.)

The arrogant old man was probably right.

Pitirim A. Sorokin was born in 1889 in Poland. He started his life as the son of a manual worker and peasant mother and, he wrote in his autobiography, 'I have subsequently been a farmhand, itinerant artisan, factory worker, clerk, teacher, conductor of a choir, revolutionary, political prisoner, journalist, student, editor of a metropolitan paper, member of Kerensky's cabinet, an exile, professor at Russian, Czech and American universities, and a scholar with an international reputation.' (Sorokin, 1963:7.) Despite the difference in his origins, his career and attitudes have interesting parallels with Pareto's. Like Pareto he became disillusioned with active politics and turned later in life to academic work and eventually emigrated; like Pareto he was an elitist, believing in the fundamental inequality of man and the impossibility of egalitarianism; and like Pareto again he had a contempt for humanitarianism and a desire instead for firm action. But despite all this he lacked Pareto's pessimism, if not his scepticism. Sorokin concluded *Social Mobility* with the words: 'The writer too much likes the mobile type of society to prophesy its funeral; therefore, he prefers to finish the discussion right here.' (Sorokin, 1927:544.) As befits a man who has risen by his own talents and efforts from obscurity to international fame, Sorokin was full of optimism and confidence, not the disillusion of the nobleman watching corruption and decline.

At the heart of Sorokin's study is a theory of stratification which might have found favour with Plato. He argues that there are (alongside various temporary bases) certain permanent and universal bases of occupational inequality. 'At least two conditions seem to have been fundamental,' he writes. '*First, the importance of an occupation for the survival and existence of a group as a whole; second, the degree of intelligence necessary for a successful performance of an occupation.*' (Sorokin, 1927:100–1; italics in the original.) Certain occupations are more important, he argues, for example in the sense that the incompetence of an individual soldier makes little difference to the success of an army whereas that of a general will be far more significant. Successful performance of those occupations which deal with the tasks of social organization and control demand a considerably greater degree of intelligence than that of routine work, while the strategic nature of these occupations in society, 'being at the controlling point of a "social engine"', enables their occupants to secure for themselves the maximum privileges and power. 'Hence, we may say that *in any given society, the more occupational work consists in the performance of the functions of social organization and control, and the higher the degree of intelligence necessary for its successful performance, the more privileged is that group and the higher the rank does it occupy in the interoccupational hierarchy, and vice versa.*' (Sorokin, 1927 : 101; italics in original.)

This theory looks very like the notorious 'functional theory of stratification' advanced by Davis and Moore (without acknowledgement to Sorokin) in 1945, but the earlier version is in fact more sophisticated than the later formulation. Whereas the later writers naively thought that high rewards were necessary to motivate the right people to undertake the functionally important positions, Sorokin more shrewdly argues that it is their strategic position of control that enables them to usurp power and privilege. He is not the unquestioning functionalist of the post-war period, glorifying the virtues of contemporary America; functionalist though he is, he also belongs to sociology's 'debunking' tradition which holds that surface appearances are not to be trusted.[5]

This greater shrewdness is brought out by Sorokin's insistence that there is nothing inevitable about the correlation between functional importance and intelligence. In Paretian style he argues that the correlation may be broken down in periods of decay, although such periods 'usually lead to an upheaval, after which, if the group does not perish, the correlation is re-established.' (Sorokin, 1927 : 102.) Social mobility, in other words, is necessary to secure the appropriate allocation of talents to occupations; failure to achieve it ends in inefficiency and disorder.

The actual distribution of talents between occupations, Sorokin holds, is determined by the specific character and functioning of the various 'channels of vertical circulation'. In a famous passage he wrote: 'Varying in their concrete forms and in their size, the channels of vertical circulation exist in any stratified society, and are as necessary as channels for blood circulation in the body.' (Sorokin, 1927 : 180.) These channels of mobility – which Sorokin also describes as 'membranes' between the strata, 'holes', 'staircases', or 'elevators' enabling individuals to move up and down – include the army, the church, the school, political organizations, professional organizations, wealth-making organizations, and the family. The last would seem an unlikely channel of mobility, but what Sorokin has in mind here is intermarriage between members of different strata. 'Such a marriage usually leads one of the parties either to social promotion or degradation. In this way some people have made their careers; some others have ruined them.' (Sorokin, 1927 : 179.) Thus, Sorokin shows, with evidence spanning the last two thousand years in Paretian vein, 'of 92 Roman Emperors, at least 36 climbed to this position from the lowest social strata up the army ladder', 'of 144 Popes, for whom the data are available, 28 were of humble origin, and 27 came from the middle classes', while 'the Chinese Mandarin government has been, perhaps more than any other one, the government of the Chinese intellectuals recruited and elevated through the school machinery.' (Sorokin, 1927 : 165, 167, 170.)

The channels of vertical mobility not only permit movement up and down the social strata but also, and perhaps more importantly, they act as a mechanism for testing, selecting and placement – sifting individuals into their places in the society. On good functionalist lines Sorokin argues that 'the essential purpose of this control is to distribute the individuals so that each is placed according to his talents and able to perform successfully his social function' (Sorokin, 1927 : 182), although more realistically he adds that there has scarcely existed any society in which the distribution of individuals has been in complete accordance with the rule: 'Everybody must be placed according to his ability.'

Some of Sorokin's most interesting comments concern the role of the school as an agency of selection. Here he anticipates the writings of the more radical social critics of the 1970s.[6] According to this modern view, the school does not really change people; rather, it sorts, labels and grades children for the labour market. In other words, schools do not make children cleverer; they merely certify for employers which ones are cleverer. It is ironic that what was put forward in the 1970s as a new and radical critique of education had been advanced nearly fifty years earlier by the more reactionary, but perspicacious, Sorokin: 'At the present moment,' he wrote, 'it is certain that the school, while being a "training and educational" institution, is at the same time a piece of social machinery, which tests the abilities of individuals, which sifts them, selects them, and decides their prospective social position.... From this standpoint *the school is primarily a testing, selecting, and distributing agency*. In its total the whole school system, with its handicaps, quizzes, examinations, supervision of the students, and their grading, ranking, evaluating, eliminating and promoting, is a very complicated "sieve", which sifts "the good" from "the bad" future citizens, "the able" from "the dull", "those fitted for the high positions" from those "unfitted".' (Sorokin, 1927 : 188–9; italics in original.)

Moreover, Sorokin, unlike the modern writers, has the grace to admit that his ideas are not new, coming as they do from Lapouge (1896) and Pillsbury (1921). And he goes on to argue that a functional fit between the channels of vertical circulation and the needs of the society is far from inevitable. Thus the educational system may select for inappropriate characteristics, with the result that the upper strata 'display a pretty intellectual ability and pretty conspicuous moral slackness' (Sorokin, 1927 : 195); or again there may be an over- or under-production of suitable recruits for the elite – 'by increasing the rapidity of production of university graduates ... our universities are preparing dissatisfied elements out of these graduates, under emergency conditions capable of supplying leaders for any radical and revolutionary movement.' (Sorokin, 1927 : 201.)

The general lines of Sorokin's argument, then, are functionalist, and although it is perhaps no longer attractive to late twentieth-century ears, it is nonetheless rather more sophisticated than some later versions. He does not hide his values beneath a veneer of scientific objectivity – he makes no secret of the fact that he prefers the open mobile society where individuals are distributed according to their own capacity and ability, regardless of their fathers' positions – and his caustic invective (rather in the tradition of Veblen) continually leads him to uncover the tensions and contradictions within the society of his day.

The positive and negative consequences of mobility that Sorokin actually enumerates are a fairly thorough list, some with a strong ring of Pareto, others that could have come verbatim from post-war writers like Blau and Duncan, Lipset, Dahrendorf or Parkin. Thus, on the positive side, mobility leads to a better distribution of talents, which in turn increases living standards and raises economic efficiency and innovation. It gives the more ambitious members of the lower classes a chance to rise and thus, 'instead of becoming leaders of a revolution, they are turned into protectors of social order' (Sorokin, 1927: 533). These upwardly mobile recruits to the elite will not have the weak humanitarian traits of the hereditary aristocracy and, 'having climbed through their personal efforts, they are sure of their rights; they are not soft-hearted. . . . If it is necessary, they will not hesitate to apply force and compulsion to suppress any riot. (Mussolini is one of the examples of this type of men.) In this way they facilitate the preservation of social order.' (Sorokin, 1927: 534.) Lines of conflict and solidarity also become much more complex and flexible. The mobile individual's face-to-face contacts become more numerous and less intense: 'he becomes like a polygamist who is not obliged and does not invest all his love in one wife, but divides it among many women. Under such conditions, the attachment becomes less hot; the intensiveness of feeling, less concentrated' (Sorokin, 1927: 539), and thus the likelihood of class solidarity and class conflict is reduced. Finally, the absence of hereditary and similar privileges decreases the validity of the arguments of the dissatisfied. 'Instead of being heroes they are regarded as failures.' (Sorokin, 1927: 534.)

But the negatives get underlined too. Mobility increases mental strain, and the likelihood of suicide. It facilitates the disintegration of morals, encourages crass materialism and individualism. In the style of Durkheim (whom he quotes with approval) Sorokin argues that in a mobile society individuals do not accept their position in life. 'He who is below wants to go up. He who is in the upper strata wants to climb further or dreads to be put down. Hence, there is a mad rush to put down all obstacles irrespective of whether it leads to social disorder or not. Hence, an increase in the "centrifugal tendencies" of present society.' (Sorokin, 1927:535.) In response there is a search for belonging, a trend 'conspiciously manifested in the social schemes of Communists, revolutionary syndicalists, and guild socialists. They contemplate a complete engulfment of an individual within the commune, or syndicate, or a restored guild. They unintentionally try to re-establish "the lost paradise" of an immobile society, and to make an individual again only a "finger of the hand" of a social body. The greater is the loneliness, the more urgent the need.' (Sorokin, 1927:544.)

Sorokin does not go on to conclude, as Pareto would have done, that these contradictory tendencies will lead to a continual oscillation from mobility to immobility. This is surprising, because one of the strongest and most persistent themes in Sorokin's book is his attack on linear theories of social progress. Empirically, he claims, there has been no consistent trend towards economic, political or occupational equality, or towards increased mobility. On this he is unequivocal. '*As far as the corresponding historical and other materials permit seeing, in the field of vertical mobility ... there seems to be no definite perpetual trend toward either an increase or a decrease of the intensiveness and generality of mobility. This is proposed as valid for the history of a country, for that of a large social body, and, finally, for the history of mankind.*' (Sorokin, 1927:152; italics in the original.)

Sorokin recognizes that this proposition may appear 'strange and improbable', and he admits that recent evidence demonstrates a short-run increase in mobility rates. He reports data collected by himself and his students on various groups of the Minneapolis population which showed that 72 per cent of the grandfathers of his respondents had the same occupation as the great-grandfathers, 38·9 per cent of the fathers had the same occupation as the grandfathers, while only 10·6 per cent of the respondents themselves had the same occupation as their fathers. But, Sorokin goes on, 'eternal historical tendencies' cannot be inferred from data covering a mere century or so; there are other indications, from the work of Levasseur (1909), that mobility may have been as high in the seventeenth century as it was in the nineteenth; and even if mobility were less in the feudal period, there is evidence of greater mobility in the Roman Empire or in primitive societies. At most, then, there has been only an alternation of periods of greater mobility with those of greater immobility.

Putting together the various arguments throughout the book, Sorokin's explanation for this pattern of oscillation would seem to have something of a Paretian character, although not going so far as postulating any inevitable contradiction in the forces operating for and against mobility. He first suggests that 'like an organism, a social body, as it grows older, tends to become more and more rigid and the circulation of its individuals tends to become less and less intensive' (Sorokin, 1927:158), presumably as the more privileged strata close ranks in an attempt to preserve their privileges. There is also a tendency for institutional lag. The mechanisms of selection do not respond quickly enough to changes in the social environment, and as a result *there almost always is a lag between the "human flour" sifted through this machinery for different social strata and between the "flour" which is necessary because of the new changed conditions.*' (Sorokin, 1927:370; italics in original.) There thus develops a defective social distribution of individuals which, on Paretian lines, eventually leads to upheaval and a subsequent increase in mobility as new and more appropriate mechanisms of selection are instituted. 'The revolutionary policemen of history' (Sorokin, 1927 : 371) then go away and the ever-revolving circle of history starts all over again.

David Glass and the national survey

Theoretical writing on social mobility has hardly progressed since Sorokin. Much of the later theory had already been clearly formulated, or equally clearly refuted, in his 1927 monograph. Indeed, one is tempted to speculate that if post-war sociologists had paid more attention to Sorokin, and less to false gods of their own such as Talcott Parsons, they would have avoided some of the darker blind alleys of the 1950s and 1960s.

But where modern sociology has progressed is in the collection and analysis of data. It is this aspect of sociology, the empirical and the technical, which really differentiates the pre- and post-war periods. Before the war Sorokin had placed great weight on careful inspection of the data, but the data available to him were on the whole unsystematic and unrepresentative. There were numerous studies of recruitment to particular occupational groups – the social origins of millionaires, men of genius, businessmen, and even saints had been studied[7] – but there were no representative surveys of the population as a whole, or even of particular areas or cities. Sorokin himself had made a beginning with his study of 'Minneapolis students, Minneapolis businessmen, and some other groups of the Minneapolis population', and in England Ginsberg had studied 'university teachers and students, teachers in training colleges, second-class civil servants, clerks and other salaried officials and wage earners' (Ginsberg, 1929 : 556). But it was not until after the war that a number of representative national samples were examined.

David Glass's team at the London School of Economics carried out the first of these, a random sample of 10,000 adult civilians aged eighteen years and over and living in England, Scotland and Wales in the summer of 1949. The work has since been heavily criticized (as I shall report in Chapter 2), but it was in its time a major pioneering study from which a host of others have taken their inspiration. The data collected in the survey consisted of basic biographical or life-history information about each of the respondents. Questions were asked about the respondents' age, sex and marital status; about the schools they attended and the qualifications they obtained; and, the central feature of a mobility enquiry, about their own and their fathers' occupations. From the latter material can be constructed the classic intergenerational mobility table comparing the occupations of the respondents with those of their fathers.

The main conclusions drawn from the resulting tables were that Britain exhibited a considerable amount of relatively short-range mobility coupled with a higher degree of rigidity and self-recruitment at the extremes, and in particular at the upper levels of the social structure where there was the strongest tendency for sons to follow in their fathers' footsteps and enter broadly comparable occupations.

Curiously, the clearest and most lucid summary of the 1949 material comes not from Glass and his team – their account is a dreary one which sticks very largely to technical issues – but from the work of Westergaard and Resler over twenty-five years later. First of all, Westergaard and Resler point out, Glass's data are sufficient 'to dispel any notion that Britain is a society in which individual position in the hierarchy of inequality is fixed at birth. Capitalism here as elsewhere allows – indeed in some respects encourages – a fair degree of fluidity of circulation.' (Westergaard and Resler, 1975 : 298.) They then go on to make the important point that high rates of social mobility can at the same time be compatible with gross inequalities of opportunity: many children from high-status origins may be downwardly mobile compared with their fathers, but at the same time children from these origins may still have *on average* a much better chance than their working-class contemporaries of getting to higher-level jobs themselves. As Westergaard and Resler put it: 'But to say that circulation is fluid is not to say that it is free. Inequality of condition sets marked limits to individual opportunities and risks of ascent and descent. People are a good deal more likely to stay at roughly the same level as their father than they would be if there were "perfect mobility". That is true especially of those fortunate enough to be born at or near the top of the scale. Men in the established professions and in high administrative jobs – including the business elite – are a tiny group of the population. If parental origin played no part in determining life chances, whether directly or indirectly, only some 3 per cent of their sons in the 1949 sample ... would have found jobs of a kind to secure them a place in this privileged minority. In fact nearly 40 per cent did so. Here is inheritance with a vengeance, even though it is not guaranteed.' (Westergaard and Resler, 1975 : 299.)

The next point which they base on Glass's material is that most social mobility is short-range, while long-range movement 'from rags to riches, or riches to rags' is very rare. In particular they see the manual/non-manual line as a barrier which hinders such long-range movement. 'Social descent from executive and professional backgrounds', they point out, 'usually stopped short of the conventional line of division between the white- and blue-collar worlds.' Again, they noticed that the social groups just above and below this barrier had distinctly different chances of movement across it. The children of routine clerical workers had better chances of advancement to higher executive positions than did their contemporaries from skilled manual homes, and they were less likely to slide down the scale into semi- or unskilled manual work.

These, then, were the main conclusions drawn from Glass's material (and drawn by many other writers besides Westergaard and Resler): there was, according to the 1949 survey, considerable short-range mobility in Britain, very little long-range movement, a high degree of self-recruitment in the elite, and a barrier to movement across the manual/non-manual line.

It is fair to say that most of the interest of Glass's work is descriptive. It provided a kind of social bookkeeping of the state of British society. But description is interesting only if it addresses specific questions which provide the *raison d'etre* of the study, and the main question which Glass's work addressed (albeit implicitly) concerned social justice. How 'open' was British society? Was there 'equality of opportunity' for those of equal talents? 'It is one of the postulates of a democratic and egalitarian society,' wrote Glass, 'that ability, whatever its social background, shall not be denied the chance to fulfil itself' (Glass, 1954:25), and he makes clear his preference for such a society. His book thus takes on something of the character of an exposé of the injustice rife in British society, of the unjustified inequalities in access to the highest strata of society. The language is always restrained and technical;

Glass is almost apologetic on the one occasion when he puts forward his own views 'which are explicitly "loaded" in that they have a value basis' (Glass, 1954:22). But the message is clear nonetheless.

There is, then, a marked shift of emphasis with Glass's work. Whereas Marx had been primarily interested in the relation of mobility to class formation and social conflict, Pareto in the bases of social order, and Sorokin in the efficient allocation of manpower to the most important positions, Glass belongs more to the traditions of the social reformers such as Tawney, concerned to expose injustice and wastage in civil society and ameliorate conditions through peaceful reform.[8]

Lipset, Bendix and comparative mobility

Glass's 1949 enquiry was the only major contribution to come from this side of the Atlantic. Thereafter the major developments come from America, issues of efficiency and order prevail again and the question of social justice recedes.

The next major milestone was *Social Mobility in Industrial Society* (1959) by Lipset and Bendix, of whom Lipset appears to have been the dominant partner.[9] Throughout his career his main concerns have been with political sociology and particularly with the sources of stable democracy. In *Political Man* (1960) he said explicitly that his basic premise was that 'democracy is not only or even primarily a means through which different groups can attain their ends or seek the good society; it is the good society itself in operation.' (Lipset, 1960:403.) The same theme dominates *Social Mobility in Industrial Society*: the ultimate reason for studying social mobility must lie in its consequences for the individual and society, and Lipset makes it quite clear that the consequences in which he is mainly interested are those for the stability of modern American democracy.

The basic lines of Lipset's argument are by now hardly novel: social mobility acts as a safety valve which can reduce the chance of radical collective action which would threaten the regime. In familiar Paretian manner he argues that 'as long as the ruling group is flexible it will allow ambitious and talented individuals to rise from the lower strata; yet an ever-present tendency towards the formation of an aristocracy tends to restrict such individual mobility in any society. If the restriction is sufficiently tight, it can provoke discontent, which may result in efforts by members of deprived groups to achieve *collective or group mobility*, sometimes through a struggle to supplant the dominant group.' (Lipset and Bendix, 1959 : 4; italics in the original.) This does not, however, provide the starting point for a cyclical view of history. Lipset does not put the proposition forward as a universal truth. Rather, it is clear that he is concerned with the role of mobility in a modern industrial society and the implication is that lack of mobility does not provide the same threat to stability in a traditional society. It is here that we have perhaps the major theoretical shift from Sorokin's work. Sorokin, like Pareto before him, took as his time-span the whole of recorded history; when he looks for trends it is over the last 2000 years that he casts his eye. But the post-war writers have been specifically concerned with analysing the conditions of contemporary industrial society, and so the time-span shortens.

Lipset does, however, share with Pareto and Sorokin the belief that, while a certain amount of mobility may contribute to stability, it is nonetheless possible for a society to have too much mobility. 'To assume otherwise is to ignore the abundant evidence of the social and psychic cost of a high degree of social mobility: a cost that is probably high in terms of the combativeness, frustration, rootlessness, and other ills that are engendered.' (Lipset and Bendix, 1959:285.) The destabilizing effect of mobility is one of the issues on which Lipset comes to place most attention. The crucial source of this, as he sees it, is the problem of status inconsistency. He takes a multi-dimensional view of stratification, the system containing a number of different hierarchies based on status, class and authority. On this view the possibility clearly arises that an individual may be mobile on one dimension but not on another. Thus he may acquire a high occupational position but find himself socially ostracized because of his lowly social origins; alternatively, an upper-class family may become economically impoverished but retain its high social position – hence terms like *nouveaux riches*, 'upstart', 'social climber', 'poor but genteel'.

Lipset sees these disjunctions or inconsistencies as sources of frustration for the individual or group, which hence predispose them to accept extremist politics. Thus, he suggests, 'the French bourgeoisie in the eighteenth century developed its revolutionary zeal when it was denied recognition and social prestige by the old French aristocracy: wealth had not proved to be a gateway to high status and power, and the mounting resentment over this fed the fires of political radicalism.' (Lipset and Bendix, 1959:268.) The converse could also be true. The threat of downward mobility which imperilled the social standing of particular groups could also be a source of radicalization, although in this case the content of the extremist politics might take a different form, threatened social groups turning to anti-democratic ideologies such as fascism rather than to communism.

In all this Lipset is quite explicitly following Michels, who had earlier argued that the Jews' leaning towards socialism could be attributed to the fact that their legal emancipation had not been followed by their 'social and moral emancipation'. 'Even when they are rich, the Jews constitute, at least in eastern Europe, a category of persons who are excluded from the social advantages which the prevailing political, economic, and intellectual system ensures for the corresponding portion of the Gentile population. Besides the sentiment which is naturally aroused in their minds by this injustice, they are often affected by that cosmopolitan tendency which has been highly developed in the Jews by the historical experiences of the race, and these combine to push them into the arms of the working-class party.... For all these reasons, the Jewish intelligence is apt to find a shorter road to socialism than the Gentile.' (Michels, 1911 : 248.)

While Lipset and Bendix's theoretical interests demonstrate the historical continuity of mobility studies, it is their attempt at comparative empirical research for which their work is most famous. Glass's study of mobility in Britain had been quickly followed by other investigations in Denmark, Sweden and Japan. What Lipset and Bendix did was to carry out a secondary analysis of the results available on nine industrialized societies – France, Germany, Sweden, Switzerland, USA, Japan, Great Britain, Denmark and Italy. They re-classified the occupations of the subjects of these surveys and their fathers as best they could into manual, non-manual and farm categories (since the finer occupational classifications used by the original studies varied considerably from one country to another). They then concentrated on upward and downward mobility across the manual/non-manual line, adding together the figures for upward and downward mobility to measure the total vertical mobility between the middle and working classes. Lipset and Bendix found that virtually all the nine countries exhibited similar, high rates of total vertical mobility. Contrary to their expectations, they found no evidence that America was more open than the traditional societies of Europe. Thus in America total vertical mobility across the manual/non-manual line amounted to 30 per cent, but in Germany 31 per cent had been mobile, in Sweden and Britain 29 per cent, and in Japan and France 27 per cent.[10]

The striking feature of these results, therefore, was the similarity of the total vertical mobility rates. Thus, to explain their results, Lipset and Bendix had to seek factors universal throughout industrial societies: factors which *varied* between societies, such as historical background, cultural patterns and national values, clearly could not be used to explain mobility rates since the rates themselves appeared to be more or less the *same*. The explanation had to lie instead in common features. 'Several different processes inherent in all modern social structures,' they therefore argued, 'have a direct effect on the rate of social mobility, and help account for the similarities in rates in different countries: (1) changes in the number of available vacancies; (2) different rates of fertility; (3) changes in the rank accorded to occupations; (4) changes in the number of inheritable status-positions; and (5) changes in the legal restrictions pertaining to potential opportunities.' (Lipset and Bendix, 1959:57.)

Of these five processes, the first and fourth are perhaps the most important. The first makes the point that industrial societies are those with expanding economies which need increasing numbers of high-level workers in managerial and administrative positions, this in turn creating an 'upward surge of mobility'. The fourth indicates that the family firm gives way to the bureaucratic enterprise with its formalized methods of selection; there is thus a change in the methods of selection and recruitment for higher status occupations – the educational system becomes, in Sorokin's language, a more important channel of vertical circulation and the direct inheritance of occupations becomes less important. In short, modern industrial societies are 'open' ones with high rates of mobility where an individual's eventual position depends more on his own merit than his personal connections.

In their emphasis on the features inherent in the working of all modern societies Lipset and Bendix were in line with a great deal of sociological thinking of the immediate post-war period. This was the era of the 'convergence thesis' and 'technological functionalism' (exemplified in the work of Kerr et al., 1961) which held that the needs of an advanced economy demanded a set of standardized features from the social structure of those societies. Advanced industrialism required small, nuclear, geographically and socially mobile families; mass education; a pluralistic power structure; high rates of social mobility on meritocratic lines; a mixed economy with a measure of government regulation. These views are now widely (perhaps too widely) attacked on the grounds that they represent ideological justifications of the state of American society; Gouldner, for example, has attacked functionalists on the grounds that they 'constitute the sociological conservation corps of industrial society' (Gouldner, 1970: 332). But in fairness to Lipset and Bendix we must recognize that they did at least start from the results of comparative research. They really did find surprisingly similar rates of total vertical mobility across the manual/

non-manual line, and so it was not entirely absurd for them to look for factors inherent in the nature of industrialism to account for this apparent uniformity. As we shall see later, they were perhaps too easily satisfied with their results, but this should not be allowed to detract wholly from their achievement.

Blau, Duncan and the determinants of attainment

Our final landmark is Blau and Duncan's *The American Occupational Structure* (1967). It is one of the most important works to be produced in the 1960s and, for the contemporary generation of sociologists, among the most influential. How it will eventually be judged by later generations remains to be seen; it may not take a place in the corpus of 'great books' but it must always be important to the historian of sociology for its influence over the 1960s and 1970s.

Unlike Sorokin's or Lipset and Bendix's works, which took a broad overview of existing research, *The American Occupational Structure* is the report of a single piece of original empirical work. It belongs to the genre of the research monograph, not the general treatise, and lies in the tradition of national surveys of occupational mobility that began with Glass's *Social Mobility in Britain*. Blau and Duncan's survey was carried out as an adjunct to the current population survey of the US Bureau of the Census and was based on a sample of 25,000 men aged twenty to sixty-four years of age and representative of the 45 million men of these ages in the civilian, non-institutional population of the United States in March 1962. Each respondent was asked about his present occupation, the occupation he had on first entry into the labour market, the occupation which his father held when the respondent was aged about sixteen, the educational attainments of both the respondent and his father, the number of siblings, and so on. No information was collected on any attitudinal or psychological data. As with Glass's, the survey was restricted to relatively 'factual', biographical information, for this can be collected reasonably efficiently on a large scale. It is the stock-in-trade of any national mobility survey.

Duncan broke new ground with *The American Occupational Structure* not in theory or data collection but in his techniques of analysis, which were both statistically sophisticated and sociologically informative, and set new standards for sociologists. The technique for which he has become famous is known as 'path analysis', a relatively simple extension of multiple regression first used in 1918 by the geneticist Sewall Wright who applied the technique extensively to population genetics and animal breeding. (See Wright, 1934, and Duncan, 1966a.) Duncan showed how an existing technique could be applied illuminatingly to sociological data. If one were being critical, one could say that Duncan had merely popularized the technique, but the popularization was in fact successful largely because Duncan's actual applications proved to be highly fruitful sociologically.

In essence, path analysis enables the sociologist to estimate the relative importance of different determinants of individuals' occupational attainment. (For a basic account, see Appendix II.) Earlier analyses of mobility had concentrated on 'interchange between the classes' (Ginsberg's phrase); thus, as in Lipset and Bendix's reanalysis of their nine national surveys, sociologists looked at the rates of upward and downward mobility between discrete social classes. There is plenty of this kind of analysis in *The American Occupational Structure* too, but it was path analysis that enabled Duncan to analyse efficiently the process of occupational attainment. This involved two shifts in focus: first, there was a shift from the analysis of *mobility* itself to that of attainment; second, there was a shift from the measurement of *rates* to that of *determinants*. Instead of asking, 'How much mobility is there in this society?' the question becomes, 'What is the relative importance of factors such as social origins and schooling as determinants of individuals' eventual occupational attainments?'

'The main reason for this reformulation,' Blau and Duncan explain, 'is that the likelihood of upward mobility depends, of course, greatly on the level from which a man starts; this makes the finding that a given factor is associated with mobility ambiguous.' (Blau and Duncan, 1967 : 10.) Consider, for example, the situation of blacks. People with low-status origins obviously have a better chance of upward mobility than those starting off from high-status positions; there simply is much more room for upward movement. Now blacks have quite a high chance of upward mobility, but it is misleading to compare black with white mobility chances. Blacks are much more concentrated in low-status positions to start with, so their relatively high rate of mobility is not a finding that reveals much, or that is a matter for complacency, being compatible with widespread discrimination and inequality of opportunity. A much more useful way to approach these problems is to control for the determinants of a man's occupational attainment and then see whether the colour of his skin has had a bearing. We need to know whether blacks end up with better or worse jobs than do whites who started off from similar social origins. For this kind of study multiple regression and path analysis provide powerful statistical tools.

The basic question which Blau and Duncan address, therefore, 'is how the status individuals achieve in their careers is affected by the statuses ascribed to them earlier in life, such as their social origin, ethnic status, region of birth, community, and parental family.' (Blau and Duncan, 1967 : 19.) And their basic strategy is to conceive of occupational status in 1962 (the survey date) 'as the outcome of a lifelong process in which ascribed status positions at birth, intervening circumstances, and earlier [educational and occupational] attainments determine the level of ultimate achievement. A formalization in terms of a simple mathematical model [path analysis] permits an appropriate assessment of the relative importance of the several measured determinants.' (Blau and Duncan, 1967 : 20.)

However, while the precise questions which Blau and Duncan ask of their data differ in important ways from those of their predecessors, their broader theoretical concerns show a marked continuity with those of the earlier writers such as Lipset and Bendix. The two passages quoted from *The American Occupational Structure* in the previous paragraph illustrate the link with broader issues. In both passages we see the contrast between *ascription* and *achievement*, between the ascribed statuses with which a man starts life and the occupation which he eventually achieves. One theme common to post-war sociological writing has been the functionalist view that a stable industrial society requires a greater emphasis to be placed on a man's achievements and a lesser one on his ascribed characteristics. It is not *who* a man is but *what* he does that matters. Furthermore, what he does is to be judged by 'universalistic' criteria, such as educational attainment, which can be applied to all and be empirically verified. Nepotism and the 'old school tie' must give way to publicly demonstrable merit.

On this view, we would expect to find that the importance of ascription has declined whereas that of achievement has increased over time. This is precisely the claim that Blau and Duncan advance, and they formulate it in explicitly functionalist terms. Industrial society, they say, is characterized by 'a fundamental trend towards expanding universalism which has profound implications for the stratification system. The achieved status of a man, what he has accomplished in terms of some objective criteria, becomes more important than his ascribed status, who he is in the sense of what family he comes from. This does not mean that family background no longer influences careers. What it does imply is that superior status cannot any more be directly inherited but must be legitimated by actual achievements that are socially acknowledged. Education assumes increasing significance for social status in general and for the transmission of social standing from fathers to sons in particular.' (Blau and Duncan, 1967: 430.)

This 'fundamental trend' Blau and Duncan see as having been brought about by the needs of industrial society. In pre-industrial society, they argue, class barriers and immobility presented no great problems since there were few positions that required scarce knowledge and skills: 'In previous periods the knowledge and skills society was able to utilize were severely limited, which made this waste of talent regrettable from the standpoint of individuals but unavoidable from the perspective of the social order.' (Blau and Duncan, 1967 : 431.) Today, however, 'technological progress has created a need for advanced knowledge and skills on the part of a large proportion of the labor force, not merely a small professional elite. Under these conditions society cannot any longer afford the waste of human resources a rigid class structure entails. Universalistic principles have penetrated deep into the fabric of modern society and given rise to high rates of occupational mobility in response to this need.' (Blau and Duncan, 1967:431.) One wonders what scathing invective such a splendid piece of teleological functionalism would have stimulated from Sorokin.

In the remainder of this book we shall look at the major issues raised by Marx, Pareto and company, seeing them in the light of recent British evidence. We shall begin in the tradition of David Glass and ask how much, and what kinds of mobility, is there in Britain today, and how does it compare with earlier periods? Was Sorokin right to talk of 'trendless fluctuation' or, as Lipset and Bendix would have us believe, does a modern industrial society exhibit greater openness than in its pre-industrial past?

From these older questions we shall then move on to Blau and Duncan's question: 'What is the relative importance of family background and schooling for a person's eventual attainment?' What role, if any, do ascribed characteristics such as race and sex continue to play in Britain? Has achievement at last replaced ascription?

In discussing these matters I shall describe the latest British material from the 1970s. But I shall then present Britain in comparative perspective, carrying out the same kind of analysis as Lipset and Bendix but relying on national surveys carried out since the publication of their work in 1959.

Finally, there is the most important but also most difficult question: What is the relation of social mobility to class formation, social conflict and social stability? Does mobility weaken class solidarity and reduce the pressure for collective action? Does mobility lead to social unrest and the consequent circulation of elites? In social science we cannot hope to find definitive answers (*pace* Sorokin) but we can at least see what light contemporary empirical work has to shed on these questions.

2 Mobility in Britain Today

For the last quarter of a century the major source on mobility in Britain has been the 1949 survey reported by Glass and his team at the LSE. There have been other, smaller-scale investigations – those of Benjamin (1958), Runciman (1966), Butler and Stokes (1969), Noble (1972) and Richardson (1977)[1] – but it is to Glass that most commentators have turned. From him they have derived the three main conclusions described in Chapter 1:

1. Most mobility in Britain is short-range, and long-range movement 'from rags to riches, or riches to rags' is very rare.
2. There is a barrier to movement across the manual/non-manual line.
3. There is a high degree of self-recruitment, 'inheritance with a vengeance', at the top of the social scale.

But Glass's work is not unassailable and has recently been exposed to blistering attack.[2] An extreme version of the offensive comes from Frank Musgrove: 'The difficulty is the 1949 (Glass) survey. It is renowned. It has been a massive international sociological datum for three decades, and it has done incalculable harm. It offers an authoritative image of Britain which shapes enquiry and social policy; important and influential books are written which draw on the evidence of "a rigid, relatively closed and stable society which the book presented". It offers a (highly statistical) picture of Britain in the first half of the twentieth century, not as a land of increasing but actually diminishing opportunity in spite of its expanding educational provision. Of course the work is thirty years old, but it is not even a good historical document; it is a serious distortion of the past. The picture of opportunity in Britain which it offers is not only empirically implausible; it is a logical absurdity and an arithmetical impossibility.' (Musgrove, 1979 : 123.)

Musgrove has a taste for hyperbole. But there are certainly some oddities in Glass's results. He found that more people had experienced downward than upward mobility even though census material suggests that higher-level occupations had actually been expanding in number. This gives Musgrove his 'arithmetical impossibility': if there is increasing 'room at the top' there must necessarily be net upward mobility – unless upper-class families are unusually prolific in their breeding habits. You cannot have a surplus of downward mobility in a period of expanding opportunity.[3]

Does this mean that the other conclusions drawn from Glass's work are equally invalid? After all, they have little to do with downward mobility. It is hard to be certain, but so much has happened to Britain in the last twenty-five years that the situation may have changed anyway. We need a new survey to tell us about the post-war period, and the problems of Glass's enquiry only become relevant when we wish to elucidate historical trends. We can therefore shelve these difficulties until the next chapter (where we look at trends) and turn for the present to more recent material.

The Oxford mobility enquiry

The most recent large-scale study of Britain was undertaken by a group of Oxford sociologists in 1972.[4] The sample consisted of 10,000 adult males who constituted a representative cross-section of all males aged twenty to sixty-four and resident in England and Wales in 1972. These respondents were asked to give an outline of their own occupational and educational biographies as well as some basic biographical information about their fathers, mothers, wives, brothers and friends. As is usual in these surveys, the material is all of a 'factual' rather than attitudinal kind, although in a follow-up in 1974 some additional data were collected on the subjective experiences of a limited number of the original respondents.

The Oxford study has been sharply criticized for its omission of women, but there is fortunately another source, the General Household Survey conducted by the government statistical service, which we can use.[5] We shall present results on the mobility of women in Chapter 4, and we can postpone until then the arguments for and against the inclusion of women in a mobility survey.

There is however another problem which we cannot postpone, namely that of classification. Any discussion of social mobility necessarily requires us to distinguish a set of categories between which mobility is to take place. This problem has received all kinds of treatments. Pareto was most interested in movement between the governing elite and the non-elite; Sorokin was more concerned with movement between occupational groups which were differentiated according to their social honour; Lipset and Bendix focussed on movement between manual and non-manual occupations, which they tended to equate with movement between the middle and working classes (classes being seen as broad social groupings with shared identities, consumption patterns and political attitudes); Blau and Duncan in contrast saw the occupational structure as 'more or less continuously graded in regard to status rather than being a set of discrete status classes' and hence rather than looking at movement between discrete categories focussed on occupational achievements as measured on a continuous scale of socio-economic status (Blau and Duncan, 1967 : 124); Glass and his co-workers looked at movement between seven 'status categories' distinguished in terms of their social prestige and based on the assumption that 'the community consists of strata arranged in the form of a hierarchy' (Glass, 1954 : 29); and finally John Goldthorpe, in his report of the Oxford project, looked at movement between seven social classes differentiated according to the market and work situations of their incumbents.[6]

The classification of occupations exhibits more disarray than almost any other issue in professional sociology and provides endless ground for argument and confusion. How a sociologist decides to categorize occupations will reflect his own beliefs about the nature of the social world, his theoretical preferences and objectives, and his own moral or political attitudes and values (and all these will themselves be interrelated). We cannot say that one categorization is 'wrong' and another 'right'. There is no neutral, objective yardstick for deciding on the correct way to classify social reality. Even if we can show that, say, functionalism involves certain empirical assumptions that are unwarranted – for example, the claim that occupations' prestige and social honour vary according to their importance for the society – we still cannot say that it is 'wrong' to scale occupations according to their prestige.[7]

We may say it is uninteresting, or unfruitful, or even perhaps that the measurement has been badly done, but these adjectives do not really mean the same thing as 'wrong'.

Despite the diversity of sociologists' attempts at classification, they can in theory be regarded as variations on two extreme positions, or world views. At one extreme come writers like Pareto, Sorokin or Blau and Duncan who see society as composed of a hierarchy of occupations in which there are no sharp breaks. True, Blau and Duncan allow that there may be some kind of 'natural break' between farm and non-farm, and between manual and non-manual occupations, but they are more impressed by the overlap between these categories and the way one category shades into another. The basis of their ranking is the occupation's 'status' or 'prestige', horribly vague concepts in Blau and Duncan's treatment, but implying simply that some occupations are 'better' or 'worse' than others as judged by the overall rewards, both monetary and non-monetary, which their incumbents receive.[8]

At the other extreme come variants on the Marxist world view. Society is seen as divided into social classes which stand in antagonistic relations to each other. The factor that creates 'class' is fundamentally economic interest, and it is held that the economic interests of, say, manual wage labourers are clearly distinct from those of the petty bourgeoisie or the landowner. The emphasis is therefore on the *cleavages* within society, not the overlaps. Instead of being ranked in a hierarchy of status or prestige, occupations are grouped into discrete categories on the basis of their distinct economic interests. And so we have 'class mobility' rather than 'prestige mobility'.

So much for the theory. In practice, the broad outlines of most classifications are quite similar, although the detail varies enormously. Thus Glass's team placed professional and high administrative occupations in the highest of their seven status categories; Goldthorpe places them in his 'top' class which possesses the most favoured market and work situation.[9] Unskilled manual work comes at the 'bottom' in both classifications. There is more disagreement in the 'middle' at the manual/non-manual borderline (which may in itself tell us something about the fuzziness of that border). Glass (or more accurately Hall and Jones) place routine grades of non-manual work in the *same* status category as skilled manual work, and place them *below* shopkeepers and foremen. Goldthorpe in contrast places clerical workers, foremen, shopkeepers and skilled manual workers in four distinct social classes, but which are in a sense at the same 'level':[10] we would regard it as inappropriate to talk about 'upward' or 'downward' mobility between these classes.

We shall be using Goldthorpe's classification in many of the tables which follow. The seven classes which it distinguishes can be set out briefly as follows:[11]

Class I: higher-grade professionals (both self-employed and salaried), administrators, managers and large proprietors.

Class II: lower-grade professionals, administrators and managers, higher-grade technicians, and the supervisors of non-manual employees.

Class III: routine clerical workers, sales personnel and other rank and file non-manual workers.

Class IV: farmers, small proprietors and self-employed workers – the 'petty bourgeoisie'.

Class V: supervisors of manual workers and lower-grade technicians.

Class VI: skilled manual wage-workers who have served

apprenticeships or other forms of industrial training.
Class VII: semi- and unskilled manual workers in industry, plus agricultural workers.

Goldthorpe sometimes groups these into three broader classes – the service class made up of Classes I and II (so called because it is the class of those who service, i.e. exercise power and expertise on behalf of, the corporate authorities); an intermediate class composed of Classes III, IV and V; and a working class combining VI and VII. Another useful division which we shall employ from time to time involves treating Classes I, II, III and IV as the white-collar classes, and V, VI and VII as the blue-collar classes.

Short-range and long-range mobility

From problems of classification let us move on to some results of the Oxford mobility study. Table 2.1 gives the conventional mobility table using Goldthorpe's classification of occupations.[12] It is an 'outflow' table showing the destinations of men from different social origins. Thus, of the men who came from Class I social origins (that is, whose fathers had Class I jobs), nearly half had themselves secured Class I positions by the time of the 1972 survey whereas the remainder had in some degree suffered downward mobility compared with their fathers. We must note that respondents have been classified according to their *present* occupations while their fathers have been classified according to the occupation which they held at the time the respondent was aged fourteen. This point in the father's career was chosen because it does enable us to talk sensibly of the respondent's social origins. Present or last main occupation would not enable us to do that since, of course, most fathers carry on working, and many change jobs, long after their children have left home.

Let us now use Table 2.1 to see if we can shed some light on the received'wisdom about the prevalence of long- and short-range mobility in Britain today. Since we must treat Classes III, IV, V and VI as being in a sense all at much the same level, we shall regard short-range mobility as any movement in or out of this group of four 'middle' classes, while long-range mobility is that from top to bottom – from Classes I and II to VII, and vice versa.

Table 2.1 Intergenerational mobility: outflow

Father's class	Respondent's class (%)								
	I	II	III	IV	V	VI	VII	Total	N
I	48·4	18·9	9·3	8·2	4·5	4·5	6·2	100·0	582
II	31·9	22·6	10·7	8·0	9·2	9·6	8·0	100·0	477
III	19·2	15·7	10·8	8·6	13·0	15·0	17·8	100·1	594
IV	12·8	11·1	7·8	24·9	8·7	14·7	19·9	99·9	1223
V	15·4	13·2	9·4	8·0	16·6	20·1	17·2	99·9	939
VI	8·4	8·9	8·4	7·1	12·2	29·6	25·4	100·0	2312
VII	6·9	7·8	7·9	6·8	12·5	23·5	34·8	100·2	2216
%	14·3	11·4	8·6	9·9	11·6	20·8	23·3	99·9	(8343)

Source: Oxford Social Mobility Group.
Sample: men aged 25–64 in 1972.

The first impression received from Table 2.1 is that the 1972 sample had indeed experienced a great deal of inter-generational mobility, more of it being upward than downward. We can apply Westergaard and Resler's earlier comment to the new material: the data dispel any notion that Britain is a society in which an individual's class position is fixed at birth. Capitalism certainly does permit a fair degree of circulation. The figures on the diagonal (sloping from top left to bottom right) give the percentage of men from each class origin who were in the same class in 1972 as their fathers had been earlier. In most cases this is less than one-third, and for the sample as a whole only 28 per cent had been intergenerationally stable. The other 72 per cent had experienced class mobility of some kind. Even if we treat Classes III to VI as being on the same level so that movement between them involves a change of class positions but not one that can sensibly be termed 'upward' or 'downward', we still find that nearly half the sample had been mobile, 31 per cent moving up and 18 per cent down.

The surplus of upward mobility is not surprising, given the expansion of professional and managerial jobs and the contraction of semi- and unskilled manual ones: 14 per cent of the respondents, but only 7 per cent of their fathers, held Class I occupations; 23 per cent of the respondents, but 27 per cent of their fathers, held Class VII occupations. Expansion at the top and contraction at the bottom means that there simply has to be some net upward mobility, and so there is.[13] There is no 'logical absurdity and arithmetical impossibility' here of which Musgrove can accuse us.

There is an important caveat which we must enter here, however. Exactly how much mobility and stability we find will depend on the number, size and character of the categories we distinguish. We could, slightly maliciously, divide the sample into just two categories – say Class I in the first and all the other six in the second. This classification would not be altogether unlike Pareto's distinction between the elite and non-elite and would yield a non-elite containing over 85 per cent of the sample. Hardly surprisingly, we would find that few people had experienced intergenerational mobility across this particular boundary; only 14.6 per cent, in fact.

Lipset and Bendix's division of the population into manual and non-manual, or working and middle classes is another one of obvious interest, and again it is easy enough to regroup the categories. If we regard Classes V, VI and VII as manual ones, and the rest as non-manual, we find that total mobility across the boundary comes to 34.2 per cent – a somewhat higher figure than Lipset and Bendix found for any of the countries they studied.[14] Does this mean that Britain has now become a relatively mobile, open society? The short answer is 'No', but the long answer must wait for Chapter 7 where we shall put this figure in an international context.

How much mobility and stability we find, therefore, depends to a large extent on the particular classification which we use. We cannot possibly take a single figure as 'the' rate of social mobility in a specific country. It would not be far-fetched to suggest that we can get almost any answer we want simply by fiddling with the categories. Fortunately, however, there are some conclusions (although not as many as some writers claim) which are going to survive any reasonably plausible rejigging of the classification. For example, no sane observer is going to doubt that there is more short-range mobility than long-range. This is pretty clear from Table 2.1. Less than 10 per cent of men from Class I origins had dropped to semi- and unskilled manual work in 1972, but over a quarter had dropped the shorter distance to Classes III – VI. There is a similar pattern if we turn to upward mobility from Class VII origins: 15 per cent achieved long-range upward mobility, but 50 per cent made the smaller distance to Classes III, IV, V and VI.

But do these figures allow us to conclude, as Westergaard and Resler did, that movement 'from rags to riches or riches to rags' is very rare? Rags, riches and rarity, like beauty, lie in the eye of the beholder. How much money do you need to qualify as rich? In the 1972 enquiry the respondents in Class I had an average annual income of £3251, over twice as much as the amount earned by those in Class VII. Will this do? And what is to count as rare? Do we draw the line at 1 per cent, 5 per cent, or 10 per cent? Westergaard and Resler's claim is one of those infuriating statements, so often found in sociology, in which the authors give no clear guide as to what would count as a confirmation or a refutation. All we can sensibly say are things like 'movement from rags to riches is rarer than that from rags to moderate affluence' – which is hardly going to make the headlines.

The manual/non-manual barrier

The notion of a 'barrier' between the middle and working classes is another that is almost as bad as 'rarity', but we can perhaps make a little more headway this time. Certainly, there is no barrier in any literal sense. If we say that Classes I, II and III are those unambiguously above the barrier, we can see from Table 2.1 that about a quarter of the men from working-class social origins (i.e. Classes VI and VII) succeeded in crossing this barrier. And the men who got across it did not collapse, exhausted from the effort, on the ground immediately beyond the barrier. Having crossed it, the working-class man was just as likely to carry on all the way into the higher-grade professional, administrative or managerial jobs of Class I as he was to end up in the routine clerical work of Class III.

True, rather fewer men from Class I were likely to cross the barrier in the other direction into the working class. This asymmetry, which has been found in other countries, has led writers like Blau and Duncan to talk of a 'semi-permeable membrane' or 'one-way screen' which it is easier to pass through in one direction than the other. They went on to say: 'Some white-collar occupations require much less skill and command considerably less income than many blue-collar occupations. This makes it possible for men with inferior abilities who want to remain in the white-collar classes to do so. Men raised in white-collar homes are often strongly identified with the symbols of white-collar status. The unsuccessful ones among them are, therefore, willing to pay a price for being permitted to maintain white-collar status. The existence of relatively unskilled white-collar occupations, such as retail sales and clerical jobs, makes it possible for the unsuccessful sons of white-collar workers to remain in the white-collar class by paying the price of accepting a lower income than they might have been able to obtain in a manual occupation. The unskilled white-collar occupations tend to absorb most of the downwardly mobile from the higher non-manual strata, which makes these occupations a boundary that creates relative protection against the danger of downward mobility from the white-collar to the blue-collar class.' (Blau and Duncan, 1967 : 63.)

This is in many ways a plausible argument, but let us look at the actual evidence for Britain. Let us compare the occupations entered by 'unsuccessful' men with inferior abilities from different social origins. For the present purposes we can define the unsuccessful as those who went to elementary or secondary modern schools and left at the minimum school-leaving age without any formal academic qualifications such as School Certificate or 'O' level. The question we now have to ask is whether these unsuccessful men from white-collar homes were largely absorbed by unskilled white-collar jobs like retail sales and routine clerical work (jobs included in Goldthorpe's Class III).

The short answer for Britain is a firm 'No'. Some of these men (rather surprisingly perhaps) managed to get Class I and II jobs, but even if we put all the white-collar occupations together, they still absorbed only 24 per cent of these unqualified offspring of white-collar fathers. This is a bit better than the unqualified children of blue-collar workers managed – 15 per cent got into these jobs – but it is hardly adequate evidence for a boundary that 'creates relative protection against the danger of downward mobility from the white-collar to the blue-collar class'. The great majority of educationally unsuccessful men with 'inferior abilities' seem to end up in some kind of blue-collar work. (See Appendix I, Table 1.)

But did they jump or were they pushed? Did these educationally unsuccessful men enter blue-collar work because they were excluded from the white-collar work they would have liked, or did they actually choose manual work for its higher pay despite the absence of 'the cherished symbol of the white collar'? The answer may tell us something about the prevalence of status snobbery in Britain, a snobbery that is often asserted by commentators on British life but rarely demonstrated.

The kind of data that is available cannot tell us about the motivations of respondents, but there are two pieces of evidence which are quite instructive. The first is the income people get from the different jobs. Table 2 in Appendix I shows that Class III jobs – the routine clerical and sales ones – do not pay at all well for these educationally unqualified men compared with *skilled* manual work (Class VI). In other words there is a considerable price to be paid for the white collar – in 1972 it was about £150 per annum. *Un*skilled manual work, on the other hand, pays even worse. The man who is left with a choice between joining the unskilled white-collar labour force or the unskilled blue-collar one is not making a financial sacrifice if he opts for the former.

The other useful piece of evidence concerns apprenticeships. These typically lead, in the beginning at least, into skilled manual work; they are quite keenly sought after – you hardly drift into an apprenticeship; and they might be taken as indicating some kind of commitment to manual work – if only for the money. Table 3 in Appendix I shows that the men from white-collar homes were actually even *more* likely to get these apprenticeships than their educationally unsuccessful peers from working-class homes. And it is a good guess that getting one helped many to avoid the low pay and low status of the unskilled manual job.

The moral is simple. Qualifications improve your chances of getting a better-paid job (although they do not ensure it). If you miss out on the qualifications to be won at school, try for the vocational ones that can be obtained after leaving school. White-collar families tend to know this lesson; they are better at securing school credentials in the first place, and they seem better at using the 'alternative route' of technical and vocational qualifications if they miss out first time round.[15] There is little sign that they allow snobbery to stand in the way of economic self-interest. It is a good bet that many of these 'downwardly mobile' men jumped into skilled manual work for the better pay and prospects which, compared with the alternatives, it offered them. But the men who ended up in unskilled manual work were pushed – or perhaps just slipped; it is hard to see what positive attractions they could have been offered.

Elite self-recruitment

Perhaps the most influential of all the conclusions based on Glass's work is that about elite self-recruitment. 'Here,' said Westergaard and Resler 'is inheritance with a vengeance.' Table 2.1 supports them. The highest levels of self-recruitment occur at the two extremes, in Classes I and VII (just as they did in Glass's table), and in Class I is the highest probability of all that sons will follow in their fathers' footsteps and maintain their privileged position in the class structure. It has become commonplace to say that the poor are 'born to fail' but if Table 2.1 is anything to go by it would be truer to say that the rich are 'born to succeed'.

True, the 1972 data do not seem to reveal quite as much 'closure' at the top as the 1949 data had done. Westergaard and Resler pointed out: 'If parental origin played no part in determining life chances, whether directly or indirectly, only some 3 per cent of their sons in the 1949 sample ... would have found jobs of a kind to secure them a place in this privileged minority [of established professional and high administrative jobs]. In fact nearly 40 per cent did so.' The ratio of the 'observed' to the 'expected' figure (sometimes called the Index of Association or mobility index) was thus 40:3 or approximately 13:1. If we repeat the calculation for the 1972 sample we observe that 48 per cent of the sons of Class I fathers had secured places in this privileged minority for themselves, compared with the figure of 14 per cent that would have been expected if parental origin played no part in determining life chances.

The 1972 data thus yield a much smaller ratio of observed to expected – less than 4 : 1 – compared with the 13 : 1 of 1949. But even if we had no reservations about Glass's material, we could not use these two ratios to conclude that the British elite has become much more open in the past quarter-century. The Index of Association is highly sensitive to the sizes of the categories being used. The 1972 Class I is much bigger at 14 per cent than the 3 per cent of the 1949 status category 1, and the index is correspondingly lower. (See Appendix II for details.) If we could take just the 'top' 3 per cent of the 1972 male population, we would probably get a very similar figure to Glass's.[16]

In another respect, however, there is a very important difference from Glass's results which has considerable sociological consequences. In Glass's table (*pace* Musgrove) there were slightly more fathers than sons with elite occupations. In the 1972 table on the other hand there are twice as many sons as fathers in Class I occupations. This reflects the fact that there was a great expansion of higher professional, administrative and managerial posts in the post-war period. There was greatly increasing 'room at the top'. This is shown clearly by the Censuses of 1951, 1961 and 1971. We cannot, of course, use the distribution of fathers in a mobility table to find out about the occupational structure in the past: their reported occupations do not relate to any single years – our oldest respondents in Table 2.1 would have been reporting the job their fathers had in 1922 while the youngest would have been reporting on 1961. But the Censuses show clearly enough that there had been a considerable expansion of higher-level jobs in the post-war period. Room at the top is not just a novelist's fiction.

The increasing room in Class I leads to an important paradox. While nearly half the men whose fathers had been in Class I had followed in their fathers' footsteps, three-quarters of the men in Class I in 1972 had come from lower social origins. The distinction is that between the destinations of those from given social origins and the current composition of a given social class. More technically, it is the distinction between an *outflow* and an *inflow* table. Table 2.1 was an outflow table where percentages are calculated across the rows, giving the destinations of men from given origins. Compare this now with Table 2.2, an inflow table, where percentages are calculated down the columns, showing where men currently in a given class came from.

Table 2.2 Intergenerational mobility: inflow

Father's class	Respondent's class (%)							
	I	II	III	IV	V	VI	VII	%
I	23·6	11·6	7·5	5·8	2·7	1·5	1·9	7·0
II	12·7	11·4	7·1	4·6	4·5	2·7	2·0	5·7
III	9·5	9·8	8·9	6·1	7·9	5·1	5·5	7·1
IV	13·1	14·3	13·3	36·7	10·9	10·4	12·5	14·7
V	12·1	13·1	12·2	9·0	16·1	10·9	8·3	11·3
VI	16·3	21·6	26·9	19·6	29·2	39·4	30·2	27·7
VII	12·7	18·1	24·1	18·1	28·6	30·0	39·7	26·6
Total	100·0	99·9	100·0	99·9	99·9	100·0	100·1	100·1
N	1197	948	721	830	969	1734	1944	(8343)

Source: Oxford Social Mobility Group.
Sample: men aged 25–64 in 1972.

The contrast between the two tables is instructive. Table

2.1 shows that the men who had the good fortune to be born into the privileged circumstances of Class I had a relatively good chance of staying there. But Table 2.2 shows that the great majority of people currently (that is, in 1972) in Class I were newcomers. The reason for the difference, of course, is the massive expansion in the size of Class I and the consequential upward mobility to which we have already alluded. *Even if every single person from Class I origins had managed to stay there, expansion would have meant that a large number would still need to have been recruited from elsewhere to fill all the new vacancies.* As some writers put it, expansion at the top 'forces' upward mobility.[17] 'Inheritance with a vengeance' is thus perfectly compatible with the arrival of large numbers of newcomers. Self-recruitment is not at all the same thing as closure.

Sociologically the contrast between Tables 2.1 and 2.2 may also be important, particularly for issues of class formation and class action. What we see from Table 2.2 is that Class I is relatively heterogeneous in its current social composition whereas Class VII is much more homogeneous. Three-quarters of Class I are upwardly mobile 'new men', 40 per cent of them having come from the three blue-collar classes. But we see a very different picture in Class VII. Nearly three-quarters of its current members are 'second generation' working class, and less than 10 per cent are downwardly mobile 'skidders' from the three white-collar classes.

It could plausibly be argued that this diversity in Class I will reduce its potential for communal class action while the similarity of origin in Class VII will increase its solidarity. In Goldthorpe's term there has been a 'maturation' of the working class which increases its potential for militant class action.[18] Whereas in many industrial societies such as Italy a large proportion of current industrial manual workers are 'green recruits', first generation members of the industrial proletariat whose fathers were agricultural workers, this is no longer true in Britain. The great majority of the British working class has been brought up in working-class homes and exposed to the culture and traditions of unions and the industrial workplace.

There is, however, an alternative and, on the surface, equally plausible argument about the relation between social origin and class action. This is the argument of Pareto and Sorokin that upward mobility into the elite turns the ambitious members of lower classes from being potential leaders of a revolution into protectors of social order 'sure of their rights, not soft-hearted, but ready to apply force and compulsion to suppress any riot'. On this line of reasoning, the expansion of Class I and the associated upward mobility has deprived the working class of potential leaders and given the elite an infusion of new blood that enables it to strengthen its hold on society.

Channels of mobility into elite occupations

We shall attempt to test these theories of mobility and class action in Chapter 8. But there is another aspect of the heterogeneity of Class I which we can pursue now. Class I, as Goldthorpe has defined it, is made up of five different occupational groups: self-employed professionals like doctors, lawyers, accountants and stockbrokers; salaried professionals such as university lecturers, scientists and engineers; senior administrators and officials in the large public and commercial bureaucracies like the civil service, local government and public utilities; industrial managers in large enterprises; and 'large' proprietors, the working owners of large shops and enterprises with more than twenty-five employees. The proportion of 'new men' in these five groups varies considerably as do the patterns of selection and recruitment. It is by no means exactly the same kind of flour that gets sifted into these five receptacles.

Table 2.3 Social origins of men in elite occupations

Father's class	Respondent's class (%)				
	Self-employed professionals	Salaried professionals	Senior administrators	Industrial managers	Large proprietors
I	40·2	24·3	20·0	18·7	44·2
II, III, IV	35·8	37·2	37·4	27·4	29·4
V, VI, VII	24·0	38·5	42·6	53·9	26·4
Total	100·0	100·0	100·0	100·0	100·0
N	92	432	446	193	34

Source: Oxford Social Mobility Group.
Sample: men aged 25–64 and in Class I in 1972.

Table 2.3 shows major differences in the social-class origins of the members of the five occupational groups. At one extreme we find that a majority of the industrial managers had come from blue-collar backgrounds while at the other only one-quarter of the proprietors and self-employed professionals had done so. To put the same result in another way, the groups which are most independent and autonomous – the self-employed – are the most exclusive in their social recruitment; it is the bureaucracies, and particularly industrial bureaucracy, which provide the main channels of upward mobility.

The extreme position of the large proprietors is hardly surprising. For them above all the direct inheritance of property is likely to be significant, and while we cannot prove that inheritance of property rather than entrepreneurial ambitions is the mechanism, it is certainly instructive that no less than 47 per cent of the large proprietors were themselves the sons of proprietors (large and small combined). The position of the self-employed professionals is different and almost certainly depends more on the inheritance of 'cultural capital' (a term taken from Bourdieu) than of material wealth and capital. They are easily the best educated of the five elite occupational groups (whereas the proprietors are the worst educated), and the 'second generation' ones among them are even better educated than the 'newcomers'. (Appendix I, Table 4.)

Another interesting contrast between the proprietors and the self-employed professionals is their career structure. Whereas similar proportions of them have Class I social origins, very few of the proprietors but the great majority of the professionals began their working careers in Class I jobs. The archetypal professional comes from a privileged social background, receives an elite education, and goes straight into a good job with a secure future. It would be wrong to talk of an 'archetypal proprietor' in the same way. There are probably two very different types, the self-made men and the inheritors. The typical inheritor goes to a private school, starts life in a subordinate position in his father's firm, and eventually takes over the business. The self-made men receive a minimal education and start life in routine white-collar or blue-collar work.

There are interesting contrasts, too, between the main channels of upward mobility, the salaried bureaucracies of industry and government. Industrial management recruits somewhat more than the other two channels from blue-collar homes, its recruits have somewhat lower educational levels, but above all there is a big difference in the proportions who have served their time on the shop floor. Well over half the managers started their careers as manual workers or technicians. In contrast nearly two-thirds of the administrators started off in white-collar jobs, routine clerical work being by far the most common starting point.

There are, then, important differences in the channels of upward mobility into these five elite occupational groups. While there will be many new recruits who will have climbed the scholarship ladder through grammar school to white-collar careers, it is also important to recognize that, particularly in management, there will be appreciable numbers of people from humble origins who went to elementary or secondary modern schools, left at the minimum leaving age without any formal qualifications, and worked their way up from the shop floor. The members of Class I have thus between them an extremely varied social experience. Let us distinguish three main routes into Class I occupations – the inheritance of privilege, the scholarship ladder into white-collar work, and promotion from the shop floor. The largest single group are the 'scholarship boys' from middle[19] or working-class homes who won places at the local authority grammar and technical schools and then entered some kind of white-collar work. The privileged route – Class I origins followed by private school and thence straight into a Class I job

– accounts for only a tiny minority, less than 10 per cent of the occupants of Class I, and is in fact more rarely followed than the promotion ladder from the shop floor. Diagram 2.1 shows the frequency with which these, and the other possible routes, are followed. It indicates once again the diversity of those in Class I.

Diagram 2.1 Routes to Class I

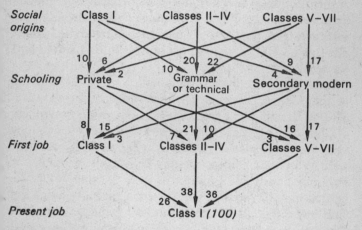

Source: Oxford Social Mobility Group.
Sample: Men aged 25–64 and with Class I jobs in 1972.
The figures give the percentage who travelled along a given path.

The governing elite

Strictly speaking, Class I should not be regarded as a governing elite in the sense in which Pareto and other elite theorists have used that term. Rather, it consists of a set of elite occupations which constitute a reservoir or recruiting market from which the members of the governing elite proper are drawn. MPs, for example, are drawn overwhelmingly from Class I occupations. The Nuffield election survey shows that of the 609 Conservative, Labour and Liberal MPs elected in October 1974, 138 were professionals (mainly barristers). A further 79 (mainly Conservative) were company directors and executives, and 92 were teachers (mainly Labour). Only 86 (all but two of them Labour) had working-class occupations. On the Conservative side of the House probably as many as 90 per cent came from the Classes I and II and even on the Labour side it is possibly not far short of two-thirds. (Butler and Kavanagh, 1975.)

However, if we look at the question in outflow instead of inflow terms we get a rather different perspective. Most MPs may come from Class I but very few members of Class I ever get anywhere near the House of Commons apart from the public galleries. In the early 1970s there were well over a million men in Class I occupations, but little more than six hundred of them became MPs. We need to move on, therefore, to examine in more detail the elite members *within* these elite occupations. After all, there may be plenty of 'new men' in the 'pool of eligibles' but few of them may actually get into the 'command posts' of industry, the civil service or parliament that make up the governing elite proper. These posts may still be reserved predominantly for established, second- or third-generation members of the elite.

The definition and identification of the 'command posts' or the 'governing elite' raise conceptual and philosophical issues that are even more complex than those involved with social class. I do not propose to discuss them at length since I have nothing to add to the existing well-known discussions.[20] All I will do is baldly express my agreement with the view that the existing social institutions confer substantial advantages on some groups rather than others, that no social groups have more than marginal power to alter these institutions (short of armed insurrection), but that such power as is available is monopolized to a large extent by a restricted set of overlapping and linked groups which, with Lupton and Wilson (1959), I would identify as 'top decision-makers' – cabinet ministers, senior civil servants at the rank of under-secretary or above, directors of major financial institutions and the like.

To what extent, then, are these top decision-makers recruited from the new men in Class I? Or are these command posts reserved for second- or third-generation members of the elite? There are a number of different sources which we can piece together to produce something like a coherent picture. First of all, Boyd (1973) has looked at the openness of the elite to those of non-elite origin, defining membership of the elite as inclusion in *Who's Who*. Thus *Who's Who* invites (among others) civil servants of the rank of under-secretary or above to submit biographies; it includes all ambassadors, high court judges and lords of appeal; all bishops of the Established Church of England are listed; directors of the clearing banks, of the Bank of England and the Bank of Scotland are all included.

Boyd listed all the members of these five groups (and some military ones) appearing in *Who's Who* in 1971 and in certain previous years in order to obtain trend data. He then checked to see what proportion had fathers who were themselves listed in *Who's Who* or *Who Was Who*. Elite succession was then taken to be any instance where both generations were listed.

Table 2.4 Elite mobility and stability

	Men listed in *Who's Who* in 1970/1 (%)				
	Higher civil servants	Ambass-adors	Judges	Bishops	Bank directors
Father listed in *Who's Who*	11·2	27·0	28·4	19·2	45·4
Father not listed	88·8	73·0	71·6	80·8	54·6
Total	100·0	100·0	100·0	100·0	100·0
N	269	74	88	125	130

Source: Boyd (1973), adapted from tables 21, 22, 23, 27, 28.

Boyd's results are given in Table 2.4. This, like Tables 2.2 and 2.3, is an inflow table telling us about the origins of men currently (that is, in 1971) occupying elite positions recognized by *Who's Who*. And it shows wide differences in the openness of the different elite groups, the civil service and the banks being the two extreme cases. At first glance, one's impression might be that all five groups are relatively open. In no case does elite succession account for a clear majority of the current group members. But it would surely be an error to take this material as evidence of openness. Boyd has taken a very restricted definition of elite origin: he requires the father to have appeared in *Who's Who* or *Who Was Who*, and of course many fathers who did not may nonetheless have come from privileged positions in society (such as the occupations that Gold-thorpe included in his Class I).

One way of putting the figures in Table 2.4 into perspective is to calculate the Index of Association, just as we did earlier. We can estimate that if elite membership were independent of social origin, only 0·15 per cent of the people in *Who's Who* would be expected to have had fathers who were also in *Who's Who*.[21] In fact, 11 per cent of the top civil servants had such fathers, giving a ratio of 'observed' to 'expected' of 75:1. And in the case of the bank directors the ratio shoots up to 300:1. Westergaard and Resler thought that a ratio of 13:1 indicated 'inheritance with a vengeance' when they were looking at Glass's material. One wonders how they would describe the bank directors.

What one does with these figures is partly a matter of choice. In the case of the higher civil servants, for example, one can either be impressed by how 'small' the figure of 11.2 per cent is or how 'large' that of 75:1 is. There is ammunition here both for those who wish to applaud the openness of the higher echelons of the civil service and for those who wish to castigate the unfair advantages given to those from elite origins.

There are, however, two points on which there is less scope for argument. First, it is clear that the home civil service is more open than the judiciary, the Church of England or the City. Second, it is highly probable that inequalities of opportunity steadily magnify the further up the ladder we go. Halsey and Crewe (1969), for example, have shown that 70 per cent of clerical officers in the civil service came from the families of manual or lower white-collar workers, 61 per cent of those in the middle and higher ranks of the executive class, and 31 per cent in the higher ranks of under-secretary and above (the ranks that obtain inclusion in *Who's Who*) of the administrative class. The aspiring bureaucrat from humble origins does not actually have doors slammed in his face; he just finds it harder to push them open as he tries to advance along the corridors of power.

Nor is this true only in the civil service. Harbury and Hitchens's study of the inheritance of wealth in Britain (1979) shows the same phenomenon. Using the Calendars of the Central Probate Registry in Somerset House, London, they sampled deceased wealth-holders and their fathers. The results yield an inflow mobility table analogous to Table 2.2, only in the present case, of course, fathers and sons are categorised according to the wealth which they left, not their occupation. The pattern within the table is also exactly like that of the conventional mobility table: the greater the wealth, the greater the extent of self-recruitment from the ranks of the wealthy. (See Appendix I, Table 5.) Thus of 'top wealth-leavers' in 1973 (those leaving estates of over £100,000)[22] 71 per cent had fathers who also left significant estates (which we are taking to be worth £10,000 or more). Put another way, only 29 per cent of these top wealth-holders would be regarded, on this criterion, as self-made men. But of the 'medium wealth-leavers' (those leaving estates between £50,000 and £100,000), 49 per cent were self-made men, and for the leavers of smaller estates the proportion exceeds one-half. Again, we can put these figures in perspective with the Index of Association. Harbury and Hitchens calculate that the chance of drawing at random an estate of over £100,000 was 0·14 per cent in 1973. In fact 36 per cent of top wealth-leavers had fathers who also fell into this category, giving a ratio of 257:1 between the observed and the expected. It is a ratio which is interestingly close to the one we obtained earlier in the case of elite succession among the bank directors. It is probably not unreasonable to conclude that the extent of self-recruitment among the wealthy and the financial elite is of much the same order of magnitude, and of course in many cases it may involve the same people. The transmission of wealth and of elite position are not so very different.

Conclusion

Britain is not a society in which individual position in the class structure is fixed at birth. The sons of foremen and technicians (Class V), for example, are spread out across the class structure in an apparently random manner. Fluidity rather than occupational inheritance seems a better characterization of this intermediate area of the British class structure. Occupational inheritance, however, is more in evidence when we look at the extremes. Almost half the sons from Class I homes followed in their fathers' footsteps into Class I jobs; well over half the sons from working-class homes likewise followed in their father's footsteps. But this still means that there were many men from these classes who experienced upward or downward intergenerational mobility. One in seven men from Class I homes were downwardly mobile into blue-collar jobs; one in five men whose fathers held semi- or unskilled manual jobs were upwardly mobile into white-collar work.

The upwardly mobile greatly outnumbered the downwardly mobile. The reason is simple. There was increasing 'room at the top'. In 1972 twice as many sons held Class I jobs as their fathers had done, and this meant there was plenty of room for newcomers to these elite occupations. Indeed, the newcomers outnumbered the 'second generation' by three to one. But the obverse of expansion at the top was contraction at the bottom. And the obverse of the heterogeneity of Class I is the homogeneity of the working class. Here it is the 'second generation' who outnumber the new recruits by three to one.

The routes which people followed into Class I were most often (but far from exclusively) educational ones. The man who went to a secondary modern school and left at the minimum leaving age with no qualifications was far more likely than his better educated peer to end up in a working-class job; the secondary modern school was a great leveller. And the most frequented route for upward mobility went via the grammar school. But the role of education in mobility can be (and often has been) greatly exaggerated.[23] It was harder, but not impossible, for men to gain access to the established professions without formal educational qualifications, but many more men with little formal schooling climbed the promotion ladder to the higher levels of industrial management.

While many 'new men' climbed the educational and promotional ladders into the elite occupations that make up Class I, progress into the very highest echelons of society – the governing elite – was harder. The bureaucracies of government and industry were the most open channels of upward mobility, and the boardrooms of the City were perhaps the most closed.[24] The *carrière ouverte aux talents* that the modern bureaucracy purports to give is neither wholly myth nor wholly fact: 11 per cent of the top civil servants whose names appear in *Who's Who* are the second generation of their families to appear in that elite publication – seventy-five times the 'chance' number; but 31 per cent were the sons of routine clerical or manual workers. These figures document one of the fundamental features of mobility in modern Britain: children from privileged backgrounds have substantial, indeed grotesque, advantages in the competition for elite positions, but when they take their place in the elite they may find that they are outnumbered by men from humbler origins.

These data also reveal that the great inequalities of opportunity are not those between children from white-collar and blue-collar homes but between the elite and non-elite. The figures cannot be estimated accurately, but the rough orders of magnitude would probably be correct if we were to say that a man from a working-class home has about one chance in fifteen hundred of getting into *Who's Who*; the man from a white-collar background has perhaps one chance in five hundred; the man from the higher professional and managerial home has one chance in two hundred; but the man from the elite home has a one-in-five chance.[25] Silver spoons continue to be distributed.

3 Trends

'In the field of vertical mobility ... there seems to be no definite perpetual trend towards either an increase or a decrease of the intensiveness and generality of mobility. This is proposed as valid for the history of a country, for that of a large social body, and, finally, for the history of mankind.' (Sorokin, 1927 : 152.)

Sorokin's proposal did not find favour with the majority of post-war sociologists. Lipset and Bendix maintained that the industrialized societies which they studied were 'comparable in their high amounts of total vertical mobility' (Lipset and Bendix, 1959 : 27), and implied that pre-industrial societies as a whole were characterized by lower rates of mobility. Blau and Duncan were even more explicit. They assumed 'that a fundamental trend towards expanding universalism characterizes industrial society', that 'universalistic principles have penetrated deep into the fabric of modern society and given rise to high rates of occupational mobility in response to this need.' (Blau and Duncan, 1967 : 429, 431.)

Two main lines of argument are employed by these post-war writers to support their contention. Lipset and Bendix stress 'changes in the number of available vacancies'. In every industrializing society, they assert, the occupational structure gradually changes its shape. There is a contraction in the proportion of unskilled manual jobs and a corresponding expansion in vacancies for professional, administrative, managerial and white-collar jobs generally. This then creates an 'upward surge in mobility'.

The changing supply of vacancies and the transformation of the occupational structure provides one basis for increased mobility. The rise of meritocracy or universalism may provide another. This is the argument on which Blau and Duncan lay most emphasis. Achievement replaces ascription – 'the achieved status of a man, what he has accomplished in terms of some objective criteria, becomes more important than his ascribed status, who he is in the sense of what family he comes from.' (Blau and Duncan, 1967 : 430.)

There are a number of different forms which the ascription/achievement argument can take. Lipset and Bendix mention the decline in the number of inheritable status positions: there are fewer family farms and family businesses and more large-scale bureaucracies. But in addition to this, the principles of selection and promotion operating *within* bureaucracies have changed over time. The nepotism and corruption of the civil service in Pepys's day, the practice of purchasing commissions in the armed forces have been swept away and replaced by a system of formal examinations, selection boards and the like. The great milestone here was the Northcote-Trevelyan Report of 1853 on the reform of the civil service. It has been described as the 'Bill of Rights of the intellectuals' and its implementation as 'their Glorious Revolution',[1] although, as Musgrove notes, 'The *Quarterly Review* at that time took a more disparaging view, complaining that over-educated young men would go into the Post Office "and other departments of inferior dignity" and claiming that: "The object, in point of fact, is to turn the sixteen thousand places in the Civil Service of the empire into so many exhibitions for poor scholars".' (Musgrove, 1979 : 109.)[2]

Alongside the spread and transformation of the bureaucracy came an increase of literacy and the rise of the public and grammar schools to prepare children for the new competitive examinations. Further demands, for greater equality of opportunity in education, culminated in the 1944 Education Act which provided universal, free secondary education in state schools. One of the fervent hopes of the reformers was that greater equality of opportunity would bring larger numbers of working-class boys into the grammar schools, opening up to them the high-status professional and administrative occupations that had formerly been closed to them for lack of the necessary education. 'The 1944 Education Act will no doubt greatly increase the amount of social mobility in Britain,' David Glass confidently asserted (Glass, 1954:22).

Sorokin would no doubt have had some caustic rejoinders to make to his optimistic successors, but for the moment let us concentrate on the historical record. First we can look at the trends revealed by the two national surveys, those of Glass and his LSE team and of the Oxford Social Mobility Group. These can in principle tell us something about 'mass' mobility – movements between Glass's seven status categories and Goldthorpe's seven classes. We can then use studies of elite recruitment to take us further back in time. There are no reliable surveys of mobility among the population as a whole for the nineteenth century or earlier, so at most we can obtain only a very partial view of trends in pre-industrial and industrializing Britain.[3] Still, we must make the best of what evidence exists in order to answer our central questions: is there a movement from ascription to achievement, to greater openness and higher rates of mobility in the advanced industrial society; or is there instead 'trendless fluctuation'?

Trends in mass mobility

We are immediately faced with two crucial problems. First, the ideal strategy for detecting trends in mobility rates would be to compare the results of similar studies carried out at different points of time. We could thus compare the mobility experience of men sampled in 1949 with that of men sampled in 1972, and indeed this was the original intention of the Oxford Social Mobility Group when they were planning their 1972 survey.

For such a replication to be successful we would need to be sure that the procedures used in the two studies were identical. We would have to be sure that the same sampling procedures, the same questions, the same methods of coding responses and the same classification of social classes had been used. Or at the very least one would want to know what procedures had been used in the earlier study so that one could correct for any differences in method. Unfortunately Glass's team left behind no clear record of how they allocated subjects to the seven status categories. The interview schedules of the 1949 enquiry have been destroyed, so there is no possibility of recoding the results; and the lack of clarity of the coding instructions means that it is impossible to recode the results of the 1972 enquiry according to Glass's status categories.

We must make do, then, with the second-best strategy, which is to divide the respondents within a given study into different 'birth cohorts'. In the case of the 1972 enquiry we could compare the mobility experience of men born, say, between 1908 and 1917 (those aged fifty-five to sixty-four in 1972) with those born in subsequent cohorts. This is only a second-best, of course, because the fifty-five to sixty-four-year-old men available in 1972 to be interviewed do not constitute a representative sample of men born in the years 1908 to 1917: many of the men born then will have died while others will have emigrated, and unfortunately for the sociologist deaths and migration do not occur at random. Life-expectation, for example, for children in working-class homes or for men engaged in certain kinds of industrial manual work is shorter than for more advantaged sections of the population (see Halsey, 1972:341), and so there will be systematic biasses in the composition of the survivors of each birth cohort. But let us remember that the best can be the enemy of the good. If we accept only the perfect research design we shall have to forego much imperfect but illuminating researches. The biasses in the present procedure are almost certainly not all that great; it is not impossible to judge how they might affect the results; and if we want to say anything about mobility trends at all, there is no better source which suggests itself. As Jencks once shrewdly remarked in a different context: 'The methods we have used may involve considerable error. In self-defence, we can only say that the magnitude of these errors is almost certainly less than if we had simply consulted our prejudices, which seems to be the usual alternative.' (Jencks, 1972:15.)

There is, however, a second major problem. Men born between 1908 and 1917 will have had much more time in the labour market than the 1938–47 cohort. This means that we will confound mobility trends with the effects of ageing. If we were to find that the older men exhibited greater work-life mobility than the younger, the obvious retort would be that they had had more time in which to be mobile. Alternatively, if we were to find that the younger men exhibited greater intergenerational mobility than the older, the immediate response would be that many men from privileged backgrounds start off their work-lives in lower-level jobs but then work their way, by various routes, back to the top during the course of their lives. The classic example of this, of course, is the boss's son who is made to start off on the shop floor in order to learn the ropes but eventually steps into his father's shoes (see Chapman and Marquis, 1912, for a notorious failure to realize this point). Many downwardly mobile young men are destined to be successful old men.

Fortunately we can circumvent this problem by asking respondents about their occupations at a fixed point in their careers. In the case of the Oxford survey, they were asked what work they were doing ten years after their entry into the labour market. In this way we can measure the work-life mobility experienced over a fixed length of time, and we have given each cohort an equal chance to experience mobility compared with their fathers. In the following analyses, therefore, we are taking as our yardstick the mobility which men had achieved ten years after entry into the labour market.[4]

We can begin with the same kind of analyses which we carried out in Chapter 2, looking at rates of upward and downward mobility. This of course means that we must group Classes III, IV, V and VI together as we cannot sensibly talk of upward or downward mobility between them. The results are given in Table 3.1.

The broad outlines should not surprise us. Over this relatively short period of the twentieth century total mobility has steadily increased, the biggest gains being in upward mobility which far exceeded downward mobility for the youngest cohort.[5] But there is a major surprise, at least for those who had dismissed Glass's work as a logical absurdity: for the oldest cohort (and these were of course men of an age to be in Glass's 1949 sample) there was a surplus of downward mobility. It now begins to look as though the scorn poured on the 1949 results was a little premature.

Table 3.1 Mobility trends: cohort analysis of the 1972 enquiry

	Birth cohort			
	1908–17	1918–27	1928–37	1938–47
% Upwardly mobile	19·9	24·5	30·5	30·5
% Downwardly mobile	25·3	23·2	20·4	21·0
Total % mobile	45·2	47·7	50·9	51·5
N	1687	1498	2019	2191

Source: Oxford Social Mobility Group.
Sample: men aged 25–64 in 1972.

True, the fact that these new results are in line with Glass's does not prove that both are correct. The same errors might vitiate both. So we must look more closely to see precisely what was going on during the early manhood of this 1908–17 birth cohort. Born just before and during the First World War, they were leaving school in the late 1920s and early 1930s; the great majority would have completed their first ten years in the labour force by the start of the Second World War; they suffered some of the worst effects of the depression and had not yet gained the benefits of post-war expansion (although of course many of them did subsequently, later on in their working careers).

And while the general trend through the twentieth century has been for increasing 'room at the top', there was a definite fluctuation around this trend during the depression. The Censuses show that in 1931 a greater proportion of the male labour force was in unskilled manual work than had been the case in 1921, while the proportion of men in professional and administrative positions had barely changed. This was no time of expanding opportunities.

It is important to realize, of course, that for many of the 1908–17 birth cohort the downward mobility will have been temporary, just as the great upward mobility experienced by the 1938–47 cohort may also be short-lived. As the economy expands or contracts, so the occupational flows may change direction, and the picture we get will depend on the time when we take our snapshot. All we can say with confidence is that over the period of their early manhood the youngest cohorts have experienced greater mobility than their predecessors. But who knows what will have happened to them by the year 2000 when they will be entering retirement?

We cannot predict the future pattern of mobility, but if we are willing to make use of Glass's data we can push the historical record a bit further back in time.[6] After all, we have covered only a brief span of the twentieth century so far, hardly sufficient to test the hypotheses of Lipset or Sorokin. Table 3.2 gives Glass's cohort analysis. Glass of course uses a different classification of occupations from Goldthorpe's, but we have reanalysed his data using four categories which are not unlike (although nor are they identical to) the ones used in Table 3.1.[7] Hence we obtain roughly comparable rates of upward, downward and total

Table 3.2 Mobility trends: cohort analysis of the 1949 enquiry

	Birth cohort				
	Pre-1890	1890–9	1900–9	1910–19	1920–9
% Upwardly mobile	16·5	23·3	23·2	21·2	20·9
% Downwardly mobile	33·0	25·9	24·6	24·6	25·3
Total % mobile	49·5	49·2	47·8	45·8	46·2
N	679	540	751	772	755

Source: adapted from Glass (1954 : 186–7).
Sample: men aged 20 and over in 1949.

mobility in the two tables, at least for the overlapping cohorts.

The main impression from Table 3.2 is that the first part of the century saw increasing *im*mobility, largely due to a fall in the rate of upward mobility.[8] And so, putting the results of the 1949 and 1972 enquiries together, the view we get is indeed one of 'trendless fluctuation', the depression years seeing greater stability, the post-war economic boom greater mobility.

Unfortunately, this is a somewhat myopic view – we do not see very far, and what we see is blurred and fuzzy. The fuzziness arises from the fact that Glass's work confuses age and cohort effects: the respondents were asked about their own and their fathers' present (i.e. 1949) jobs or about their last main job if they were already retired.

And since many sons will still have been at early stages in their careers whereas most of the fathers will have been retired or towards the end of their working lives, this means that like is not being compared with like. It is not obvious how this will affect the rate of *total* mobility – hence the fuzziness. It means that there will be less upward mobility in the younger cohorts, promotions coming later in one's career, but there might equally be more downward, too, as the sons of high-status fathers enter the labour market at lower levels preparatory to promotion back to high-status destinations (the phenomenon of 'counter-mobility', as it has been called). If we plot the career paths over time of men from upper- and lower-class backgrounds, they appear as in Diagram 3.1.

Diagram 3.1 Career paths over time[9]

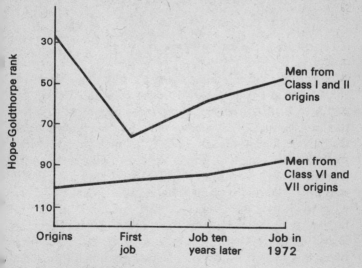

Source: Oxford Social Mobility Group.
Sample: men aged 40–59 in 1972.

The second source of myopia is our limited view of the past. Even with Glass's oldest cohorts we do not get back beyond the end of the nineteenth century. But the theory of ascription and achievement is in principle dealing with a much longer time-span than this. At heart it is a theory of the transformation of pre-industrial into advanced industrial societies, and any protagonist of the theory could reasonably assert that the fluctuation which we think we have discerned is but a movement around a longer-run rising trend. One fluctuation does not make a generalization about the history of mankind.

I do not think we are ever going to produce valid generalizations about the history of mankind, but studies of elite recruitment do enable us to push the historical record a little further back into the nineteenth century, a rather shorter time period, perhaps, but not a wholly uninteresting one.

Trends in elite recruitment

Whatever their limitations, the studies by Glass's team at the LSE and by the Oxford Social Mobility Group are the only British ones based on large and representative national samples. They are our only sources of information about the mobility experience of the 'man in the street'. We can supplement them, as we did in Chapter 2, with studies of elite recruitment which cover varying periods in the past. Boyd (1973) takes his study of *Who's Who* back to 1939, Kelsall (1955 and 1974) takes the study of the higher civil service back to 1929; Harbury and Hitchens (1979) take their study of the wealthy back to 1924; Morgan's (1969) study of bishops goes back to 1860; Stanworth and Giddens's (1974) study of the chairmen of major corporations starts with chairmen in office from

1900; Erickson's (1959) study of executive directors in steel-manufacturing and hosiery takes her steelmen back to 1865 and her hosiers to 1844; Compton (1968) looks at changes in recruitment to the Indian civil service in the mid-nineteenth century; Otley's (1970) study of recruits to Sandhurst goes back to 1810; and Razzell's (1963) study of Indian army officers to 1758.

We can certainly use this material to produce some kind of story about mobility patterns in the second half of the nineteenth century, but it is a story interspersed with long silences. The coverage of elite groups is, to put it mildly, patchy; and all the studies are based on *inflow* analyses in contrast with the *outflow* analyses we have reported from Glass and Goldthorpe. Boyd's is a good example of the techniques used. A list of the elite members is compiled from some written source, and a search is then conducted for information about their fathers. Boyd had the easiest job. He merely had to turn up back copies of *Who's Who* or *Who Was Who* (although even he had to face problems of misidentification). The problems were much worse for Erickson or Stanworth and Giddens. They had to rummage through whatever biographical information was available about their subjects, and they are of course totally at the mercy of the fragments that have survived the passage of time. In turn, we are totally at the mercy of the thoroughness with which the search has been conducted. All the standard problems of contemporary survey research – non-response, interviewer bias, misinterpretation of the question, coding errors – have an equally or even more serious equivalent in historical research.

With this general warning that historical research is not a soft option for sociologists dissatisfied with survey research, let us proceed to the results. They are set out below

Table 3.3 Trends in elite recruitment

Author	Group studied	Time period	Results
Boyd (1973)	Higher civil servants, ambassadors, judges, admirals, generals, air marshalls, bishops and bank directors	1939–70	A slight increase over time in the openness of the higher civil service, but no change recorded with any of the other groups.[10]
Kelsall (1955, 1974)	Higher civil servants	1929–67	'A certain, if not spectacular, broadening of the band of types of social and educational background from which top civil servants were drawn over this period of nearly 40 years' (Kelsall, 1974:174), the proportion with fathers in routine non-manual or in manual work increasing from 12 per cent in 1929 to 31 per cent in 1967.
Morgan (1969), Thompson (1974)	English diocesan bishops	1860–1960	'[A] decline in landed and peerage connections, and [a] shift in terms of parental occupation from old landed ruling class to a more professional background (especially worthy of note being the increase in the number of bishops whose fathers were themselves clergymen).' (Thompson, 1974:200.)
Harbury and Hitchens (1979)	Wealth-leavers	1924–73	'The importance of fathers' wealth for substantial wealth-leavers (those leaving over £50,000 in 1956–7 prices) did not appear to change greatly between the mid-1920s

			and the mid-1950s. Thereafter a decline was observable in 1965, which appeared to continue in 1973.' (Harbury and Hitchens, 1979:67.)
Stanworth and Giddens (1974)	Chairmen of major corporations and banks	1900–72	'Our data do not indicate that there has occurred a process of increasing "openness" of recruitment to the Chairs of the largest corporations but, if anything, something the contrary of this.... But these phenomena vary to some degree according to the type of economic sector in question. Banking is clearly shown to be the most fixed and unchanging.' (Stanworth and Giddens, 1974:89.)
Erickson (1959)	Executive directors in steel manufacturing	1865–1953	No change during the nineteenth century but an increasing proportion with fathers in routine non-manual and manual occupations in the first half of the twentieth century.
Erickson (1959)	Executive directors in hosiery	1844–1952	Fluctuations in recruitment throughout the period, with the twentieth century slightly more open than the nineteenth.
Otley (1970)	Entrants to Sandhurst, Entrants to Woolwich, Lieutenant-generals and above	1810–1939 1880–1939 1913–59	'There seems to have been a slow trend towards the "democratisation" of recruitment, but it was only really during war-time that the lower social strata sent really substantial numbers of boys to Sandhurst and Woolwich.' (Otley, 1970:231–2.) 'Open competitive entry undoubtedly helped to break the stranglehold the upper class had on the officer corps, but it also helped to establish, in its turn, a new stranglehold – that of the upper middle class.' (Otley, 1970:234.)

Table 3.3 (cont.)

Author	Group studied	Time period	Results
Razzell (1963)	Officers in the Indian army	1758–1834	'The purchase system ensured that the British army was never closed to the wealthy middle classes – the Indian army allowed lesser lights to quench their thirst for social status.' (Razzell, 1963:259.)
Razzell (1963)	Officers in the British home army	1780–1952	'Perhaps the most surprising finding of the study was the way the landed upper classes maintained their position within the army throughout the nineteenth century and even into the twentieth. The great watershed was of course the First World War. After this war members of the landed classes were remnants; although very important remnants.' (Razzell, 1963:259.)
Compton (1968)	Entrants to the Indian civil service	1854–76	'Those who profited most from the abolition of patronage were the clergy and the professional classes whose sons together made up nearly a half of the "new competitives". Representation of the landed interest was cut from a quarter to a tenth whilst Indian civilians who might formerly have pushed their sons in as "hard bargains" found such a channel of automatic employment blocked.' (Compton, 1968:283.)

in Table 3.3. Trendless fluctuation is not so evident in elite recruitment. The general movement has been towards greater openness, although the slow pace and unevenness of the development is perhaps the most striking feature. The British elite is not a homogeneous one; its different sectors have had varying success in resisting, or adapting to, the pressures for reform. In the mid-nineteenth century the aristocracy and landed gentry dominated the upper echelons of the 'gentlemanly' professions of the City, the church and the armed forces. The civil service and manufacturing industry were probably never quite so aristocratic in their connections, although steel, at least, was already an industry requiring large amounts of capital investment, and its leaders were certainly men of substance and privilege.

In the hundred years after 1850, however, a variety of reforms and social pressures opened some of these elite occupations, but to varying degrees. The direct reform of the forces, through the introduction of open competitive examinations, loosened the stranglehold of the upper classes and landed gentry and opened up a route for the children of the professional middle classes. The new educational requirements gave birth to some, and new lease of life to other, so-called 'public' schools. By 1900 they provided 85 per cent of Sandhurst entrants, and even in 1936 they provided 84 per cent (see Otley, 1978). Similarly in the civil service, competitive examinations and the abolition of patronage probably reduced the intake from the landed gentry and gave new opportunities to the professional middle classes who were able to make use of the public schools. In Otley's words, 'Open competitive entry undoubtedly helped to break the stranglehold [of the upper class] ... but it also helped to establish, in its turn, a new stranglehold – that of the upper middle class.' (Otley,

1970:234.) On the Indian civil service, Compton remarked that 'the abolition of patronage came as a gift to the clergy [but] the Service was hardly wide open to the sons of drapers, undertakers, and gamekeepers.' (Compton, 1968:283.)

But while the latter part of the nineteenth century saw the rise of the upper middle classes and the public schools in the civil service and the military, and the first part of the twentieth century saw its consolidation, the period since the Second World War has seen the beginnings of a new transformation of the civil service – the rise of the grammar-school boy from the lower middle or working classes. It has been a slow rise and one that has not yet threatened the ascendancy of the professional classes, but by 1967 a third of the higher civil servants came from state schools compared with a tenth in 1939, and a third came from routine white-collar or manual working-class homes. It has not yet achieved the *carrière ouverte aux talents* but it is nonetheless a radical transformation from the position of the 1850s.

The civil service has probably been the success story of direct governmental or educational reforms on access to elite positions. Here, if anywhere, has been increasing openness and the replacement of ascription by, to a limited extent, achievement. Indeed, in a formal sense, the abolition of patronage, the institution of competitive examinations, and the spread of universal secondary education so that all could sit the exams, is what some writers mean by a shift from ascription to achievement. There is now *formal* equality of opportunity for all in the civil service, although whether there is *effective* equality of opportunity is another matter: it is a familiar cliché (that will be examined more rigorously in Chapter 5) that home background still affects one's educational achievements.

In the other sectors of the elite the move from ascription to achievement is not so clear-cut. There is prima facie evidence in Erickson's material of greater openness in industry, but examination of the career paths of her industrialists reveals a rather more subtle picture. In 1865 56 per cent of her steel manufacturers were 'independents', men who had founded the firms which they controlled (or who had established and led a firm in another business before entering the steel industry); 30 per cent were 'heirs', men who had taken over their fathers' firms or gained control through the investment of inherited wealth; only 14 per cent were salaried professionals or administrators. By 1953 the independents had been almost wholly eliminated by the salaried administrators, reflecting the growth of bureaucracy; the independents were down to 3 per cent, the salaried administrators and professionals up to 57 per cent. But the 'heirs' had more than held their own, comprising 40 per cent of the total in 1953. (See Appendix I, Table 6.)

The concentration of industry and the spread of large-scale bureaucracies has undoubtedly squeezed out the individual entrepreneur, not only in steel manufacturing but probably in industry generally. But here bureaucracy and its principles of achievement and meritocratic selection and promotion has triumphed not over patronage and nepotism as it did in the civil service but over a different kind of achievement, that of the self-made man in the competitive market. Bureaucracy has replaced the market, not the family. In the boardroom (although probably not lower down in the middle ranks of management) the family seems to have long retained its position.

The civil service, the armed forces and industry provide the best case for a shift from ascription to achievement. The City provides the worst case. Here there have been no government reforms and competitive examinations, and while the clearing banks have clearly become vast bureaucracies which are probably as meritocratic as any throughout their lower ranks, the merchant banks remain relatively small and, it would appear, even more exclusive (Stanworth and Giddens, 1974:92). If Blau and Duncan are right in general that 'society cannot any longer afford the waste of human resources a rigid class structure entails. Universalistic principles have penetrated deep into the fabric of modern society and given rise to high rates of occupational mobility in response to this need' (Blau and Duncan, 1967:431), we must conclude nevertheless that one particular part of that fabric – the City – has proved remarkably resistant to penetration.

Mobility in pre-industrial Britain

None of the studies we have looked at so far takes us any further back than the mid-nineteenth century, to the high point of Victorian capitalism. If we wish to go back further we are even more pressed to find reliable historical sources. We have contemporary testimony from a number of periods. Waterhouse in 1665 produced what was probably the first ever monograph on social mobility with his *Gentleman's Monitor or a Sober Inspection into the Vertues, Vices and ordinary Means of the Rise and Decay of Men and Families*. Gaskell (1833) and Cobbett (1827) both demonstrate that there was certainly some long-range upward mobility in the early nineteenth century. Cobbett was responsible for that famous phrase, 'from the dunghill to the chariot'. He wrote: '. . . this hatred to the cause of public liberty is, I am sorry to say it, but too common amongst merchants, great manufacturers, and great farmers; especially those who have *risen suddenly* from the dunghill to the chariot. If we look a little more closely into the influence of riches . . . we shall be less surprised at this apparently unnatural feeling in men who were, but the other day, merely journeymen and labourers themselves. . . . Such men are always seeking to cause their origin to be forgotten. . . . Their chief aim is to trample into the very ground all who are beneath them in point of pecuniary circumstances, in order that they may have as few equals as possible, and that there may be *as wide a distance as possible between themselves and their labourers.*' (Cobbett, 1827:86; italics in original.)

We also have a number of studies of particular groups and periods. Grassby (1978) has looked at the social origins of apprentices in the seventeenth century, the successors of Dick Whittington whose rise from apprenticeship to be Lord Mayor of London is probably more than simply heroic legend. Everitt (1966) has studied recruitment to the gentry in the seventeenth century, too, and Stone has contributed a more general (and speculative) piece on the same century, arguing that it saw 'a phase of unprecedented individual mobility, upwards and downwards, followed by a fresh period of stability' (Stone, 1966:33).

There are two main planks to Stone's case. The dissolution of the monasteries in the sixteenth century made large quantities of land available for purchase. Since landownership was the key to social status, wealthy merchants and traders could thus buy their way in, and while they may not have acquired social acceptance for themselves, their descendants inherited the land and joined the ranks of the hereditary landowner. The second plank rests on the principle of primogeniture. The English practice in the seventeenth century was not to divide the estate equally between all offspring. Instead, the eldest son inherited the property and the other male offspring (if there were any) had to look elsewhere for a living. The proposition that the second son went into the army and the third into the church was probably not without foundation, but there is also evidence that some landowners' sons went into commerce, joining the great livery companies as apprentices. Since there seemed to be a high rate of fertility among the landowners in this period, there was a surplus of younger sons and thus an exodus from the elite into lower-status positions. Subsequently, Stone claims, fertility declined among the elite and no new sources of land became available. The elite thus tended once more to closure and, as Everitt puts it, 'within a couple of generations, however, the flowing lava of local society had solidified' (Everitt, 1966:65).

On the eighteenth century we have Pollard's (1965) study of the genesis of modern management and Sanderson's (1972) brave effort to look at 'mass' mobility using the Lancaster Charity School Registers for 1770–1816. Again, both saw evidence of considerable mobility and Pollard concluded that in the industrial revolution 'society was at least as open to the talents, in the industrial commercial sphere, as it has been at any time since' (Pollard, 1965:128).

Management, it seems, may have been a hopeful avenue of upward mobility in the late eighteenth century for the man of talent but no financial resources, just as it is today. Pollard documents the way in which the salaried manager could use profit-sharing schemes to join the ranks of the industrial capitalists. By giving the manager a small salary but a large share of the profits, the capitalists ensured that his interests were intimately linked to their own but at the same time enabled him to build up his own stake in the company. Pollard gives the example shown in Table 3.4, from the firm of Newton Chambers.

Table 3.4 The rise of the salaried manager

	1799		1802		1817	
	Capital £	Share of profits	Capital £	Share of profits	Capital £	Share of profits
Active (managing) partners:						
G. Newton	1577	$\frac{1}{4}$	1740	$\frac{1}{5}$	16,360	$\frac{1}{3}$
T. Chambers	668	$\frac{1}{4}$	931	$\frac{1}{5}$	14,852	$\frac{1}{3}$
Sleeping partners:						
H. Longden	6247	$\frac{1}{2}$	7215	$\frac{2}{5}$	—	—
R. & T. Scott	—	—	4746	$\frac{1}{5}$	19,878	$\frac{1}{3}$
	8492		14,632		51,090	

Source: Pollard (1965 : 179).

In 1799 Newton and Chambers were clearly getting a much larger share of the profit than their capital holdings alone would have warranted, but by ploughing back these profits into the business they both built up the firm and achieved parity with the sleeping partners. It is probably this kind of man that Gaskell had in mind when he wrote: 'Men who did establish themselves were raised by their own efforts – commencing in a very humble way, and pushing their advance by a series of unceasing exertions, having a very limited capital to begin with, or even none at all save that of their own labour.' (Gaskell, 1833 : 45.)

We have to be careful with these historical accounts however. The only hard evidence we get are particular *examples* of, say, landowners' sons who were apprenticed into the livery companies or of salaried managers who became capitalists. This can be quite illuminating about the processes at work, but we do not really know how common they were, even in their own period, much less how they compared with other periods. Historians often refuse to generalize; their evidence is such that generalization is usually unwise. What we need are proper time-series where a standard set of information has been collected about a well-defined population over a long period of time. There are two such data sets: university admissions records (Jenkins and Caradog Jones, 1950; Stone, 1975),[11] and the marriage records of the peerage (Hollingsworth, 1964; Thomas, 1972). Let us see what we can make of them.

With this kind of historical material, problems of data interpretation become crucial and the hazards involved with, say, cohort analysis of the modern social survey pale into insignificance. Take Oxbridge admissions records, for example. While studies of educational background are currently very popular among elite theorists and close links have been found between elite membership and an Oxbridge education (Boyd, for example, finding that around three-quarters of his top civil servants, ambassadors and judiciary in 1970 had been educated at Oxford and Cambridge), the relation between Oxbridge and the elite has undoubtedly changed over time. In the eighteenth century, for example, Oxford and Cambridge fell into decay. The numbers attending dropped and Gibbon's caustic comment about the idleness of Oxford dons was probably not far off the mark: 'From the toil of reading, or thinking, or writing, they had absolved their conscience.' Oxford was at that time an intellectual and political backwater and it is probable that the only elite institution to which it gave regular access was the Church. Jenkins and Caradog Jones show that 60 per cent of the Cambridge alumni of the second half of the eighteenth century became clergymen, compared with 6 per cent in 1937–8, and Oxford would not have been so different.

The other crucial problem, which will apply to almost any long-term historical study, not just to university admissions, is that social categories will change their meaning. For most of the period with which he deals, Stone reports, the Oxford records distinguished between the sons of peers, baronets, knights, esquires (armigers), gentry and clergy. Everyone else was indiscriminately labelled 'plebeian' – 'a word which covered all social categories from the prosperous yeoman or wealthy merchant downward – meaning over 90 per cent of the population of the country' (Stone, 1975 : 14).

In the sixteenth century the term 'armiger' meant someone authorized to bear a coat of arms, while gentry were supposed to be country gentlemen resident in country houses. Over the succeeding centuries there was a debasement of these categories. By the middle of the seventeenth century, says Stone, 'the term "gent" was being increasingly used by men engaged in middle-class occupations and earning middle-class incomes, but who had no serious pretensions to gentility. Thus in 1624 H. Willett was registered as the son of H. Willett of Exeter, "woollen draper, generosae conditionis", which suggests that the registrar himself had lingering doubts about the compatibility of the two descriptions.' (Stone, 1975 : 14.) Similarly there was a collapse in the seventeenth century of all attempts by the College of Arms to regulate heraldic claims, so that 'by the days of Charles Dickens, successful members of the commercial classes and the professions were calling themselves esquire, without any recollection of its original meaning'.

I mention these really rather devastating problems on the principle that it is better to know the extent of our ignorance, and why we are ignorant, than to believe erroneously that we are or could be knowledgeable. So when Stone shows a dramatic decline in the proportion of plebeians entering Oxford over the three-and-a-half centuries that he encompasses, we do well to be on our guard. In the sixteenth century over half the matriculants admitted to being plebeians; virtually none did so by the end of the nineteenth. But given the debasement of status categories that was taking place, it would be a foolish man who believed the story these figures tell. On the other hand, if Stone is correct in supposing that 90 per cent of the population were plebeian in the sixteenth and seventeenth centuries, the fact that about half the Oxford matriculants then admitted to plebeian status does make Oxford look relatively open even by modern standards. It is very doubtful whether the 'bottom' 90 per cent of the population were getting more than half the places at university (leave alone Oxford) even in the mid-twentieth century (see Halsey, Heath and Ridge, 1980: Table 10.4).

But while university admissions records warn us of the pitfalls that lie in wait for the unwary sociologist who meddles in historical research, the records of peers' marriages may offer us firmer footing. There is a clearly defined universe of peers to be studied, and virtually all of them have left behind some biographical information. There can be little argument about whether someone was or was not a peer, and while some governments may have been more liberal in their creation of peerages it can reasonably be argued that this will reflect real changes in society and social relations rather than changes in language use.

Hollingsworth's results are given in Table 3.5. We should regard these figures much as we did those for elite stability in Chapter 2. On the other hand, the fact that

Table 3.5 Marriages of the peerage

Cohort born	Males' marriages		Females' marriages	
	N	% noble	N	% noble
1550–74	64	25·0	58	34·5
1575–99	359	37·6	404	29·5
1600–24	554	41·3	701	31·2
1625–49	552	38·0	636	33·0
1650–74	516	36·6	626	30·8
1675–99	492	33·3	532	32·0
1700–24	513	23·2	461	27·3
1725–49	428	25·0	395	26·6
1750–74	669	26·5	617	26·1
1775–99	739	27·5	708	28·5
1800–24	915	24·3	800	26·2
1825–49	986	23·7	833	28·2
1850–74	1067	20·2	971	22·5
1875–99	862	18·7	842	21·9
1900–24	295	12·5	284	14·1
1925–49	9	11·1	11	9·1
All	9020	26.9	8879	27.2

Source: adapted from Hollingsworth (1964).
Sample: legitimate offspring of peers who died between 1603 and 1938.

only in about a quarter of the marriages were both partners from the peerage indicates substantial female mobility both in and out of the peerage; but on the other hand, it is a proportion that is probably much more than a hundred times greater than would be expected if marriage partners were chosen without regard to their social origins.

Whereas Oxford admissions records, if we take them at

face value, seem to give evidence of trendless fluctuation, the marriages of the peerage show a clear and long-run trend towards greater openness. It is not of course a completely smooth trend but looks more like a series of downward steps. The first major step occurs in the first half of the eighteenth century as the birth cohort of 1700–25 were contracting their marriages (a step that may seem to contrast oddly with Everitt's assertion that the flowing lava of local society solidified at that time). The second major step occurs in the second half of the nineteenth century, and thereafter follows a headlong downward flight, paralleling the increasing openness that we have seen from other studies of elite recruitment over this period.

We should not make the mistake, however, of supposing that all these marriages made outside the peerage involved long-range mobility for either of the partners. Thomas (1972) has shown that in the eighteenth century the majority of these out-marriages were with knights, baronets and the landed gentry, perhaps reflecting the gradual social acceptance of those new landed families whose rise Stone described. And in the nineteenth century, as marriage within the peerage and gentry declined, their places were taken by foreign and military families. The greater openness of the peerage to marriage with commoners over these two centuries, it appears, did not extend to those whose fathers actually had to work for a living in 'ordinary' jobs in Class I such as the professions and business. The common belief that wealthy heiresses of commoner stock were acceptable to the peerage even if their ill-bred fathers were not does not stand up to the evidence. Rather, when peers went outside the aristocracy and gentry for their brides, they turned either overseas or to the armed forces. It is hard to resist the thought that imperialism rather than industrialism is what mattered to the aristocracy.

Conclusions

There is little support here for any simple thesis. The memorable slogans of 'trendless fluctuation' and 'expanding universalism' offer us half-truths at best. Certainly we have seen fluctuations in mass mobility during the twentieth century, the depression years bringing greater immobility and the expanding opportunities of the post-war years reversing the trend. But these were almost certainly fluctuations around a long-run rising tendency. The sheer arithmetic of the occupational structure means that if we go back to, say, the seventeenth century, when manual workers and farm labourers came to far more than 50 per cent of the population and the urban middle class to less than 10 per cent, total mobility rates across the manual/non-manual line must necessarily have been far lower than they are today.[12]

If we turn to elite mobility we find some support for the rival thesis of expanding universalism. The reforms of the civil service and the military were the embodiment of a shift from ascription to achievement. Open competitive entry instead of patronage and purchase gave new opportunities to the educated offspring of the upper middle classes and there can be little doubt that the nineteenth century saw greater access to these particular elite occupations.

But the City, on the other hand, was not reformed (and still has not been), nor is it obvious that expanding universalism is the best characterization of the changes in the higher echelons of industry. The spread of bureaucracy has seen the rise of the salaried employee to the boardroom, but the group which has lost out is that of the independent entrepreneur. It is not the victory of achievement over ascription but of one kind of achievement over another – that of the salaried bureaucrat over the self-made man.

Further back in time we lose sight of the underlying trends in a mist of patchy data and shifting definitions. Each historian seems to think that his own particular time or group were unusually open, and perhaps they were. The same story of expanding opportunities that explains the increase in mass mobility in the mid-twentieth century may also account for the accessibility of the gentry in the seventeenth, as land flooded on to the market, and of management and capitalism in the eighteenth as the industrial revolution got under way. Fluctuations there may well have been as new opportunities arose, were filled, and closed.

But our one long-run time-series of any credibility, the marriage records of the peerage, shows a continuous if uneven move to greater openness. This has little to do with universalism and achievement and does not mean that social barriers between the different strata of society have crumbled. Rather, it suggests that the exclusivity of the hereditary peerage has declined as the aristocracy has gradually merged with an only slightly broader grouping – the landed gentry, the military and the financial elite.[13] The English elite has never been completely impermeable, and has become slightly less so over time, but its different sectors have not all opened their doors equally wide and they are not equally happy about whom they will let in.

4 The Mobility of Women

Until now in this book women have been conspicuous by their absence. This has been the usual fate of women in research on mobility and stratification. Apart from his remark that through marriage 'some people have made their careers; some others have ruined them' (Sorokin, 1927:179), Sorokin has virtually nothing to say about women; Lipset and Bendix's international comparisons deal exclusively with the mobility of adult males; Glass had data available on women but analysed only the mobility of men (although Kelsall and Mitchell, 1959, subsequently did report the material); Blau and Duncan, and the Oxford Social Mobility Group restricted themselves to male samples (although also collecting some data on their male respondents' wives and mothers).

The usual justification for the omission of women from these studies is that in Western capitalist societies married women are primarily involved in domestic labour within the household and are economically dependent upon their husbands. The man's job is the major articulation between the family and the class structure. Thus 'inequalities associated with sex differences are not usefully thought of as components of stratification' (Parkin, 1971:14), and: 'Given that women still have to await their liberation from the family it remains the case in capitalist societies that female workers are largely peripheral to the class system. . . .' (Giddens, 1973 : 288.)

Perhaps the clearest treatment of this problem is given by John Goldthorpe. He begins by pointing out that throughout the period covered by the 1972 survey, the majority of married women were not in paid employment. In 1931 the figure was only 10 per cent, in 1951 around 20 per cent, and even in 1971 only about 40 per cent of married women had paid jobs. Of those who had paid jobs, perhaps only half were in full-time employment, and the kind of employment conditions they had were either 'similar to those of their husbands, or inferior – so that the "dominance" of the latter's class position is rarely affected'. Goldthorpe then concludes: 'In other words we would wish to maintain the view that – whatever current trends of change in women's work and family life may portend – during the decades preceding our enquiry, and to which our data relate, it has been through the role of their male members within the social division of labour that families have been crucially articulated with the class structure and their class "fates" crucially determined. Or conversely, one could say, the way in which women have been located in the class structure has reflected their general situation of dependence.' (Goldthorpe, 1980 : 288.) If there is sexism in sociology, then, it is because it accurately reflects the sexism within the wider society.

Not altogether surprisingly, the other major commentators on mid-century Britain – Westergaard and Resler – hold the same position. 'The conclusion is then plain that the inequalities of the female labour market – internally and in relation to the male labour market – in no sense take away from or cut across the general pattern of class inequality. On the contrary, they sharpen class divisions.' (Westergaard and Resler 1975 : 104.) Women in manual work, they argue, are recruited almost exclusively from working-class families while women in higher-level white-collar jobs come from middle-class families. Only in the routine grades of non-manual work – typists, secretaries and shop-assistants – are class lines blurred. 'There may well be consequences of some social significance arising from that meeting: from the fact that increasing numbers of wives, and especially daughters, of manual workers get a foot inside the world of non-manual work. But the social implications are probably limited by a number of other factors. It is likely that working-class women are concentrated disproportionately in the most routine grades of clerical and saleswork, with the least opportunities for promotion and for contact with their superiors.' (Westergaard and Resler, 1975 : 105.) Their main thesis is thus rescued, and they finish their chapter on women in the labour market with the final, insistent message that 'class divisions, to repeat, are accentuated by the heavy incidence of sex discrimination in the lower ranges of the labour market. There is no neutralization or contradiction here of one form of inequality by another: the two are linked.' (Westergaard and Resler, 1975 : 106.)

Where there is such unanimity among the sociologists, it is a good idea to be wary.[1] There is a danger that the self-evident character of the premises will distract us from the need to check the conclusions. It is not in dispute that for the first half of this century (except in wartime), most married women's work was domestic labour while many of those in wage labour worked part-time and for low wages, and in similar class positions to their husbands. (See Kelsall and Mitchell, 1959; DoE, 1974; Halsey, 1972 : 116.) Nor is it in dispute that important changes in female employment may now be occurring. But what is not clear is the *significance* of women's employment and mobility for class action and class formation. Does the fact that 'increasing numbers of wives, and especially daughters, of manual workers get a foot inside the world of non-manual work' have any impact on the social cohesion of the working class? Westergaard and Resler give an *a priori* argument for supposing that it does not, but *a priori* arguments are no substitute for evidence.

A second reservation is that all our major commentators have defined patterns of class stratification as their central concern. But even if they are right in asserting that 'female workers are largely peripheral to the class system', other issues remain. The liberal issue of equality of opportunity is the foremost candidate. How do women's chances of upward and downward mobility compare with those of men from similar social origins? Is it true for Britain, as it seems to be for America, that 'patterns of marital mobility of women are more similar to the occupational mobility of men than to the occupational mobility of women' (Tyree and Treas, 1974: 300)? And what are the relative chances of women from different social origins? Do the same inequalities of opportunity hold among women that we have already seen among men? Or does class divide men but sex bring women together?

There are, then, three main questions which concern us in this chapter. First, how do women's marital and occupational mobility chances compare with the social mobility of men? Secondly, how great are the inequalities of opportunity which divide women themselves? Thirdly, what is the significance of women's occupational and marital mobility for class action and class formation? We may find that there are more questions than answers, I should warn the reader now, but the questions should nonetheless be posed.

Mobility through marriage

The expression 'marital mobility' is a rather unfortunate one, although it has now become something of a technical term in American sociology.[2] It assumes that a woman's status or class position is determined by her husband's occupation, and it implies that the woman's own achievements have little to do with her husband's fate. The assumption is questionable: if we are concerned with status (in the strict sense of the term) rather than class, we could well maintain that the woman's education will be paramount. And the implication is unsound: there is evidence that a woman's educational achievements have a considerable effect on the British man's occupational attainment (see Kerckhoff, 1978). The woman should not always be treated as the passive beneficiary of her husband's activity. Doubtless this will be true in some cases, but in others it might be much better to talk of the *husband's* marital mobility.

Nonetheless, it may be of considerable interest in its own right to examine the relationship between a man's social class and that of his father-in-law, for this is in fact all that tables of women's marital mobility record. What interpretation is placed on the table is, as always, a matter for the reader's discretion, but the table itself bears some study.

Table 4.1 takes all the men in the Oxford Social Mobility Group's 1972 survey who were, or had been, married, and cross-tabulates them according to the occupation which their father-in-law held when the respondent's wife was aged fourteen. It is thus analogous to the inter-generational mobility table presented in Chapter 2, Table 2.1, and the figures in italics show the differences between the two tables.

Table 4.1 Marital mobility

Father-in-law's class	Respondent's class (%)								
	I	II	III	IV	V	VI	VII	Total	N
I	42·2	18·9	7·2	7·4	7·8	7·0	9·6	100·1	488
	−6	=	−2	−1	+3	+3	+3		
II	29·7	20·2	8·0	11·1	10·3	11·4	9·3	100·0	377
	−2	−2	−3	+3	+1	+2	+1		
III	19·7	16·5	10·2	9·1	11·0	18·5	15·0	100·0	547
	+1	+1	−1	+1	−2	+3	−3		
IV	15·8	11·9	8·8	18·2	10·6	15·2	19·5	100·0	1048
	+3	+1	+1	−7	+2	=	=		
V	15·4	15·2	9·6	9·5	12·1	19·2	18·9	99·9	676
	=	+2	=	+2	−5	−1	+2		
VI	10·3	8·8	8·1	9·1	13·0	26·7	24·0	100·0	2221
	+2	=	=	+2	+1	−3	−1		
VII	8·0	7·6	7·7	8·6	13·9	24·5	29·8	100·1	2020
	+1	=	=	+2	+1	+1	−5		
%	14·7	11·3	8·3	10·3	12·2	21·1	22·1	100·0	(7377)
	=	=	=	=	+1	=	−1		

Source: Oxford Social Mobility Group.
Sample: married men aged 25–64 in 1972.
The figures in italics give the deviation from the corresponding cell in Table 2.1.
For details of the social class classification, see Chapter 2, pages 52–3.

Two main features are immediately apparent from Table 4.1. First, there is no large-scale net tendency for women to 'marry up'. The class distribution of the married men is almost identical to that of the total male population given in Table 2.1 whereas marrying-up would leave a surplus of single men in low-status occupations (and a balancing surplus of single women in high-status occupations). The similarity between the two distributions is hardly surprising given that the great majority of adults do at some point get married. However, if we look at the social origins of the small minority of single people (see Table 4.3) we do find an imbalance, and it does seem that a few high-origin women remain single rather than marrying down while low-origin men may be at a slight competitive disadvantage in the marriage market. But the differences are small and, quantitatively at least, the problem of high-status spinsters and low-status bachelors is not a major one in modern Britain.

On the other hand, we see that there is a great deal of 'marrying up' that is balanced by other women 'marrying down'. This interchange is very extensive, more so indeed than the father–son interchange of Table 2.1. The British class structure would appear to be rather more fluid than consideration of father–son mobility alone would have us believe. The typical father from Class I is more likely to see his daughter downwardly mobile than his son, or, to be more precise, to have a son-in-law of lower social class than his son. Conversely, the girl from Classes VI or VII is more likely to be upwardly mobile than her brother.

But again the differences are not all that great. This can be seen if we compute some summary indices. In Table 4.1, total mobility between the seven classes amounts to 76 per cent, compared with 72 per cent for Table 2.1. Upward mobility (treating movement between Classes III to VI as being neither up nor down) comes to 36 per cent instead of 31 per cent; downward mobility to 19 per cent instead of 18 per cent, and manual/non-manual mobility (treating Classes V–VII as manual and the rest as non-manual) to 37 per cent instead of 34. Both tables give an impression of considerable openness, and the differences between them are much less remarkable than the similarities.

If we restrict ourselves to marital mobility, therefore, we find slightly greater movement for women than for men, or, to put it more strictly, a man's class position is likely to be more similar to his father's than to his father-in-law's. There is both more downward and more upward mobility through marriage for women than there is through the labour market for men. In this sense a woman's 'class fate' is more loosely linked to her social origins than is a man's.

Occupational mobility: inequalities between men and women

Marital mobility is, we have implied, a somewhat sexist concept. But occupational mobility may fall into the opposite trap. The occupations of many married women are part-time; they affect, for many people quite crucially, their overall standard of living but will not be the major component of family income. And if, as many sociologists argue, we should take the family as the unit of stratification, the relationship between a married woman's own occupation and her position in the class structure will be in many cases a loose one.[3] Again, however, I would argue that the relation between a woman's social origins and her occupational position is of interest in its own right, and we shall present such evidence as is available on it.

Despite the general omission of women from mobility surveys, there is fortunately one recent source which we can utilize. This is the General Household Survey conducted for the government by the Office of Population Censuses and Surveys.[4] It is mainly used to obtain information required by government departments but the

1972 and 1975 surveys also obtained the basic biographical information required for mobility studies from representative national samples including both men and women. Unfortunately, the data on fathers' occupations are not coded in the same way as in the earlier studies we have used, and so in addition to the Hall–Jones classification and Goldthorpe's schema, used respectively by Glass and the Oxford Social Mobility Group, we must now get used to a third one based on the socio-economic groups distinguished by the OPCS. I have grouped these into seven classes not entirely dissimilar from Goldthorpe's, but they differ in detail and the reader should check the small print carefully.[5]

Table 4.2 cross-tabulates the current (i.e. 1975) occupation of employed women by their fathers' occupations. It includes both married and single women, both full-time and part-time workers. To compare women's occupational mobility with men's the corresponding table was calculated for the male respondents in the General Household Survey (see Appendix I Table 7) and the differences between the two are given in italics in Table 4.2.[6]

Table 4.2 provides a major if unsurprising contrast with Table 4.1. The occupational distribution of women is very different from that of men: it is a 'bimodal' one with women heavily concentrated in lower white-collar work and semi- or unskilled manual work and grossly under-represented both in higher-grade professional and managerial and in skilled manual work. Not surprisingly, then, women from Class I and II origins tend to be downwardly mobile in large numbers, and there is nothing like the tendency for daughters to follow in their fathers' footsteps that there was for the sons from Class I. There appears to be a gross inequality of opportunity between men and women here. Among both there is a surplus of upward over downward

Table 4.2 Women's occupational mobility: outflow

Father's class	Respondent's class (%)							Total	N
	I	II	III	IV	V	VI	VII		
I & II	8·4	24·1	52·7	0·4	0·0	2·9	11·6	100·1	490
	− 23	*+ 4*	*+ 37*	*− 1*	*− 4*	*− 15*	*+ 2*		
III	4·4	21·8	54·8	0·8	0·0	2·4	15·7	99·9	248
	− 17	*+ 3*	*+ 38*	*+ 1*	*− 6*	*− 20*	*+ 1*		
IV	2·6	16·2	47·2	0·4	0·8	5·1	27·7	100·0	235
	− 11	*+ 5*	*+ 35*	*− 1*	*− 8*	*− 28*	*+ 7*		
V	2·3	10·9	55·8	0·8	0·8	1·6	27·9	100·1	129
	− 10	*− 1*	*+ 45*	*=*	*− 12*	*− 31*	*+ 8*		
VI	1·6	11·2	49·6	0·2	1·6	6·4	29·3	99·9	1101
	− 9	*+ 1*	*+ 39*	*=*	*− 7*	*− 33*	*+ 9*		
VII	1·2	10·3	47·4	0·0	1·5	5·2	34·3	99·9	842
	− 6	*+ 1*	*+ 38*	*=*	*− 6*	*− 31*	*+ 4*		
%	2·9	14·3	50·0	0·3	1·1	4·9	26·6	100·1	(3045)
	− 11	*+ 2*	*+ 38*	*=*	*− 6*	*− 28*	*+ 6*		

Source: GHS, 1975; a special tabulation prepared by George Psacharopoulos.
Sample: women aged 25–64 in 1975 who reported income.
The figures in italic give the deviation from the corresponding cell in Appendix I, Table 7.
For details of the social class classification see Note 5 to Chapter 4.

mobility, but the surplus is much smaller for the women, 27 as against 32 per cent moving up and 26 as against 19 per cent moving down.

Our first view of the material, then, suggests that women have considerably poorer mobility chances than men – if we take their own occupational achievements rather than their husbands' as the yardstick. They are more likely to be downwardly mobile and less likely to be upwardly mobile than men from the same class origins. And this, of course, is due to their enormous concentration in 'women's work' – their employment as secretaries, shop assistants, clerks, telephone operators, waitresses, cooks and hairdressers.[7]

This pessimistic conclusion about women's chances, however, is particularly sensitive to the assumptions we make about what counts as 'upward' and 'downward' mobility. Many women from working-class homes cross the manual/non-manual line to enter 'white-blouse' jobs, and we could do a good cosmetic job on the ugly face of sexual inequality by counting Class III as 'higher' than Class VI and thus generating a large number of apparently upwardly mobile women.

This raises the conceptual questions about occupational classification that we described in Chapter 2. If we are interested in questions of class formation and class action, as Westergaard and Goldthorpe are, then movement across the manual/non-manual borderline becomes of considerable potential interest and makes it vital to differentiate Classes III and VI. What are the political and social consequences, we have to ask, of increasing numbers of wives and daughters of manual workers getting a foot inside the world of non-manual work? But if we are interested in questions of equality of opportunity to obtain rewarding jobs, the relevant distinctions are rather different. It is by no means obvious that junior white-collar jobs are 'better' than skilled manual ones in terms of their general desirability. They command considerably less pay (as we have already seen), and while it is one of the clichés of contemporary British sociology that white-collar workers make up for this with their improved working conditions, fringe benefits, promotion prospects and job security, no one has quantified these properly even for men and it is highly doubtful whether these advantages apply to anything like the same extent to women. Nor should one ignore the not negligible attractions of skilled manual work. We saw something of its attractiveness to the 'educationally unsuccessful sons of high-status fathers' in Chapter 2, and we might add that the skilled manual worker may enjoy considerable respect and status within the working-class community. We have no study comparing the 'general desirability' of these junior white-collar 'women's jobs' with those of 'men's jobs' such as skilled manual work, but it is a reasonable guess that they rank lower. The results of Goldthorpe and Hope's enquiry on the social grading of occupations may be relevant here, although not conclusive as it was intended to cover men's jobs only. Judgements were obtained from a national sample of respondents about the social grading of a number of selected occupations, and Goldthorpe and Hope interpret the results as indicating the general desirability of the various jobs. They found that fitters and tool-makers ranked markedly higher than clerical workers and cashiers; setters and sheetmetal workers ranked higher than cooks and hairdressers; machine-tool operators and assemblers ranked higher than shop assistants. One suspects that the differences would be magnified if the respondents had been asked to consider female shop assistants, for example, rather than male.[8]

We should not, then, overturn our initial conclusion that women have inferior chances of occupational mobility than men. The 'losses' experienced by the daughters of high-status fathers are not balanced by 'gains' accruing to those from low-status origins. The concentration of women in lower white-collar work of 'intermediate' status works to the disadvantage not benefit of women as a whole. To think otherwise would be a kind of middle-class 'ethnocentrism' which saw white-collar jobs as intrinsically superior to manual ones and which failed to recognize that women's exclusion from skilled manual work, from those jobs which command the greatest pay, power and respect within the working-class community, constitutes yet another disability attached to their sex.

There is, however, a second and more cogent objection to our analysis. If we are considering women's mobility chances or *opportunities* rather than their *experiences*, is it fair to include the jobs, often part-time, of married women? It could be argued that women have the opportunity in a formal sense to obtain good full-time jobs but opt instead for low-level part-time work, marriage and a family. The point is another important conceptual one. Mobility data do not tell us about opportunities for advancement but about the actual *use* made of such opportunities as exist. To talk of an opportunity is to assume that people could refuse to make use of it if they wished; it implies a voluntaristic approach to social action. And so we cannot reject out of hand the objection that the opportunities are there for the women who wish to use them. True, we might want to argue that women have been socialized into stereotyped role-expectations and are thus not free to choose a career rather than a family, but then the language of opportunities becomes inappropriate. We are adopting a deterministic rather than a voluntaristic model.

It is not important in the present context which side we come down on. The reader is free to reinterpret and translate the evidence into his own preferred language of choice or determinism. I do not wish to get embroiled in semantic and philosophical questions about the meaning of free-will and determinism. However, if, for the sake of argument, we grant the point made by the voluntaristic critic, there is a simple empirical test which we should make: we should look at the mobility of single women, at those women who have made (or had forced upon them) a different choice, opting for career rather than family and marriage.

The number of single men and women in the 1975 General Household Survey is too small for us to present a detailed mobility table on the lines of Table 4.2. Instead we shall report the social origins and present occupations of the single people, together with some summary statistics. Table 4.3 gives the occupational distributions.

Table 4.3 sheds a very different shade of light on the inequalities between men and women. There is, to be sure, the expected concentration of women in lower white-collar work and their exclusion from skilled manual labour, but they also do much better than the men in gaining access to Class II and in avoiding Class VII. Overall (using our usual definition of upward and downward) 37 per cent of the single women but only 27 per cent of the single men were upwardly mobile; and 17 per cent of the single women as against 25 per cent of the men were downwardly mobile. The picture we now see is the mirror image of the earlier one. True, the upwardly mobil women tended to enter a small range of 'women's' jobs – school-teaching, nursing and social work – all of which are included in Class II (both in the present classification and in Goldthorpe's). I do not therefore deny that there is still considerable sexual segregation (and probably discrimination) even within higher levels of non-manual work which may be of great importance both socially and individually. But if we concentrate simply on questions of *vertical* mobility, it would seem to be the case that the 'helping professions' provide a definite channel of upward mobility for career-orientated women (if such we can take the single to be). Nor do I deny that women are still under-represented at the very highest levels, both of the helping professions and of white-collar work generally (PEP, 1971). The most that

Table 4.3 Single men and women: origins and destinations

	Father's class		Respondent's class	
	Men	Women	Men	Women
I ⎱	17·5	23·5	10·2	13·1
II ⎰			12·1	24·9
III	9·8	12·2	16·5	40·3
IV	6·7	4·1	1·0	0·0
V	4·8	5·4	4·1	1·4
VI	34·6	27·6	28·6	4·5
VII	26·7	27·1	27·6	15·8
Total	100·1	99·9	100·1	100·0
N	315	221	315	221

Source: GHS, 1975; a special tabulation prepared by George Psacharopoulos.
Sample: single men and women aged 25–64 in 1975 who reported income.
For details of the social class classification see Note 5 to Chapter 4.

the present data suggest is that single women have been able to make use of such opportunities as are available to them to obtain jobs of generally higher social standing than their male equivalents.

We now have two radically different accounts. The first, based on the comparison of employed women with employed men, suggests that the former have markedly inferior opportunities for occupational mobility; the second, based on the comparison of single women and single men suggests that the former have rather better chances. Is it then fair to conclude after all that the employment opportunities facing women are as good as those for men (at least in terms of their general desirability) but that only this tiny minority of career-oriented women choose to make full use of them?

The question may seem simple but, as so often, the answer is not. Even if we accept the evidence at face value, there is still a crucial complication which arises if we take the notion of opportunity seriously. There may be occupational opportunities for a few women, but if everyone chose to take them up the opportunities would vanish. We all have the same formal opportunity to walk down, say, the High Street, but if we all choose to do so at once, the street becomes jammed and no one can get through. Similarly, the current supply of 'women's work' may give excellent opportunities to the few women who want continuous full-time careers at the moment, but if the great majority of married women were to opt out of domestic labour and seek paid employment instead, the demand for jobs would far outrun the supply and the opportunities facing women would be much reduced. The problem does not apply to men, since the great majority are already in full-time employment or actively seeking it. And the problem would not apply specifically to women if there were not the barriers which effectively exclude women from skilled manual or managerial jobs in industry. Sexual discrimination in the labour market may only reveal itself clearly if more women sought work, but the very existence of such discrimination may itself deter more women from seeking work.

There is a second problem, too. In comparing single men and women's occupational mobility we assume that the two groups have the same qualifications and aptitudes, in other words that we are comparing like with like. But is this a fair assumption? For most men the choice of work or marriage does not present itself as a dilemma; the two are complementary not antagonistic. But for most women it is a dilemma.[9] The typical role-expectations confronting a wife and mother reduce her ability to pursue a career effectively. She cannot usually maximize her contributions in one role without sacrificing those in the other. This suggests that the woman who actually does opt for a career by staying single may have a greater commitment to work than the single man who has not had to make the same sacrifices. This might be reflected in the single woman's seeking and obtaining higher educational qualifications than the single man (a point which we shall take up in Chapter 6 when we look at the determinants of occupational attainment for men and women). The single women, therefore, may well differ markedly from the married women in their greater occupational ambitions; but there is no reason to expect that the single men differ likewise from their married counterparts.

All we have really managed to do, therefore, is to set upper and lower bounds to our estimates of male/female differences in mobility chances. The decidedly poor chances of employed women taken as a whole mark the lower bound; the moderately good chances of the single women represent the upper bound. The truth lies somewhere in between, and Chapter 6 will help us decide where.

Inequalities between women

So far we have been concerned with a comparison of the opportunities facing men and women, but another question of great interest is the extent of the inequalities of opportunity which divide women themselves. Do differences of social background divide women in the same way that they divide men, and to the same extent? Does the woman from a privileged home have the same relative advantages over her working-class contemporary that her brother has over the working-class male?

As is often the case in mobility studies, the answer one reaches will depend crucially on the kind of data one has collected (or borrowed) and the technique of analysis that one brings to bear. The best course, although one rarely followed, is to share the dilemma with the reader and to give him as much information as possible so as to allow him the option of alternative analyses. This is particularly important in the case of statistical techniques. These tend to go in fashions, and today's vogue is often tomorrow's heresy.

Of all the statistical techniques for measuring *relative* mobility rates, the disparity ratio is the simplest and the one with the readiest interpretation. It simply tells us the relative chances of people from different social origins of getting to a given destination. Thus in Table 4.1 we see that 42 per cent of married women from Class I origins had husbands also in Class I in 1972 whereas this was true of only 8 per cent of women from Class VII origins. This gives us a disparity ratio of 5·3 : 1. In other words, the women from Class I origins were over five times as likely as those from Class VII to have husbands in Class I in 1972.

We could, if we wished, go on to calculate disparity ratios for all other possible pairs of origin class and for all possible destinations. To carry out all these computations would generate a vast quantity of statistics and produce a most indigestible diet. Fortunately, in the case of marital mobility, the pattern is quite simple and can easily be stated without recourse to yet more tables. The differences are small but consistent: the disparity ratios are generally closer to unity than they were for men's occupational mobility. In other words, the relative chances for women from different class backgrounds are more equal than those for men. Thus instead of the five-fold advantage which women have, men from Class I have a seven-fold advantage over those from Class VII in the competition to stay in Class I. And whereas the woman from Class VII is four times more likely to end up with a husband there than is her Class I rival, the man is six times more likely to get a job there than his Class I competitor.

Unfortunately the picture is not so clear when we move on from marital to occupational mobility, and we must therefore give more details. The crucial figures are presented in Table 4.4. One peculiarity of the presentation should be noted: we have not calculated the relative chances of getting to, say, Class II on its own because what is actually important to the participants themselves is the chance of getting to Class II *or somewhere better*. There may be pretty equal chances of getting lower white-collar work, for example, but this may be the case only because so many people from favoured backgrounds have already secured better positions for themselves in higher-level professional work; it is hardly indicative of equal opportunity. Table 4.4 presents a set of disparity ratios where we take as our base the likelihood of a woman from Class VII getting to a given destination (or the likelihood of a woman from Classes I and II in the case of a destination in Class VII). Thus we see that a woman from Classes I and II origins is seven times as likely as someone from Class VII to get a Class I job herself.

That there is inequality of opportunity among women in the labour market, just as there is for men, is quite evident from Table 4.4, although there are also some interesting differences between the male and female

Table 4.4 Relative class chances among women

Father's class	Relative chances of obtaining a job in:			
	Class I	Classes I, II	Classes I, II, III	Class VII
I & II	7·0 (4·7)	2·8 (3·3)	1·4 (2·7)	Set at 1
III	3·7 (3·1)	2·3 (2·6)	1·4 (2·3)	1·4 (1·5)
IV	2·2 (2·1)	1·6 (1·6)	1·1 (1·5)	2·4 (2·1)
V	1·9 (1·8)	1·1 (1·5)	1·2 (1·4)	2·4 (2·0)
VI	1·3 (1·6)	1·1 (1·3)	1·1 (1·3)	2·5 (2·1)
VII	Set at 1	Set at 1	Set at 1	3·0 (3·2)

Source: calculated from Table 4·2 and Appendix I, Table 7.
Figures in brackets give the corresponding ratios for men.

patterns. There are greater inequalities between women than among men in access to Class I, but then as we move downwards to include Class II and then Class III the pattern reverses and it becomes the women who are more equal. Moving on to Class VII the picture changes once again with women tending to become less equal. The differences are small and we should not perhaps make too much of them. They are however quite intelligible. The great concentration of women in lower white-collar work almost inevitably means that they will have quite similar chances of ending up there whatever their social class origins. But in the competition to secure one of the few high-status vacancies (and to avoid the low-status ones) social origin comes into its own.

Finally, if we are to be thorough, we must consider the relative chances among single women too, and this yields broadly the same picture. Look at Table 4.5. Because of the small numbers involved we have had to group categories rather drastically and to compare chances of getting to white-collar and blue-collar destinations respectively.

But the picture is nonetheless clear. Single women from different origins have relatively equal chances of achieving white-collar work but *un*equal chances of avoiding blue-collar work. The explanation for the discrepancy is simple: in the case of single women, those from non-manual origins almost without exception manage to find non-manual work to do themselves; manual working-class jobs are the exclusive preserve of those from manual origins.

Table 4.5 Relative class chances among single women

Father's class	Relative chances of obtaining a job in:	
	Classes I–III	Classes V–VII
I & II	1·5 (2·5)	Set at 1
III	1·5 (1·9)	— (1·5)
IV & V	1·2 (1·8)	6·2 (1·5)
VI	1·0 (0·9)	8·5 (2·3)
VII	Set at 1	9·1 (2·2)

Source: GHS, 1975; a special tabulation prepared by George Psacharopoulos.
Sample: women aged 25–64 in 1975 who reported income.
Figures in brackets give the corresponding ratios for men.
For details of the social class classification see Note 5 to Chapter 4.

This provides an interesting contrast with the situation among men from white-collar backgrounds, some of whom at least find their way into manual work. Does this mean that women are more snobbish than men and that, to paraphrase Blau and Duncan, 'women raised in white-collar homes are more strongly identified with the symbols of white-collar status ... the existence of relatively unskilled white-collar occupations, such as retail sales and clerical jobs, makes it possible for the unsuccessful daughters of white-collar workers to remain in the white-collar class by paying the price of accepting a lower income than they might have been able to obtain in a manual occupation'? (See Chapter 2 above.)

This is probably an unfair slur on womanhood. Remember that women tend to be excluded from the better-paid skilled manual jobs and so, if they enter manual work, are doomed to the badly paid and insecure semi- or unskilled jobs. In avoiding these, women from white-collar backgrounds are not paying a price for the cherished symbol of white-collar status. 'White-blouse' jobs may not pay very well either, but I doubt if they entail much of a sacrifice given the inferior conditions offered by unskilled manual work.

The overall impression, then, is that there is greater equality of opportunity among women than there is among men in competition for lower white-collar jobs. *But this equality may simply be a consequence of the inequalities between women and men.* In other words, sexual discrimination in the labour market may be a great leveller of women, but if women were given the same opportunities as men to enter jobs in industrial management or skilled manual work, the same class differences that divide men might reappear among women. Indeed, the overall class differences might be magnified as the women from privileged backgrounds who are at present excluded from top jobs compete successfully with men from less-privileged backgrounds.

Women and class formation

From questions of equality of opportunity we now return to class formation. The central problems are those raised by Westergaard and Resler. They accept that there is a great concentration of women in lower white-collar work and hence a potential blurring of class lines as women from manual backgrounds undertake the same kinds of jobs as those from non-manual homes; 'there may well be consequences of some social significance arising from that meeting,' they allow. But they then argue that this potential blurring is limited by two factors. First, working-class women are likely to be concentrated disproportionately in the most routine grades of clerical and sales work with fewest opportunities for promotion, and the meeting is thus more apparent than real. Second, away from 'white-blouse' work the class divisions are as clear as ever: 'Women in manual work are almost certainly still recruited practically exclusively from working-class families; women in non-manual work above the routine grades no doubt very largely from middle- and upper-class families.' (Westergaard and Resler, 1975 : 104.)

We can effect a partial test of these assertions by turning from outflow to inflow analysis, and asking what the social mix is within each of the main categories of 'women's work'. For Table 4.6 we have divided lower white-collar work into two categories. Class IIIa consists of what the Office of Population Censuses and Surveys calls junior non-manual workers – clerks, typists, shop assistants and the like; Class IIIb on the other hand contains what are called personal service workers – cooks, waitresses, hairdressers and the like. The distinction is not quite the one Westergaard and Resler had in mind but is nonetheless

Table 4.6 Social origins of women employees

Father's class	Respondent's own class (%)			
	I & II	IIIa	IIIb	IV–VII
I & II	30·4	20·3	8·2	7·3
	− 3	− 2	− 14	− 2
III	12·4	10·3	5·4	4·7
	+ 1	=	− 17	=
IV	8·4	6·9	8·2	8·0
	+ 3	+ 1	− 3	+ 2
V	3·3	5·2	3·5	4·0
	=	+ 1	+ 3	− 1
VI	27·0	34·6	39·1	41·4
	− 4	− 2	+ 13	− 2
VII	18·5	22·6	35·5	34·6
	+ 3	+ 2	+ 17	+ 3
Total	100·0	99·9	99·9	100·0
N	523	1097	425	1000

Source: GHS, 1975; a special tabulation prepared by George Psacharopoulos.
Sample: women aged 25–64 in 1975 who reported income.
The figures in italic give the deviations from the corresponding percentages for men (see Appendix I, Table 8).
For details of the social class classification see Note 5 to Chapter 4.

instructive. The recruitment patterns and social mix of the personal service workers are almost identical to those of manual work generally. There is a negligible representation of women from white-collar backgrounds, and an overwhelming predominance of women from manual backgrounds. Indeed, many of the jobs that go into Class IIIb, jobs such as cooks and hairdressers, one might want to regard as the 'woman's equivalent' of skilled manual work (and they are in a strict sense manual, even if one can wear a white blouse while doing them).

Westergaard and Resler are right, then, thus far. Some of the blurring of class lines which we thought we saw in Class III is illusory after all. But an equally striking feature of Table 4.6 is the heterogeneity not only of Class IIIa but also of Classes I and II, a heterogeneity which parallels that to be found among men.[10] The same story that we heard in Chapter 2 therefore has to be retold – diversity of origin at the higher levels but similarity at the lower levels of the class structure. True, the 'higher levels' are not that high. The kinds of job that many of the women in Classes I and II will be doing, for example, are nursing and teaching. They are hardly ladders into the governing elite, but they do provide something of a channel for upward mobility just as industry and administration do for men.

What are the implications of this for class formation? First, it is clear that there will be a substantial minority within the working class whose wives, husbands and parents will all hold manual jobs. They will constitute a sort of 'core' to the working class where the work experience of all family members will be in line. They will suffer no cross-pressures as the result of white-collar affiliations,[11] whether through marriage or the work place. We cannot unfortunately put a figure to the size of this core for we do not have cross-tabulations showing own job by spouse's job by father's job and so on. But we can calculate that over a quarter of the women from blue-collar backgrounds have married white-collar workers (see Table

4.1) and that, of those who work, at least a half are engaged in white-collar jobs (see Table 4.2).[12] From the 1971 Census we can also calculate that over a third of the employed women whose husbands were blue-collar workers had white-collar jobs themselves.[13] At the very most, then, this 'core' of the working class can hardly come to more than 50 per cent of the total, and it may be considerably less.[14]

At the other extreme we will find a small core in the elite, outnumbered by newcomers, where both husbands and wives come from privileged backgrounds and the wives either do not work or have secured a professional or administrative job for themselves.[15] Again, they will experience no cross-pressures. The husbands' work will take them into the almost exclusively masculine world of the professions and business management and their wives will be spared the necessity of taking paid employment in the more heterogeneous world of teaching or nursing.

In between these two homogeneous cores will come a variety of cross-pressured groupings: white-collar workers whose fathers or fathers-in-law held working-class jobs; manual workers with wives in 'white-blouse' work; senior officials whose wives hold junior positions. These cross-pressured groupings will almost certainly contain a majority of all families, and the overwhelming majority of what we might call middle-class families. The extent of women's marital mobility, and the concentration of employed women in lower white-collar work, ensures that cross-class affiliations of some kind will be extremely common. And the recent rise in upward mobility, the expansion of white-collar work, and increasing tendency for women to seek paid employment will ensure that these affiliations become even more common.

What we now need to know are the *consequences* of these

cross-class affiliations, and on these there is a surprising silence. First of all, however, we must make the distinction (alluded to earlier in Chapter 2) between 'market' and 'work' situation. The 'market' situation of many of these women in junior clerical work – their size of income, degree of job security, and opportunity for upward mobility – will be poor. Their economic interests, broadly conceived, will not be so very different from those of their fathers or husbands in blue-collar work. They are clearly in subordinate positions in the class structure and have a shared interest in *collective* action through trade unions or left-wing political parties to improve that position.

On the other hand, as Lockwood made clear in his classic work on the clerk, the 'work situation' – that is, 'the set of social relationships in which the individual is involved at work by virtue of his position in the division of labour' (Lockwood, 1958 : 15) – *may* be very different. What we need is a modern study of the work relationships of the female white-collar worker and their influence on her own, and thence on her husband's, political attitudes and class identity. It is frequently asserted that wives tend to vote the same way as their husbands, but is this equally true of working wives? We do not know. But it is not wholly out of the question that the increasing volatility of the electorate over the last two decades has something to do with the greatly increased number of working wives, exposed to a greater number of conflicting pressures than before.

There are in fact a number of ways in which the mobility of women into white-collar work might affect class identity. Perhaps the most common view is that these women will be exposed to, and to some extent assimilate, the mores and life-styles of the middle class. Thus Goldthorpe and his colleagues argued: 'The long-run trends for white-collar employment to expand more rapidly than blue-collar work and for women to take up an increasing proportion of white-collar jobs must mean that more manual wage-earners will have siblings and wives who are "middle class" in terms at least of occupational status. Consequently it is precisely such changes in the occupational structure, rather than affluence itself, that must be regarded as possibly the most influential factor in encouraging the spread of middle-class values and lifestyles among the working class.' (Goldthorpe et al., 1968:81.)

Another possibility is that the involvement of these women in their work may be minimal; they may have little contact with fellow-workers from other social backgrounds; their contact with supervisors may be formal and distant. The cross-pressures may thus be illusory, or they may evade them by taking a calculative, 'nine-to-five' approach to their work, treating it as a straightforward effort-bargain with no strings attached.

Yet another possibility is that working wives take with them into their jobs something of the culture of the working class. Rather than being the passive recipients of the middle-class attitudes and values which we imagine dominate the white-collar world, they may bring with them a sympathy for trade unions and collective action. White-collar unionization may reflect the increasing number of women workers with manual affiliations.

We do not know what the net effect of these different processes will be, but it is a fair guess that all will play some part. Overall they may tend to produce that same 'normative convergence' of the middle and working classes that Goldthorpe and his colleagues argued for in the Affluent Worker series (Goldthorpe et al., 1969). In this respect women's mobility will work in the same direction as the men's mobility that we documented in Chapter 2. It will tend to generate a blurring of class boundaries and a growing 'middle mass' with no clear class identity and an instrumental attitude to work and politics, seeing employers, unions and both the major political parties as remote bodies with alien ideologies and pursuing other people's interests.

Conclusions

The general tendency of women's mobility patterns is to increase the openness of the class structure. Through marriage women experience slightly more mobility than men do through the labour market; their husbands' class position is less closely linked to their fathers' than to their father-in-laws'. And this means that there is, in a sense, greater equality between women in their prospects of advantageous life-chances than among men.

Women's occupational mobility shows a much more radical departure from the male patterns, with the enormous concentration of women in lower white-collar employment. Again, womanhood is a leveller. The restrictions on women's job prospects means that they are much less divided by their social origins than are men. Class discrimination divides men, but sexual discrimination brings women together. Doubtless, if sexual discrimination and segregation within the labour market vanished, class divisions might reassert themselves more strongly; but at present women's chances of occupational mobility are relatively poor and relatively equal.

The chances of *single* women, however, provides an interesting contrast with those that face the majority of employed (often part-time) women workers. They are more likely to be upwardly mobile and less likely to be downwardly mobile than single men, and middle-class single women are particularly good at avoiding the drop into manual work. But whether this means that the opportunities are there for women if they choose to take advantage of them is uncertain (if not improbable): single women are a distinctive group who may well have had to make a definite choice between work and family; they may be more committed to their work than the typical man; and they are only a small minority – if the majority of women followed their example, sexual discrimination in the labour market might well result in chances for women, on average, being distinctly worse. The few good 'women's jobs' would simply not go round as far.

The overall consequence of women's mobility patterns is to increase the number of families with cross-class affiliations and thus to increase the proportion of the population experiencing cross-pressures. The outcomes for class solidarity and class conflict have yet to be studied but it may well have the effect of increasing the size of the 'middle mass' with no strong class allegiance and a more calculative orientation to employers, unions and parties. It may well increase the instability and unpredictability of class action and political preference.

5 Who Gets Ahead (or Stays Behind)?

Who gets ahead and who stays behind are questions that have always fascinated Americans, and one of the dominant schools of American sociology – perhaps the most influential new school to appear in the 1960s – has made this its focus. The inspiration behind this school was Otis Dudley Duncan, whose re-orientation of mobility research was briefly described in Chapter 1. In the restrained and formal language fashionable in this most 'scientific' of all contemporary sociological schools, the central questions become those of the determinants of individuals' status attainment and more specifically of the relative importance of ascription and achievement. 'How and to what degree do the circumstances of birth condition subsequent status,' asks Duncan, 'and how does status attained (whether by ascription or achievement) at one stage of the life cycle affect the prospects for a subsequent stage?' (Blau and Duncan, 1967 : 164.) More crudely, is it *who* your parents are that matters or is it *what* you can do?

As we described earlier, Duncan's re-orientation of mobility research involved two shifts in focus. First, there was a shift from the analysis of mobility itself to that of attainment, and second there was a shift from the measurement of rates to that of determinants. Instead of asking, 'How much mobility is there in this society?' the question becomes, 'What is the relative importance of factors such as social origins and schooling as determinants of individuals' eventual occupational attainment?' Attainment itself is measured by a socio-economic index of occupational status. As we argued in Chapter 2, when Duncan's classification of occupations was contrasted with Goldthorpe's class schema, this ranks occupation in a single hierarchy of status or prestige and it can in practice be treated as a measure of how good, or desirable, different jobs are.[1]

We can, then, treat Duncan's work as telling us about access to more and less desirable jobs rather than about issues of class formation. Coser (1975) rather rudely says that this school is obsessed with the problems of 'making it', but there is no need to put it in such a negative light.[2] It is probably fairer to say that it is the liberal concern with inequalities of opportunity that underlies Duncan's work. The modern liberal believes that inequalities which stem from a man's own achievements are fair in a sense that those stemming from the ascribed characteristics of birth are not. Do people of equal merit have equal chances of success (or failure) irrespective of their ascribed characteristics such as their social origins, race or sex? These are fundamental questions in the contemporary liberal and social democratic tradition, and they are questions to which Duncan's work has provided some important answers.

Duncan's basic model is a processual one which looks at the determinants of individuals' attainment at different stages of the life cycle. First of all, an individual's social origins and family circumstances (as measured by his father's occupation and educational level) may be expected to influence his own educational achievement; next, educational achievement and social origins may both be expected to affect the kind of jobs which the individual gets when he enters the labour market for the first time; and his first job, educational achievement and social origins may all be expected to influence his subsequent career. This can be set out diagrammatically, as in Diagram 5.1, in a so-called 'path diagram'. Each arrow or path represents the postulated effect of one factor on another.

Diagram 5.1 The basic model of the attainment process

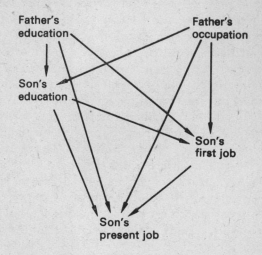

There are some interesting questions to be asked about the various 'effects' postulated in this model. First, just how important are they? How far do social origins actually condition one's educational attainment? How far does educational attainment affect one's prospects in the job market? Are there tight bonds at each stage so that people from advantaged social origins are 'born to succeed' while those from deprived backgrounds are 'doomed to failure', or is there a second chance for those who missed out in the lottery of birth? Put somewhat differently, is there a 'cycle of deprivation' (and a corresponding 'cycle of privilege') which means that those who start off at the very top or bottom of the social scale are inevitably bound to follow in their parents' footsteps?

Second, what is the relative importance of ascribed and achieved characteristics? Do ascribed characteristics like social origins continue to have a direct effect on one's chances of getting a good job even after one has passed through the educational system? Or is the influence of social origins on one's career wholly mediated by one's own educational achievements? In a liberal world of equality of opportunity where achievement had replaced ascription we would expect people of similar educational attainments to compete on equal terms for jobs in the labour market irrespective of their family connections and advantages. The only way in which a high-status father could help his son to follow in his footsteps would be to encourage him to succeed at school. He could not pass on his position directly. As some writers (for example, Bourdieu) have put it, the inheritance of 'cultural capital' – knowledge and skills – becomes a more important mechanism for the intergenerational transmission of status than the inheritance of property.

We can also complicate Duncan's basic model. We can look at additional ascribed characteristics such as sex and race. Do men and women, or blacks and whites, compete on equal terms in the labour market? Duncan had pointed out (as we described in Chapter 1) that blacks have quite a high chance of upward mobility, but since they are much more concentrated in low-status social origins, it is misleading to compare black with white mobility chances. What we need to know instead is whether the colour of a man's skin is an additional handicap over and above other handicaps which he may suffer such as low-status social origins and poor educational attainment. We shall tackle this in Chapter 6.

Circumstances of birth and subsequent status

The first part of our answer to the question, 'To what extent do the circumstances of birth condition subsequent status?' comes from an estimation of the different 'effects' represented in Duncan's basic model. We shall carry out the analysis on the 1972 survey of England and Wales rather than on the 1962 American survey originally used by Duncan, although in practice the results for the two countries are remarkably similar and most of Duncan's comments on America apply equally well to Britain. The British results are given in Diagram 5.2.[3]

The precise technical meaning of the numbers (usually called path coefficients) entered in the diagram is slightly complicated, and is described in Appendix II. The usual sociological interpretation of them is that they represent the size of the direct effect which one variable has on another, *controlling for other variables already included in the model.*[4] Consider, for example, the effects which son's education has on his career. We see from Diagram 5.2 that his educational level has a powerful effect on the kind of job which he gets on entering the labour market; indeed the link between education and first job is the tightest in the whole causal chain. First job then influences present job, and this means that people whose original educational success had given them a step up the ladder continue to maintain something of their initial advantage. However, we also see that there is a direct effect of education on present job which has nothing to do with initial job place-

Diagram 5.2 The attainment process in England and Wales

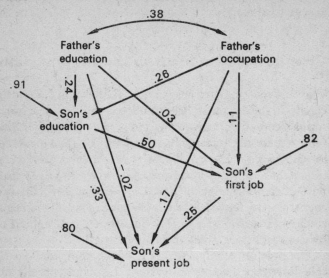

Source: Halsey (1977).
Sample: men aged 25–29 in 1972 and resident in England and Wales at age 14.
For details of the variables, see Note 3 to Chapter 5.

ment. It tells us that, *among people who entered the labour market at the same level,* those with more education got more promotion. Education thus brings a double benefit; it helps you get a good first job, but then it also gives you a competitive advantage in the promotion stakes compared with the less educated people who had managed (despite their lack of education) to start off on the same rung of the ladder. Putting the matter slightly differently, education has an *indirect* effect on present job via first job and it also has a separate *direct* effect. The numbers in Diagram

5.2 tell us about the two separate effects, not about the combined or *total* effect of education or occupation (although this can in fact be calculated quite easily with the aid of some additional information).

We should not, however, adopt too deterministic an interpretation of these 'effects'. In the first place, statistical manipulation of the data can never *prove* a causal connection. To do so, we would need to conduct an experiment in which we gave some (randomly chosen) people extra education and then monitored their subsequent careers, comparing their achievements with those of a 'control group'. Non-experimental data, such as those provided by a social survey, only give us the pattern of relationships among the measured variables. It is the sociologist who then imputes causation in order to make the statistical results understandable. Thus the strict interpretation of the direct effect of education on present job in Diagram 5.2 is that, among members of the sample with similar first jobs and social origins, those with higher levels of education tended on average to have higher-level jobs in 1972. We do not actually know for sure that they got the higher-level jobs *because* of their educational achievements; this *causal* interpretation is one which the sociologist provides.[5]

In the second place, even if we are happy with this causal interpretation of the model, we must remember that there are plenty of other causes which the sociologist has not been able to measure and enter in his diagram. These are represented by the various arrows, and their associated numbers, which so to speak come out of nowhere into Diagram 5.2. Thus as well as the arrows from father's education and father's occupation leading to son's education, there is also a third arrow which comes out of the blue. This arrow represents all the unknown factors which affects a man's education but which have not been included in the model, and it is usually termed the 'residual'. It could include his genes, sibling rivalry, how well he got on with the teachers at school, what kind of friends he made, whether he got marked down because the examiner could not read his handwriting or because the topics he revised did not come up in the examination. The list of potential influences is almost endless, their effect enormous.

Perhaps the most striking feature of the model, indeed, is that these unknown or unmeasured factors are much more important determinants of educational and occupational achievements than are the known ones. One way to put this is to say that there is extensive variation in the educational achievements of men from identical social backgrounds. One's education is powerfully influenced by a wide variety of factors other than one's father's occupation and education, and one is not therefore doomed to failure (or success) by the circumstances of one's birth (at least, not by those circumstances included in the basic version of the model).

Furthermore, as we proceed along the life cycle we find at each stage that there are wide variations in the educational and occupational achievements of people with similar social origins and similar antecedents (as measured by the model). But educational achievements turn out to be the ones which are most influenced by these unknown factors (witness the size of the 'residual path') and hence least affected by the factors explicitly included in the model. While education has quite a powerful effect on first job, it clearly cannot be acting to any great extent to perpetuate the individual family's position within the job structure. As Duncan rightly observes, 'Far from serving in the main as a factor perpetuating initial status, education operates *primarily* to induce variation in occupational status that is independent of initial status. The simple reason is that the large residual factor for [education] is an indirect cause of occupational status.' (Blau and Duncan, 1967 : 201.)

The importance of the unknown factors is the dominant feature of Diagram 5.2 – as is the case in most path diagrams of occupational attainment. As Duncan points out, sociologists are often disappointed at its size, 'assuming that this is a measure of their success in "explaining" the phenomenon under study'. But such sociologists, he goes on to say, 'seldom reflect on what it would mean to live in a society where nearly perfect explanation ... could be secured by studying causal variables like father's occupation or respondent's education. In such a society it would indeed be true that some are "destined to poverty almost from birth ... by the economic status or occupation of their parents". Others, of course, would be "destined" to affluence or to modest circumstances. By no effort of their own could they materially alter the course of destiny, nor could any stroke of fortune, good or ill, lead to an outcome not already in the cards.' (Blau and Duncan 1968 : 174.)

If the unknown factors truly represent causes like men's 'efforts of their own' to alter their fate, then these results are perhaps encouraging – at least for Americans who believe in the virtues of self-help. At any rate the general message would seem to be clear: the measured aspects of social origin which have been included in the model do not condition subsequent status at all tightly. This expresses in another way the conclusion we had already drawn from the mobility tables in Chapter 2 – Britain is not a society in which individual position in the hierarchy of inequality is fixed at birth.

Expanding the model

It can, of course, be objected that Duncan's basic model has only a rudimentary coverage of the influences on men's attainment. What happens if we try to expand it?

The most ambitious attempt to include additional determinants of educational and occupational attainment in the model is that of the American sociologist Christopher Jencks in his study *Inequality: a Reassessment of the Effect of Family and Schooling in America*. To expand the model, Jencks has to engage in various practices which upset the purist. He synthesizes data from a variety of disparate sources; Blau and Duncan, for example, did not have any IQ data on their respondents, so Jencks incorporates the results of other studies on IQ instead.[6] Second, he engages in various statistical manipulations in order to get even more out of the existing data. The most interesting of these is his use of data on brothers' achievements in order to extract further information about the influence of family background on attainment. The technique is an ingenious one (already pioneered by Duncan),[7] and is worth explaining briefly.

If we take people from the same social origins (as measured by the variables included in the model, namely father's occupation and education), we shall find that there is some similarity in their educational and occupational achievements. However, if we take brothers, who by definition have the same social origins, we shall find that they are even more similar. This additional similarity exhibited by the brothers clearly must have some sources which we have not yet included in the model, but which Jencks attributes to unmeasured aspects of the family environment and genetic endowment shared by the brothers. Moreover, the extent of this additional similarity enables us (if we make certain assumptions) to estimate the importance of these unmeasured aspects of family and heredity as determinants of attainment.[8]

Jencks's main conclusion is that while IQ and the un-measured aspects of family environment may have important effects on educational attainment, they have less influence on later stages of one's career and very little indeed on income. As he observes, the wryness with which the question, 'if you're so smart, why aren't you rich?' is usually asked 'suggests that most people see the connection between cognitive skill and economic success as rather problematic. This scepticism is well-founded.' (Jencks, 1972 : 220.) Nor is it just the connection between cognitive skill and economic success that is problematic. According to Jencks there is very little evidence from the American studies that family background or education have much effect on income either. There is, he says, almost as much variation in the income of men who come from similar backgrounds, have similar educational qualifications, and have similar IQ scores as there is among men in general. Income is even more unpredictable than other outcomes like educational or occupational achievements.

This leads to one of Jencks's most controversial con-clusions, namely that income depends above all on luck and on-the-job competence that has little to do with family background, IQ or schooling. By luck he has in mind such things as 'chance acquaintances who steer you to one line of work rather than another, the range of jobs that happen to be available in a particular community when you are job hunting, the amount of overtime work in your particular plant, whether bad weather destroys your straw-berry crop, whether the new super-highway has an exit near your restaurant.' (Jencks, 1972:227.) And by on-the-job competence Jencks has in mind such things as 'the ability to hit a ball thrown at high speed, the ability to type a letter quickly and accurately, the ability to persuade a customer that he wants a larger car than he thought he wanted, the ability to look a man in the eye without seeming to stare.' (Jencks, 1972 : 227.)

We do not have British data which would allow us to look at the connection between IQ, family environment and income, but the general picture is probably not too different from the American one. Brothers, for example, are quite similar in their schooling (although the significance of even that can be exaggerated), but the further they get away from their origins, the more their paths diverge. Thus the 1972 Oxford survey shows that, of those respondents who gave details about a brother's education, 70 per cent went to the same type of school; but of those who attended similar schools, only 30 per cent had the same social class destination (using the seven-fold class schema).

Measuring additional aspects of family environment, therefore, is not going to help us very much in explaining occupational success. But what about IQ? Combining evidence from a number of sources we can construct Diagram 5.3, a somewhat speculative, path diagram.[9] IQ proves to be a distinctly more important influence on one's educational attainment than on one's occupational success, but its effect on occupation is still by no means negligible. Our (not particularly reliable) sources[10] suggest the encouraging conclusion that clever men, even if they miss out in the educational system, get a second chance in the labour market and can do quite well for themselves. What we make of this, as usual, is partly a matter of individual preference. We can either be impressed by the fact that IQ has any effect at all – that the path coefficient is actually greater than zero. Or we can be depressed by the fact that we

Diagram 5.3 IQ and the attainment process

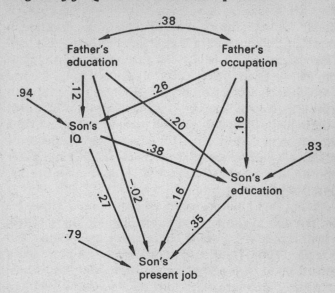

Sources: see Appendix 1, Table 10.

have not made any very great inroads into the residual – its fall is very meagre. The unknown factors still dominate the scene, and it is not obvious that adding further sociological variables to our path model is going to make things any better.

Cumulation and redundancy

Duncan uses this first major finding to attack the concept of a 'vicious circle of poverty' or 'cycle of deprivation' as it is more often called in Britain. Earlier writers such as Lipset and Bendix had argued that: 'Occupational and social status are to an important extent self-perpetuating. They are associated with many factors which make it difficult for individuals to modify their status. Position in the social structure is usually associated with a certain level of income, education, family structure, community reputation, and so forth. These become part of a vicious circle in which each factor acts on the other in such a way as to preserve the social structure in its present form, as well as the individual family's position in that structure. . . . The cumulation of disadvantages (or of advantages) affects the individual's entry into the labour market as well as his later opportunities for social mobility.' (Lipset and Bendix, 1959 : 198–9.)

All this, says Duncan, is grossly exaggerated. He agrees that position in the social structure is indeed associated, *to some extent* with level of education, social origins, and so forth. People from poor homes really are more likely than others to leave school early; people who leave school early really are more likely to enter the lowest level jobs when they go into the labour market.[11] The path coefficients in Diagrams 5.2 and 5.3 suggest that these factors do influence subsequent attainment. But there is a difference between influence and self-perpetuation. People from deprived social origins are indeed handicapped, but they are not born to fail, for social origins are not the only, or even the most important, influences on an individual's subsequent career.

That even people who suffer from multiple handicaps are not destined to poverty is encouraging but at first sight puzzling. Why is it that even when we take account more fully of family background we are still left with widespread variation in men's fates?

Duncan's answer is based on a paper written early in the century by Karl Pearson with the splendid title, 'On

Certain Errors with Regard to Multiple Correlations Occasionally Made by Those Who Have Not Adequately Studied This Subject'. The main error that concerns us is that if the various determinants of, say, educational attainment are highly correlated with each other, 'their combined effect will consist largely in redundancy, not in "cumulation"' (Blau and Duncan, 1967:203). If low income, large families, overcrowding, poor health and periods of unemployment are all substantially correlated with the antecedents already included in the model – father's education and occupation – then adding them as additional antecedents of the children's educational attainment (or lack of it) brings little extra in the way of explanatory power. Why is this the case?

The point is easiest to make with the aid of Venn diagrams. Suppose that the small circle in Diagram 5.4

Diagram 5.4

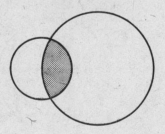

represents all those whose fathers were unskilled manual workers and the large circle represents all those with low educational attainment. The shaded section then gives those who fall into both categories simultaneously and indicates that roughly one-third of the children from unskilled manual origins were low attainers at school. This figure is purely hypothetical – the actual figures for Britain will be given in the next section.

We might now proceed to repeat this exercise for children with low-paid fathers, from overcrowded homes, with large numbers of siblings, and so on, finding each time that around a third (at a guess) of the children with the specified 'handicap' were low attainers. But what happens when we put the various handicaps together and look at their combined effect? One possibility is that un-skilled manual work is strongly associated with low income. (It would be rather surprising if it were not.) The two circles representing unskilled manual parentage and low family income will thus overlap substantially – the two measures of social deprivation will get at much the same people. Where the two circles overlap we have the children who suffer from the double handicap, but we can see from

Diagram 5.5

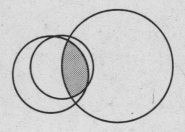

Diagram 5.5 that the proportion of these doubly handi-capped children who are low attainers is not going to be all that much greater than was the proportion when we picked out those with only one handicap. All we are doing by adding extra 'handicaps', therefore, is picking out the same set of people and discovering that they have

multiple handicaps instead of the single one we started with – hence the redundancy.

Similarly, the many other variables such as family size, overcrowding, health and employment record which we believe will correlate with educational attainment may add very little if they are strongly correlated with the variables we have already included. Each new variable may increase our explanatory power a bit, but sociologists usually find that diminishing returns soon set in in a big way. If we are to make more substantial inroads into the unknown sources of variation in educational attainment we must find variables which are *un*correlated with the background variables already included in the model – although of course at the same time correlated with the variable of interest whose outcome we wish to predict. But if we do find such a variable, Duncan suggests, it will not be one that provides a mechanism for the perpetuation of the cycle of deprivation from one generation to another. By definition it is uncorrelated with parental poverty and so can hardly act to transmit it.

This is all very well, one may object, but all Duncan has really done is show that new background variables may not help very much. But it is one thing to show that an argument *may* be fallacious; it is quite another, and rather harder, to show that it actually *is*. Sociologists too often stop when they have cast doubt on an argument, but we ought to carry on and look at the evidence. There are two crucial issues here which must be investigated. First, we need to check whether new variables such as overcrowding really are all that highly correlated with parental occupation and education – how substantial, in other words, is the overlap between the different handicaps? Second, a serious defect of Duncan's argument is that it is based on correlations, which are measures of the strength of associa

tion between two variables *for the population as a whole.*
What we want to know about, however, is the association
at the *extremes* of the social scale. Thus it is quite possible
that there is a great deal of variation in the educational
attainments of children from, say, skilled manual and
routine white-collar homes and that all kinds of unknown
factors are at work producing this variation. But at the same
time there may be very little variation in the destinies of
children from deprived or privileged backgrounds. Duncan fails to check this.

Let us then try to check these arguments for ourselves
using the Oxford Social Mobility Group's 1972 data. We
can begin with the first stage of the basic life-cycle model
of Diagram 5.1 and look at the overlaps between father's
occupation, father's education and son's education.
Diagram 5.6 gives the picture at the lower end of the social
structure.

Diagram 5.6

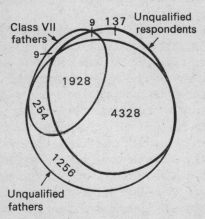

Source: Oxford Social Mobility Group.
Sample: men aged 25–64 in 1972 with at least one of the named attributes.

The meaning of the three circles should be self-explanatory. We have simply taken the people with low scores on the three measured variables which come at the start of the life cycle. They are (1) respondents whose fathers were in Class VII;[12] (2) respondents whose fathers left school without obtaining School Certificate or 'O' level (and who obtained no qualification of this or any higher level thereafter); and (3) respondents who themselves obtained no school or higher-level academic qualifications.[13]

The startling feature of the diagram is the vast number of respondents and their fathers without any formal academic qualifications. This is one of the most important characteristics of British education in mid-century.[14] The distribution of educational credentials was extremely highly skewed, the bulk of the population leaving school at the minimum leaving age without having sat or passed any of the main public examinations. If we go by formal academic credentials, then, we find at the bottom of the scale a huge undifferentiated mass.

Not surprisingly, we also find enormous overlap between our three circles. With very few exceptions the fathers in Class VII had obtained no academic qualifications and so we find redundancy not cumulation – 88.0 per cent of respondents with fathers in Class VII obtained no qualifications; and of the doubly handicapped – those with unqualified fathers from Class VII – the percentage was 88·4. All we have done by adding the extra 'handicap' is to pick out the same set of people rather than to isolate a specially deprived sub-group.

At the other, privileged, end of the social structure we see the mirror image of our first picture. The parent with a high-level qualification is a rare breed; the highly qualified members of Class I are a distinctive, particularly

Diagram 5.7

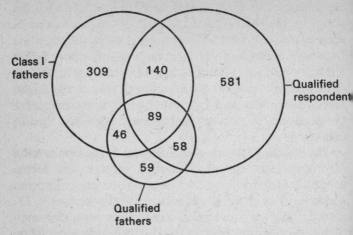

Class I fathers · 309 · 140 · 581 · Qualified respondent · 89 · 46 · 58 · 59 · Qualified fathers

Source: Oxford Social Mobility Group.
Sample: men aged 25–64 in 1972 with at least one of the named attributes.

privileged sub-group; and we get cumulation instead of redundancy. Diagram 5.7 gives the new picture.

Again, the three circles should be self-explanatory. They give (1) respondents whose fathers were in Class I, (2) respondents whose fathers had post-school qualifications (mainly degrees and certificates in education),[15] and (3) respondents who themselves had these higher, post-school qualifications. This time we have isolated much more select groups, the overlaps are much smaller, and hence there is scope for cumulation: 39·2 per cent of respondents from Class I backgrounds obtained post-school qualifications but 65·9 per cent of the doubly advantaged did so.

That we get redundancy at the bottom, but cumulation at the top, warns us to be careful. A good argument in one context may be bad in another. This is equally evident if we think about cycles of deprivation and privilege.

Despite the redundancy which we have just observed, there does seem to be some merit in the idea that the poor are born to fail – educationally at least. With nearly nine out of ten boys from Class VII origins leaving school with no formal qualifications to their name, talk of 'destiny' does not seem so inappropriate after all. To be sure, they share their educational fate with many others, and if they can compete with them on equal terms in the labour market their eventual fates may be more equitable. But it is none-theless a striking indictment of our educational system that so many children 'failed' – or rather were never allowed to succeed since few were ever entered for the major public examinations. For much of the century the British educational system was geared to the needs of the academic and social elite; by its very structure it destined the great majority to fail.

Cycles of deprivation and privilege

We must now extend our analysis in two ways: we must take account of a wider range of handicaps (and advantages), and we must take our respondents through the life cycle from the educational system into the labour market. The extra background variables which we can include from the 1972 survey are family size, domestic amenities and housing. Family size has often been shown to have an association with deprivation: it is the large working-class family which is often the poorest (income per head of family member almost inevitably falling where there are more children of school age) and which suffers most overcrowding. Lack of domestic amenities is not so obviously an important causal factor, but it is worth including to see what role, if any, it plays. In the Oxford

Social Mobility Group's survey, questions were asked about four amenities: telephone, refrigerator, inside flush lavatory and fixed bath or shower. People who had none of these at home when they were growing up would certainly now be regarded as 'deprived', although it is rarely clear whether these amenities are needed for their own sakes or because of the long-run benefits which they bring. Do we need an inside flush lavatory because it is part of our conception of a 'civilized standard of living' or because it actually improves, say, health? (The two need not, of course, be exclusive alternatives.) Finally, we have data on type of housing, the major divisions being between owner-occupation, council housing and rented accommodation. We might guess that this would show substantial overlap with the other conditions which we have already included, but there is never any harm in checking.

These, then, give our background handicaps and advantages. For our outcomes we can take four: educational attainment, first job, 1972 job and 1972 income. Table 5.1 tells the story of the 'deprived' group. The table may need some explanation. The first row tells us that there were 2236 respondents whose fathers had been in Class VII, and that of these 2236 people 87·9 per cent obtained no formal academic qualifications, 42·9 per cent found themselves in a Class VII job on entering the labour market, 34·5 per cent were again in a Class VII job in 1972, and 17·2 per cent were low paid (which we define as an income below £1200 in 1972 – an income that put them towards the bottom 10 per cent of the men in our survey[16]). So far so good. The second row is where the complications begin. It tells us that there were 7184 respondents, both of whose parents were unqualified (in the sense we have described) but that there were only 2005 with the double disadvantage of unqualified parents *and* Class VII social

Table 5.1 Cycles of disadvantage

'Disadvantage' (column 1)	Number of respondents with disadvantage (column 2)	Number with cumulated disadvantages (column 3)	% of column 3 themselves unqualified (column 4)	% of column 3 with first job in Class VII (column 5)	% of column 3 with 1972 job in Class VII (column 6)	% of column 3 with low pay (column 7)
Father in Class VII	2236	2236	87·9	42·9	34·5	17·2
Neither parent qualified	7184	2005	88·4	43·4	34·8	17·3
More than four siblings	2115	569	94·0	54·3	41·8	21·6
No domestic amenities	3449	339	95·6	58·1	44·5	27·1
Rented accommodation	4162	262	95·4	56·9	46·6	26·7

Source: Oxford Social Mobility Group.
Sample: men aged 25–64 in 1972 with one or more of the listed 'disadvantages'.

origins; of these 2005 respondents 88·4 per cent were themselves unqualified, 43·4 per cent took first jobs in Class VII, 34·8 per cent were still there in 1972, and 17·3 per cent were among the low paid in 1972. Similarly with row three. Here we find 2115 respondents from large families (which we define as those containing five or more children) but only 569 who suffered the treble handicap of coming from large families, having unqualified parents and Class VII origins; of these 569 respondents 94 per cent were unqualified, and so on.

The first feature to notice in Table 5.1 is that all the 'disadvantages' which we can identify from our material were relatively widespread among our respondents. They were common features of British life (particularly working-class British life) in the first half of the century. Remember that we are describing the conditions which our respondents experienced when they were growing up; we are dealing with social history and would find a distinctly different picture if we collected data on the *present* conditions of the sample. The middle years of the century were a period of relatively rapid economic and educational progress, and even if that progress has now been brought to a halt it has nonetheless left the map of social deprivation in Britain with different contours.

The overlap between the different disadvantages is the next significant feature of the table. We have already seen how parental education overlaps with social class, but overlap is not the only story told by column three. Most importantly, we find that large families were not a prerogative or even a commonplace of Class VII. Less than a third of our respondents with the first two disadvantages also experienced the third of a large family. Large families were still quite common among higher social classes where, one suspects, their disadvantageous side-effects of overcrowding and poverty would be much less marked; and even in Class VII there were plenty of people, a majority in fact, who followed what are usually thought of as 'middle-class' norms of family limitation.[17] As a result of this lesser degree of overlap we are picking out a definite subgroup with the 'trebly disadvantaged' and we find a moderate degree of cumulation rather than our erstwhile redundancy. The same happens to a lesser extent with domestic amenities, while housing itself adds nothing to our analysis.

Despite all our labours, however, we have not managed to find a great deal of transmitted deprivation. The group of people that we have isolated with multiple disadvantages come to less than 5 per cent of the population, and it is a fair guess that they are effectively the most deprived 5 per cent of the male population; but over half of them, despite their poor start in life, experienced upward mobility and even of those who remained in Class VII the majority avoided the extremes of low pay. To put the matter differently, there is still widespread variation in the economic fates of these from disadvantaged origins. The disadvantaged, even those with multiple disadvantages, are in no way born to fail. Duncan's argument is sustained.

There are a number of rejoinders which can be made; academic arguments always leave loose ends. First, it can be objected that poverty particularly affects two groups omitted from the survey – the old and women (especially divorced or separated women with young children). The objection is sound, but mention of the old reminds us that poverty is to a large extent associated with specific stages of the life cycle – it is not the permanent fate of those from disadvantaged origins, nor is it uniquely their fate; old age and its problems of poverty and physical infirmity visit large numbers in all social classes. And mention of single-parent families (not all of which are headed by women) prompts me to suggest that poverty and its problems may have more to do with one's *current* role in life than the conditions of one's upbringing.

The second objection is the inevitable one that there may be some other handicaps which the 1972 survey did not cover but which might have a significant bearing on its victims' chances of poverty. There is no need to rehearse Duncan's arguments about redundancy; the point is at heart an empirical one to be settled by evidence not argument – is there such a factor (or group of factors) or not? The most likely candidate once again is a broken home, although we should remember that divorce was much less common when our respondents were growing up than it is now. In a sample survey of the kind run by the Oxford Social Mobility Group there might well have been too few cases of divorce among the respondents' parents who were in Class VII to permit any worthwhile analysis.

We must make do with what we have, and this suggests strongly that economic deprivation is not transmitted ineluctably from generation to generation. There is no evidence, at least for Britain, that 'Being poor ... is a rigid way of life. It is handed down from generation to generation in a cycle of inadequate education, inadequate homes, inadequate jobs, and stunted ambitions.' (Shriver, quoted in Duncan, 1968b.) The first part of the cycle may hold (if we make the rather arrogant assumption that anyone who fails to get 'O' level has received an inadequate education), but the latter stages do not. The 262 men in our multi-disadvantaged group certainly have relatively poor chances in the competition for jobs and income, but they are by no means doomed to a life of unskilled manual labour.

The general conclusion to be drawn from this study (and others) of transmitted deprivation is that it is not part of a rigid way of life handed down from generation to generation. Its root is not always to be found in the culture or character of the home. As Rutter and Madge concluded from their survey of the literature: 'At least half of the children born into a disadvantaged home do not repeat the pattern of disadvantage in the next generation. Over half of all forms of disadvantage arise anew each generation. . . . In short, familial cycles are a most important element in the perpetuation of disadvantage but they account for only a part of the overall picture.' (Rutter and Madge, 1976 : 304.) Rather, I suspect that deprivation is a vicissitude (sometimes transitory) which strikes broadly and unpredictably across the working class (and indeed white-collar groups) as the vagaries of economic policy and fortune eliminate overtime in a particular industry or factory, throw men out of work, or drive them into the low-wage sectors of the economy. It is an ever-present hazard of working-class life, more likely to strike some than others but never far away.

But just as our Venn diagrams showed that redundancy among the disadvantaged was matched by cumulation among the privileged, so Table 5.2 tells a different story from Table 5.1. The two tables have the same form, but their content is very different. Our criteria of advantage are the mirror of those we used earlier: instead of Class VII we take Class I; instead of unqualified parents we take those with higher-level academic qualifications (although there are so few cases where both parents had reached such educational levels that we have satisfied ourselves with cases where only one did); instead of large families we take small – those respondents with one sibling or none; instead of tenants we take owner-occupiers; instead of those with no domestic amenities we take those who grew up in homes with all four.

The first contrast with Table 5.1 is that most of our categories of advantage distinguishes a much more select group than those we had before. By and large they were not common features of British life, even of British middle-class life. Indeed, this is one of the keys to understanding

Table 5.2 Cycles of advantage

'Advantage' (column 1)	Number of respondents with advantage (column 2)	Number with cumulated advantages (column 3)	% of column 3 themselves highly qualified (column 4)	% of column 3 with first job in Class I (column 5)	% of column 3 with 1972 job in Class I (column 6)	% of column 3 with high pay[18] (column 7)
Father in Class I	595	595	39·3	26·7	47·4	28·2
Highly qualified parent(s)	429	162	62·3	37·7	53·7	39·5
One sibling or none	3051	85	68·2	41·2	58·8	47·1
All four domestic amenities	613	38	65·8	47·4	60·5	47·4
Owner-occupier	2387	33	69·7	51·5	60·6	45·5

Source: Oxford Social Mobility Group.
Sample: men aged 25–64 in 1972 with one or more of the listed 'advantages'.

the distribution of life chances in Britain today. Society, from this point of view, is not divided into two large homogeneous blocks of the middle class and working class, nor is it shaped like a diamond – that would give a quite erroneous symmetry between top and bottom. A better analogy is with a pear, with its broad, flattish bottom and tapering upper parts.

The second contrast with Table 5.1 is the lack of overlap

between the different advantages. As we cumulate them we are quickly reduced to smaller and smaller numbers, and so their effects are cumulative too (at least before we run out of numbers). Multiple advantages, then, seem to operate in a rather different way from multiple dis-advantages. We are not simply picking out the same group of people each time, discovering that they grew up with two, three or four advantages. Rather, we are narrowing it down to a smaller and smaller, but more and more privileged, group whose members may not have been born to succeed but certainly had an unusually high probability of doing so. These results are the counterpart of those we found in Chapter 2 where, as we focussed on a smaller and more select elite, we found grotesque inequalities of opportunity. There may be considerable variation in the fates of people from 'deprived' or 'ordinary' backgrounds; there seems to be distinctly less among the privileged.

Conclusions

We started from the question, 'Do the circumstances of birth condition subsequent status?' and our answer must now be that 'it all depends on where you are born.' Path analysis tells us about the factors which influence the 'man in the street's' attainment, and for him it seems clear that those circumstances of birth which we can measure do not exert a very powerful constraint on his later achievements. The variations in the fates of men from similar social origins, even brothers, are impressive. This variability seems to extend to the 'deprived', and we have been unable to discover a group who are 'born to fail' (except education-ally). The 'deprived' are not, as far as we can tell, a distinctive sub-group within the working class with a culture and way of life handed down from generation to generation that sets them apart from the rest of the working class. Rather, deprivation is a common mischance that afflicts many, almost at random, within the working class, and those with multiple handicaps do not differ greatly from the rest in the chances of ending up in unskilled jobs or with low pay.

But if there is little evidence for cycles of deprivation, cycles of privilege have a firmer basis. Sociologists have typically devoted more research to the poor than to the rich – they tend on the whole to be more accessible – but the culture of privilege may be more worthy of investigation than the so-called culture of poverty.[19] Certainly, we have seen that advantages cumulate in a way that disadvantages do not, and even if the numbers involved may be small their social significance may be great.

6 Ascription and Achievement

'Heightened universalism has profound implications for the stratification system. The achieved status of a man, what he has accomplished in terms of some objective criteria, becomes more important than his ascribed status, who he is in the sense of what family he comes from. This does not mean that family background no longer influences careers. What it does imply is that superior status cannot any more be directly inherited but must be legitimated by actual achievements that are socially acknowledged. Education assumes increasing significance for social status in general and for the transmission of social standing from fathers to sons in particular. Superior family origins increase a son's chances of attaining superior occupational status in the United States in large part because they help him to obtain a better education, whereas in less industrialized societies the influence of family origin on status does not seem to be primarily mediated by education. Universalism also discourages discrimination against ethnic minorities....' (Blau and Duncan, 1967 : 430.)

I have quoted this passage at length because it is their clearest and fullest statement of the 'expanding universalism' thesis. Today it has a rather naively optimistic ring, but the basic ideas are not self-evidently unsound. We have already seen in Chapter 3 that certain elite groups, such as the higher ranks of the civil service, have slowly become more open under the pressures of competitive examinations and expanding educational opportunities, although other areas like the City have remained impervious to change. But while the bastions of privilege at the apex of the class structure may be able to use their resources and their strategic positions in society to maintain their positions for themselves and their children, it is less obvious that the mass of the population in white-collar and blue-collar jobs can successfully resist the spread of bureaucracy, the use of impersonal selection procedures, the demand for academic qualifications and the like. It is this mass of the population that Blau and Duncan's models tells us about and to which their thesis should be restricted.

We shall begin this chapter, then, by considering whether 'expanding universalism' has characterized Britain, at least in the middle and lower reaches of society, during the twentieth century. We shall then ask whether it has also discouraged discrimination against ethnic minorities and women.

Expanding universalism?

As in Chapter 3, our main sources for trends over time in the twentieth century are the 1972 survey by the Oxford Social Mobility Group and the 1949 survey by Glass's LSE team. The caveats which we raised before will necessarily apply again: we are simply using the same material, with its strengths and weaknesses, to look at the changing determinants of attainment over time. We shall start with the 1972 survey and divide the sample into two cohorts, the older consisting of men born between 1913 and 1932 (and aged forty to fifty-nine in 1972) and the younger consisting of those born between 1933 and 1947 (aged twenty-five to thirty-nine in 1972). We shall use the same basic model as in Chapter 5, with one exception: our final variable will be the job obtained ten years after entry into the labour market rather than 1972 job. Diagram 6.1 gives the results for the two cohorts, the figures for the older cohort being placed first.[1]

Diagram 6.1 The changing attainment process: 1972 enquiry

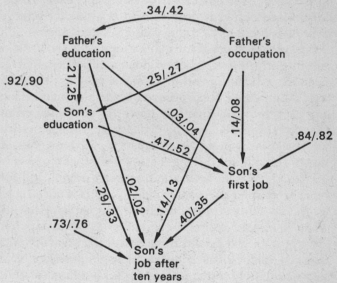

Source: Oxford Social Mobility Group.
Sample: men aged 40–59 and 25–39 in 1972.

The two cohorts can be thought of as dividing the sample into those who were educated and grew up before the Second World War and the 1944 Education Act, entering the labour market in the years of depression, wartime and post-war austerity, and those who benefited from the educational reforms of the 1944 Act and the expanding economic opportunities of the post-war labour market. They grew up in very different times, and this is reflected in the changing nature of the attainment process. For the post-war cohort education is indeed of increased significance for the transmission of social standing from fathers to sons. Education, or rather formal academic qualifications for this is what we have measured, has a larger effect on one's occupational career, while the direct effect of one's father's occupation is reduced.[2] In this respect achievement does seem to be triumphing over ascription.

The second major feature of Diagram 6.1, however, is that the influence of social origins on educational attainment has actually *increased*. It is not just that there has been a tightening bond between academic qualifications and job prospects; education itself has at the same time become more influenced by social background, particularly by these aspects which are tapped by the variable 'father's education'. Taking these two findings together we see that the *overall* association between origins and first job has remained effectively unchanged.[3] It is not so much the extent of transmission as the mechanism that has changed; instead of direct inheritance, nepotism or pulling strings, privileged parents try to ensure that their offspring have acquired the educational advantages needed to compete successfully in the new, more achievement-oriented labour market. As Karabel and Halsey suggest, 'With the decline of the family firm, the privileged no longer reproduce their positions solely through property but also through the acquisition of superior education for their children. Rather than describing this process as heightened universalism it would seem more accurate to view it as a new mechanism performing the old function of social reproduction. Social inheritance, whether through the transmission of property or through the transmission of cultural capital, is still social inheritance.' Karabel and Halsey, 1977 : 19.)

To take the historical record further back we must return to Glass's 1949 survey. This has been reanalysed by Ridge (1974a) using the techniques of path analysis. Ridge does not divide the sample into cohorts as we have just done. Instead he makes use of an unusual feature of the survey, namely that respondents were asked about both their fathers and their eldest sons. He selects all the married men with a son aged twenty or more in 1949 and carries out two separate analyses on them. In the first he looks at their own educational and occupational attainments and relates them to their fathers' attainments. In the second he looks at their sons' careers, relating these in turn to the positions of the respondents themselves. The respondents thus appear in both analyses, the first time as 'sons' and the second time as 'fathers'. We thus have, in effect, 'data on two loosely defined cohorts a generation apart' (Ridge, 1974a : 27) – the first generation growing up and receiving their education in the first twenty years of the century, the second generation doing so mainly in the 1930s and early 1940s (and thus more or less coinciding with the older cohort of the 1972 study).

Ridge does not employ the basic model constructed by Duncan but a more complex one which among other things differentiates several elements in the educational process – the type of school attended, the school examinations passed, the further education undertaken and the qualifications obtained. Unfortunately the only information on jobs related to the subjects' current (that is, 1949) job and we thus have all the problems of confusing life cycle with secular changes discussed in Chapter 3. All our interpretations of the material must therefore be tentative. Diagram 6.2 gives a somewhat simplified version of the model.[4]

Diagram 6.2 The changing attainment process: 1949 enquiry

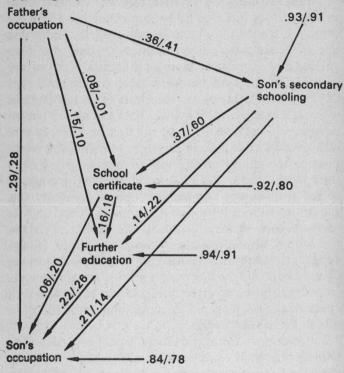

Source: Ridge (1974a).

The remarkable aspect of Diagram 6.2 is that, despite all the differences in the samples, the methods of distinguishing cohorts and generations, and the construction of the variables, it tells exactly the same story as Diagram

6.1. Occupation becomes much more dependent on the academic qualifications which the individual has acquired, while the direct effect of social origins on occupational attainment is reduced but that on secondary schooling is increased: Once again we find that education has been playing an increasing role in the transmission of social status. The trend which we had already observed appears to have been in operation throughout the century.

The second notable feature of Diagram 6.2 is the way in which the bonds within the educational system were also tightening. This is in fact the most securely founded of all the inferences to be drawn from the model, for it is the one least affected by problems of timing. It means that the first part of the century saw the British educational system becoming increasingly rigid as the type of secondary school one attended became increasingly consequential for success in the School Certificate examination. This trend, too, continued into the post-war period and the ensuing rigidity of the tripartite structure of grammar, technical and secondary modern schools is documented by Halsey, Heath and Ridge (1980). The pre-war years saw the gradual evolution of this structure but the 1970s its rapid destruction. Whether comprehensive reorganization will witness a general loosening of bonds not only within the educational system but between the educational and class structures remains to be seen, but if it does it will be the reversal of a long-established trend.

John Ridge rightly observes that a thick hedge of reservations grows around any inferences that spring from the 1949 survey, but so far all the evidence points in the same direction, that Blau and Duncan were right in claiming that education has been assuming increasing significance for the intergenerational transmission of status.

There are problems enough in trying to establish what the trend is, but the difficulties are even greater when we turn to the causal processes that generate the trends. As we observed in Chapter 5, path analysis tells us about the pattern of relationships among the variables, but it is the sociologist who provides the causal interpretations. There are plenty on offer. Karabel and Halsey, we saw, argued that with the decline of the family firm the privileged reproduce their positions through the transmission of cultural capital instead of property, but is it this simple? Could there not be other mechanisms which also tend to reduce the direct, but increase the indirect, effects of social origin on occupational attainment?

Consider, first, the direct effect. To be sure, inheritance of the family firm would almost certainly show up as a direct effect in the model, but so would the nepotism and corruption that characterized the eighteenth-century bureaucracy and the practice of purchasing commissions in the forces. So too might the practices, widespread once in the docks, of restricting recruitment to the families of existing employees. The use of family contacts and resources to secure jobs for their offspring can occur in all kinds of ways and at all levels in society. The actual inheritance of property has probably never been the major source of the direct effect, and it certainly is not now; if we exclude the self-employed (the ones most likely to inherit) from the analysis, the effect remains almost as strong as before.[5]

Inheritance, nepotism and the use of contacts all represent ways in which the family tries to use its resources to protect its members; they are efforts made by the *suppliers* of labour to exploit opportunities in their own interest. But the consumers of labour, the employers, may also have their practices and preferences which produce the same

net effect although by a different mechanism. In recruitment and promotion employers may show a preference for
those who share the same cultural and social characteristics
as themselves – the predominance of Oxbridge graduates
on the selection boards of the civil service and the high
success rate of Oxbridge candidates might be a reflection
of this. One of the main selection procedures for the
administrative grade of the civil service involved written
examinations, marked impersonally and with no knowledge of the candidate's social background, but also an
interview conducted by the selection board, where differences in accent and manners, articulacy and composure
would be manifest. Kelsall was given access to the gradings
made in one pre-war year, 1938, and was able to carry out
a unique analysis. He found that 'the effect of the interview
marks was to eliminate 24 per cent of the original successful
group, whose marks in the written part of the examination
would have brought them the offer of a post in the
administrative class, and to replace them by an equal
number of candidates with slightly poorer results in the
written examination but with better interview marks.
These two groups of eighteen men, one of which changed
places with the other as a result of the interview, were
found to be very different in social origin, type of school,
and university.' (Kelsall, 1974: 180.)

This argument has nothing to do with individual
families. There is no suspicion that the members of the
selection board were related to the successful candidates.
Rather it is a matter of broader social groupings with their
differences in culture and way of life. A more explicit
version of the theory has been produced by Collins who
presents a 'conflict theory of stratification' in which the
basic units of society are 'associational groups sharing
common cultures (or "subcultures")'. There is, then, a

continual struggle between these 'status groups' for wealth, power and prestige, the struggle being carried out primarily through organizations. Collins continues: 'Once groups of employees of different status groups are formed at various positions (middle, lower, or laterally differentiated) in the organization, each of these groups may be expected to launch efforts to recruit more members of their own status group. This process is illustrated by conflicts among whites and blacks, Protestants and Catholics and Jews, Yankee, Irish and Italian, etc. found in American occupational life. These conflicts are based on ethnically or religiously founded status cultures; their intensity rises and falls with processes increasing or decreasing the cultural distinctiveness of these groups. . . . Parallel processes of cultural conflict may be based on distinctive class as well as ethnic cultures.' (Collins, 1971 : 126.)

We have, then, a variety of possible explanations for the decline of the direct effect of social origin on attainment during the present century. The abolition of purchase and the curbing of blatant corruption had already done their work by the beginning of the century, but since then the decline of self-employment, the spread of large bureaucracies with more impersonal selection procedures giving less scope to families pulling strings, and even a diminution of status-group conflict as the distinctiveness of class cultures declines may all have played a part. We cannot sensibly adjudicate between these rival explanations, and there are more, too, as we shall now see.

Consider the *indirect* impact of social origins on attainment running via education. One option is that the conflict between status groups has simply found a new battlefield (and this I suspect is the one that Collins would prefer). The 'screening function' of education may have increased as the larger-scale, more bureaucratic employers find it a convenient and cheap yardstick (for it is provided free by the state) for selecting recruits with the appropriate ability and personality. As Sorokin suggested, *'the school is primarily a testing, selecting, and distributing agency.* In its total the whole school system, with its handicaps, quizzes, examinations, supervision of the students, and their grading, ranking, evaluating, eliminating and promotion, is a very complicated "sieve", which sifts "the good" from "the bad" future citizens, "the able" from "the dull", "those fitted for the high positions" from those "unfitted".' (Sorokin, 1927 : 189; italics in original.)

As Sorokin implies, this selection may not be along lines of ability and achievement alone, but may screen for personality and motivation, culture and manners as well. The interview, with its almost inevitable cultural biasses, is an entrenched part of selection procedures in the educational system, and this may suit employers very well: 'Educational requirements for employment can serve both to select new members for elite positions who share the elite culture and, at a lower level of education, to hire lower and middle employees who have acquired a general respect for these elite values and styles.' (Collins, 1971 : 127.) The use of educational criteria in selection may thus have the guise of universalism but the reality of particularism, since those with the highest levels of achievement will differ in their social character and culture – the real ingredients which employers are seeking.

The main rival hypothesis is of course the one that Blau and Duncan espouse, sometimes called the 'technological functionalism' theory. On this view, technical progress has created a need for more and more members of the labour force to have the advanced knowledge and skills which the modern educational system is designed to provide. The emphasis is on the school as a 'training and educational'

institution rather than as a 'testing, selecting and distributing' agency. The needs of the economy for qualified
manpower have changed over time, as can be seen from
the declining numbers of workers in semi- and unskilled
manual work and the growth of technicians, semi-
professionals and the like. The expansion of these technical
jobs requiring formal knowledge and skills, it can be
argued, is what has led to the tightening bond between
education and occupation.

There is no need for these different interpretations to
be mutually exclusive, but some version of Collins's conflict theory would seem to have the most pull. If the
cultural distinctiveness of the social classes were declining,
we would have expected the effects of social origin on
educational attainment to fall too but, as we have seen,
these effects have instead become *more* important. Similarly, a strong version of the technological functionalism
thesis would have expected these effects to have declined
as universalistic forces penetrate the educational system,
developing talent wherever it can be found. Blau and
Duncan hold that 'society cannot any longer afford the
waste of human resources a rigid class structure entails'
(Blau and Duncan, 1967 : 431), but one suspects that plenty
of wastage still exists. The balance of evidence would seem
to come down on the side of the view that the locus of
the conflict has been shifting and that 'the game is increasingly played through strategies of child rearing refereed
by schools through their certifying arrangements' (Halsey,
1977 : 184).

Blacks and whites

Universalism, said Blau and Duncan, discourages dis-

crimination against ethnic minorities. Ascribed characteristics such as the colour of one's skin should become less
and less relevant to one's educational or occupational
opportunities. Indeed, that there should be equal opportunity for people of equal talent irrespective of their
ascribed characteristics such as race and sex is a fundamental tenet of modern liberal democracies, not merely
a hypothesis of the sociologists.

To show that there is discrimination on the lines of
colour or sex we have to show at the very least that people
with the same aptitudes and qualifications get treated
differently in the labour market. It is not enough to show,
for example, that West Indians or Pakistanis are disproportionately concentrated, as indeed they are, in manual
jobs. The obvious retort would be that their qualifications
may be, on average, inferior to those of whites and that
their effective opportunities are really no worse than those
of equally qualified whites. If there really is discrimination,
on the other hand, we would find that equally qualified
blacks and whites get different levels of occupation and
income – in short, that the effect of qualifications on
occupational achievement is different for the two groups.
Even this, of course, would not *prove* discrimination.
Other mechanisms – lack of ambition or ignorance about
the job market – could always be postulated. Only actual
field experiments of the kind reported by Daniel (1968)
and McIntosh and Smith (1974) can be conclusive, but
statistical analysis of the kind Duncan employs can tell us
what the maximum effect of discrimination might be.

The basic point, then, is that if blacks have poorer
parents and lower educational levels than whites, then on
this account alone they will tend to end up with worse jobs.
The problem is to determine how much of the black/white
occupational differential can be attributed to these handi-

caps and how much remains to be explained by factors like discrimination. In one of his most famous articles Duncan showed that roughly half the black/white occupational difference could be attributed to educational differences, family size and family background. The remaining half he labelled 'occupational discrimination' and said that 'it is due literally to the fact that Negroes equally well educated as whites (in terms of years of schooling) and originating in families of comparable size and socioeconomic level do not have access to employment of equal occupational status.' (Duncan, 1968 : 99–100.)

The nearest comparable work to Duncan's in Britain has been carried out by the economists McNabb and Psacharopoulos (1981) using data from the General Household Survey. Being economists, they focussed on income rather than occupational attainment, and they included a wide range of economic determinants of income such as the number of hours worked each week, length of experience in the labour force, and the industrial sector in which the respondents worked.

They found that the 6701 white males in the sample had average annual earnings of £1519 in 1972 whereas the 172 non-whites whom they could identify earned only £1294. Grouping together West Indians, Pakistanis, Indians and East African Asians in a single category in this way is hardly ideal, for there are important cultural differences between the different groups and also some important variations in the level of education and occupation. But with a total of only 172 non-whites in the sample, amalgamation into a single category is unavoidable.

McNabb and Psacharopoulos then set out, in much the same way as Duncan, to see how much of this gap of £225 could be attributed to the poorer qualifications and experience of the non-whites, and how much remains to be explained by factors such as discrimination. Their first attempt led to a surprising result. They found that their non-whites had actually received on average *more* years of schooling than their white colleagues – they were actually better qualified in this sense – unlike the American experience. If people with equal amounts of education were paid equal amounts of income, therefore, the non-white workers would have earned considerably more than their white counterparts. McNabb and Psacharopoulos calculated that if there were no discrimination, non-white earnings might have been as much as £60 per annum greater than the white earnings, and non-white workers might thus in effect have been suffering a financial handicap on account of the colour of their skin to the tune of £285 per annum.

But this first result is somewhat misleading. Three-quarters of the non-white workers in the sample had been educated overseas, and it could be argued, not altogether unreasonably, that we are not comparing like with like. If, for example, university degrees from the Third World are of a lower standard than British ones, the earnings of holders of overseas degrees might also be expected to be lower. A year of British education on this line of argument is worth more than a year of education in the new commonwealth, and the analysis ought to take account of this.

To meet this objection McNabb and Psacharopoulos tried some alternative measures of education, namely the type of school attended and the level of qualification obtained. Among both white and non-white workers qualifications affected earnings in exactly the way one would expect. The holders of degrees received substantial earnings premiums over those who had only 'A' levels. Holders of 'A' levels in turn had a substantial (although slightly smaller) premium compared with those whose highest qualification was 'O' level, and these in turn received a premium over the unqualified. The premiums that the non-whites received were slightly less than those of the whites, but the differences were not all that great. For the non-white, as for the white, it paid to get qualified.

The type of school that the worker attended, however, had a more surprising impact on his earnings. It transpired that, among the whites, those who had been to independent schools earned substantially more than equally qualified peers who had only been to grammar, secondary modern or foreign schools. The old school tie seemed to be alive and well and bringing its wearers definite financial benefits. For the remainder of the whites, however, the type of school they attended made little difference to their earnings once the level of qualifications that they had achieved had been taken into account. The unqualified boy from a grammar school fared very little better than the unqualified leaver from a secondary modern; if the grammar school is a passport to success, this is only because it provides a surer path to the qualifications that employers want, not because it provides any particular social cachet of its own. (See also Heath and Ridge, 1980.)

Very few of the non-whites, of course, had been to English independent schools – indeed, to be precise, only one of the 172 non-white workers in the sample had done so – so there was no real scope to determine whether they would have received the same benefits from the old school tie. Their exclusion from the independent schools, like that of the white working class, thus represents a subtle form of discrimination. But the more striking result was that the non-whites who had attended British secondary modern schools earned considerably less than those who had been educated overseas and indeed received a large financial penalty compared with similarly educated white workers. The lower earning of the non-whites, therefore, could not be put down simply to the fact that they had attended in many cases foreign schools of supposedly lower standard than their English equivalents. True, some of the income gap could be attributed to this foreign education of the non-white workers, although whether these foreign schools they had attended really were inferior and really did justify lower earnings is not something we can determine from the available statistical evidence. It may or may not reflect discrimination. But there can be much less doubt that the lower earnings of the non-white secondary modern school leaver compared with his white equivalent are discriminatory, and that such discrimination accounts for a fair proportion of the income gap between the two groups. The mere colour of one's skin seems to affect one's earnings in Britain in much the same way, and probably to much the same extent, as it does in America.

McNabb and Psacharopoulos give a variety of estimates of the proportion of the income gap that can be attributed to discrimination of the kind suffered by the non-white leaver from a British secondary modern school. There is some uncertainty as to the correct answer, but it is at least one-third and possibly the whole of the gap.[6] In 1972 the cost of being non-white was at least £100 per annum. Moreover, this figure excludes the cost of any prior discrimination that takes place in school. It tells us that non-whites earn £100 a year less than equally qualified and experienced whites, but if they are penalized by the colour of their skin in the competition for educational credentials, the true cost is higher still.

Men and women

Whatever the problems of comparing blacks and whites, those with men and women are bound to be rather different. At least most white women, like most white men, will have been educated in British schools. But the basic problem is still the same. Men typically earn more than women, but the gap cannot be attributed wholly to discrimination. Women tend to have fewer or lower level qualifications, they are more likely to undertake part-time work (particularly if they are married), and they are likely to have had less work experience (notably if they have children). Part of the gap therefore must be attributed to women's lower levels of educational achievement and their lower levels of participation in the labour force; direct discrimination may account for the remainder. The central question again, then, is how much of the income gap can be explained by overt discrimination on the grounds of sex alone.

Inevitably, the problem is rather more complicated than this first quick overview allows. In the first place, we could argue that women have lower educational achievements, work fewer hours or stay at home to look after the children because of various forms of discrimination at home or at school before they ever reach the labour market. Sex-typing and the associated cultural pressures and expectations are in themselves discriminatory, it could be argued, since they lead women into domestic labour and inhibit their acquisition of those attitudes or qualifications that make for success in wage labour.

As we observed in Chapter 4, this argument is largely a semantic one. The point is that there are two different processes at work, whether or not one chooses to call either or both 'discrimination'. On the one hand girls typically experience different patterns of socialization from boys so they are already differentiated as potential workers by the time they leave school. But on the other hand, over and above this, their experiences in the labour force may vary. It seems worthwhile to separate the two processes.

The second problem concerns the identification of the precise mechanisms operating within the labour force to produce 'discrimination'. Equally qualified men and women, with equal amounts of experience and working similar hours, may still vary in their attitudes towards, say, promotion. Married women, for example, because of their domestic responsibilities, may not be as ambitious in their own careers as their husbands. Their lower earnings, therefore, could not be laid at the door of sexist employers. It could reflect the wider patterns of sex differentiation embodied in contemporary culture.

One way of dealing with this is to follow the strategy outlined in Chapter 4 and compare the earnings of *single* men and women, although this runs the opposite risk of underestimating the true extent of discrimination. Better still, we can compare the earnings of both single and married men and women, and this is what has been done by the economist Christine Greenhalgh (1977).

Greenhalgh used data from the General Household Surveys of 1971 and 1975, thus obtaining some leverage on the problem of whether the sex discrimination legislation of the early 1970s had had any effect. Let us begin with the situation in 1971. Greenhalgh found that the average annual earnings of British married men then were £1625, of their wives £523, of single men £1355, and of single women £1097. This pattern of raw income differentials is in itself quite interesting. Thus the gap between single men and women is rather bigger (both in absolute and in percentage terms) than that which McNabb and Psacharopoulos found between white and non-white male workers. The gap is £258 per annum, the single men thus earning 23·5 per cent more than the single women, whereas the white workers earned only 17·2 per cent more than the non-white workers. When we also take into account the enormous gap between married and single women, and the substantial gap between married and single men, the problem of sex and sex-role differences in earnings seems to be of a quite different order of magnitude from the ethnic differences.

It is not perhaps all that surprising that married men should earn three times as much as their wives, for it is well known that the majority of wives work part-time. In 1971 the husbands in this study worked more than forty hours a week on average (rather more than the single men or women), while their wives typically carried out less than thirty hours each week of paid market labour. How much domestic labour in the home they undertook each week is a different matter, but not one that we can pursue from these data. If we restrict our interest to wage labour, however, it is clear that *hourly* earnings may be a better starting point from which to investigate overt discimination, and this is what Greenhalgh uses. She found that in 1971 these were 71 pence for married men, 36 pence for their wives, 61 pence for the single men and 52 pence for the single women. These constitute the raw differentials which Greenhalgh sets out to explain.

There are a number of factors apart from overt discrimination which could account for these raw differentials, most obviously educational levels. There were more unqualified wives, for example, than husbands, and those of the wives with educational qualifications tended to have somewhat lower ones than their husbands. Sex roles have already played their part long before women enter the labour market. The single women, on the other hand, were the *most* qualified of all the four categories, and although a very large proportion had diplomas (particularly, one imagines, teaching diplomas) they were also more likely to have degrees than either group of men. This is in line with the suggestion we made in Chapter 4 that single women may be more ambitious and more committed to a career than their male equivalents.

It further follows from this that the effective discrimination against single women is even bigger than the raw differential with which we started. Single women earn markedly less than single men, but if they got the same returns for their qualifications and experience as men do, the gap would be reversed. Interestingly, almost all the gap between the single and married women could be explained by their differences in hours worked, qualifications obtained and so on. There was thus little evidence of discrimination against women because they are *married* – a common, although not, it would seem, a well-founded complaint in 1971. They share the same 'cost of being a woman' as do the single, but most of the enormous gap between their earnings and their husbands' can be explained by the fact that they obtain fewer qualifications, work fewer hours and take on the responsibility of children. Processes outside the labour market would seem to be crucial here.

Finally, and on a more optimistic note, Greenhalgh found that the discrimination against single women had declined in 1975, although the position of married women had not greatly improved. As she suggests: 'An explanation for what appears to have been a differential impact of the Equal Pay Act may be that single women were more likely to be doing jobs at senior level, for which obvious comparisons between men and women doing similar work were possible. Married women, especially those working part-time ... were more likely to be in sex-segregated employment in which the Equal Pay Act was less effective.' (Greenhalgh, 1977 : 19.) The ascribed characteristics of sex and race still have their cost.

Conclusions

Path models tell us about the factors which influence the attainments of the 'average man', and the main lesson to be drawn from Chapter 5 was that there is wide variation in the fortunes of ordinary people from similar social backgrounds; social origins and educational attainment may influence the kinds of job we get and the levels of income we earn, but the known influences like these which we have been able to measure are greatly outweighed by the unknown or unmeasured. So when we ask about the relative importance of ascription and achievement we should remember that luck may be far more important than either. And while the evidence of this chapter shows that ascribed characteristics such as class, sex and race still affect men and women's fortunes, an apologist for the status quo could argue that their actual importance is small. He could point out that in the early 1970s white men earned, on average, 17 per cent more than non-white, men from Class I origins earned 71 per cent more than those from Class VII origins,[7] and single men earned 23 per cent more than single women, but that men whose *current* job was in Class I earned 120 per cent more than those whose current job was in Class VII,[8] while men in the top tenth of the income distribution earned over 200 per cent more than those in the bottom tenth.[9] On this view, the circumstances of birth do not have much influence on our eventual fate.

At heart this is the same issue as the one we discussed in Chapter 2 when we asked whether movement from rags to riches was rare or not. Whether something looks big or small, important or unimportant, depends on what we compare it with. A gap of 20 per cent looks rather small if we juxtapose it to one of 200 per cent, but if we hold that there should not be any gap at all, one of 20 per cent looks much more serious. The contrast is also between *inequality of opportunity* and *inequality of outcome*. To say that the income gap between blacks and whites is 'only' 17 per cent compared with the 200 per cent gap between rich and poor is in a way to point out that the inequality of outcome is a larger problem than the inequalities of opportunity to achieve good or bad outcomes. It reminds us that wealth and poverty are recreated anew in each generation although the chances of becoming rich or poor are not distributed wholly at random. And so how much importance we attach to these gaps between blacks and whites or men and women is almost more of a political issue than a sociological one.

It is, however, a sociological task to identify the sources of these inequalities and the processes that generate them. The figures of 17, 71 and 23 per cent give the *overall* differences between blacks and whites, and so on, but why do blacks earn less than whites – is it because they are less intelligent, less educated, or less ambitious? Or is it due to discrimination? The kind of evidence we have reported only makes a start at answering these notoriously difficult questions. That there are innate differences between the sexes, classes or ethnic groups cannot be doubted, but that these differences have any direct impact on their occupational fortunes is implausible and certainly has never been demonstrated. But what we can sensibly say is that *none* of the gap between single men and women can be explained by women's inferior educational attainments (since in fact they are superior); that *some* of the gap between blacks and whites can be attributed to their different educational histories; and that about *half* of the gap between those from Class I and Class VII origins is educational in character.[10]

Of the gaps that remain between single men and women, blacks and whites, or men from different class origins even after we have taken account of their qualifications, a variety of explanations are possible. We could put it down to overt discrimination against women, blacks and the working class; or we could argue that these groups have characteristics which we have failed to measure – lack of ambition or intelligence, for example. In the case of single women the latter argument looks implausible in the extreme: if they are less ambitious and less intelligent, why do they have higher levels of educational attainment than single men? In the case of blacks, too, we know from the studies of Daniel (1968) and of McIntosh and Smith (1974) that overt discrimination is at least part of the story. Only in the case of class is there really much scope for argument. It is certainly quite reasonable to hold, as Collins does, that there is a struggle between status groups in the labour market, the dominant groups showing a preference for their fellow-members in recruitment and promotion, but this has not been demonstrated quite so unequivocally as it has been for women and blacks.

But while direct discrimination against women, blacks and, probably, the working class still persists, such evidence as we have suggests that it may be on the wane. Here, however, our material on the changing importance of the direct and indirect effects of class origins on occupational attainment may be particularly instructive.

Education has come to play an increasing role in the transmission of status (loosely defined) from father to son; the *direct* influence of social origins – whether through patronage, nepotism, inheritance or some other mechanism – on occupational attainment has declined, but simultaneously its *indirect* influence via the educational system has increased as family background has become more closely linked to educational success and failure. One possible interpretation of our results is this: under the impact of governmental reforms, the spread of bureaucracy and of a meritocratic ideology, the long-run trend has been away from patronage, nepotism and direct inheritance; the struggle between the different status groups has therefore moved to a different arena, competition for educational resources and qualifications taking the place of that for favours and patronage. The new terrain offers different advantages and hindrances to the protagonists so the outcomes are slightly different from before – just as competitive examinations for the civil service gave an unexpected advantage to the children of the clergy – but the struggle most emphatically continues, each group trying to improve its position or make the best of a bad one.

It is one of the paradoxes of a free society that privileged groups must retain the freedom to fight in protection of their privileges. As society tries to become 'fairer', with equal pay legislation and the like, new 'unfairnesses' may arise as the dominant groups try to find new ways of perpetuating their position. Direct discrimination in the labour market may decline but competition for schooling and credentials may intensify. How the different groups are equipped for this new battle remains to be seen, but it would not be surprising if the most affluent sectors of society found that the independent schools could act as a bulwark to their position while within the state system neighbourhood comprehensive schools evolved to satisfy the ambitions of the (residentially segregated) middle classes. Discrimination may decline, but new mechanisms to perpetuate unequal opportunity may take its place. Blacks and women may gradually secure equal treatment from employers as do similarly qualified white males, but they may begin to lose out even more in the struggle to acquire qualifications.

7 International Comparisons

Ever since the publication of Lipset and Bendix's book, international comparisons have been one of the most challenging, but also most frustrating, areas of mobility research. Comparisons promise to help answer one of the central questions of stratification theory: do class systems tend to converge as societies industrialize, the needs of a modern industrial society demanding and creating high rates of mobility? Or do values and culture, political regime and deliberate political action shape patterns of stratification, producing distinctively different kinds of modern industrial society? Unfortunately, to date, the answers have got lost in a morass of technical complexities and statistical sophistication.

Let us begin with the theories. The first contender is the theory of technological functionalism which we met in Chapter 6. This comes in various guises, but the central thrust, as John Goldthorpe explains, concerns the '... standardizing effects upon social structures of the exigencies of modern technology and of an advanced economy. These factors which make for uniformity in industrial societies are seen as largely over-riding other factors which may make for possible diversity, such as different national cultures or different political systems. Thus, the overall pattern of development which is suggested is one in which,

once countries enter into the advanced stages of industrialization, they tend to become increasingly comparable in
their major institutional arrangements and in their social
systems generally. In brief, a convergent pattern of
development is hypothesized.' (Goldthorpe, 1964: 97.)

This was in essence the theory that Lipset and Bendix
had advanced to account for their finding that the industrial societies they surveyed had broadly similar rates of
total vertical mobility across the manual/non-manual line.
They stressed processes 'inherent in all modern social structures', notably the expansion of professional, managerial
and white-collar work, creating a surge of upward mobility:
'more and more people are needed to manage industry,
to distribute goods, to provide personal services, and to
run the ever-growing state bureaucracy.' (Lipset and
Bendix, 1959: 57–8.) They mention other processes, too,
such as the decline in the number of inheritable status
positions, but the changing shape of the occupational
structure which industrialization brings they see as a major
source of the high rates of mobility which they observed.

Against this, various writers have argued that cultural
and political diversity can produce variations in mobility
rates, or indeed in the occupational structure itself.[1] One
of the main empirical bases for their claims was provided
by Miller's (1960) comparison of mobility rates in seventeen different countries. Whereas Lipset and Bendix
concentrated on 'mass' mobility across the manual/non-
manual line, Miller looked also at mobility into and out
of the 'elite' and found here much more national variation.
Indeed, this is something that even technological functionalists such as Lipset and Bendix or Blau and Duncan have
emphasized. The latter, for example, claimed that upward
mobility from manual backgrounds to the professional and
managerial stratum was particularly high in the USA

compared with other countries, and they concluded: 'There is a grain of truth in the Horatio Alger myth. The high level of popular education in the United States, perhaps reinforced by the lesser emphasis on formal distinctions of social status, has provided the disadvantaged lower strata with outstanding opportunities for long-distance upward mobility.' (Blau and Duncan, 1967 : 435.)

A variety of cultural and political sources of variation in mobility rates, whether 'mass' or 'elite', can be suggested. Implicit in Blau and Duncan's remark is the idea that there are fewer barriers to mobility in a less status-conscious 'new' society like America than in the 'old' societies of Europe with their heritage of aristocratic and feudal pasts. It is an hypothesis we could extend to embrace Australia and Canada as well: we might expect this group of new societies to exhibit higher rates of mobility, particularly into the elite, than those which boast a traditional ruling class anxious and able to retain its privileges.

Another hypothesis (advanced by Parkin, 1971) is that among Western European countries those where left-wing parties have had long periods of power will exhibit higher rates of mobility. The main argument underlying this thesis is that such governments can use the educational system as a tool for social reform. Education is directly under the control of the state; it has a close link with occupational attainment; and measures such as free secondary education or maintenance grants for students at university can, in theory, enable larger numbers of working-class students to obtain the educational qualifications needed for entry into elite occupations. By reforming the educational system, therefore, it is claimed that the state can widen opportunities both educationally and socially; political action increases equality of opportunity and upward mobility increases accordingly.

The most dramatic experiments in social reform are, of course, those of the communist countries, and Parkin goes on to argue that one of the most significant differences in the reward systems of socialist and capitalist societies is the 'range and extent of upward mobility' in the communist countries of Eastern Europe (Parkin, 1971 : 154). There are a number of reasons why the socialist societies might be more open. One is the transformation of some Eastern European countries from largely peasant and agricultural societies to modern industrial economies, achieved if not overnight then at least within a couple of generations. Their occupational transformation has been particularly rapid and their 'upward surge of mobility' accordingly large. Another reason would be educational reform, aimed at securing equality of opportunity, which one might expect a totalitarian government to be able to effect more thoroughly than its reformist counterparts in a 'free', Western society. Yet another might be the same 'low degree of status deference between social strata' that Blau and Duncan attributed to America. In the supposedly 'classless' societies of the communist bloc the ideology that 'all men are equal' might be expected to perform the same function that that of 'individual liberty' does in the United States.

At all events, it is possible to think of reasons why industrialized nations should differ in their rates of social mobility, particularly in rates of mobility into the elite. The most closed societies, we might expect, would be the traditional and conservative societies of Western Europe; the most open, paradoxically, might be on the one hand the USA, the land of opportunity and aggressive individualism, and on the other, their ideological rivals of the communist bloc.

Unfortunately, before we turn to the evidence, there are

some thorny technical questions with which we have to tangle. First, there are problems over the comparability of data. Enquiries, even national random sample surveys conducted by trained sociologists, are unlikely to employ identical procedures. If there are difficulties of comparability between the 1949 and 1972 enquiries in Britain, where the investigators spoke the same language and did indeed talk to each other, how much greater are the problems likely to be in comparing studies from different cultures.[2]

The comparability of the occupational classifications used is one of the most visible problems. Not only does everyone seem to devise their own individual schema so that it is not practicable to construct any common framework, but also, quite aside from practicability, it is not even clear that a common framework is *theoretically* appropriate in societies with different class structures. For example, it is frequently asserted that clerical work has lower status in the socialist societies of Eastern Europe than it has in the West. Thus Parkin has argued that '... we cannot represent the reward structure of socialist society as a dichotomous class model on exactly the Western pattern, since there is much less of an obvious "break" between manual and non-manual positions. The lower non-manual categories in socialist society could not be said to enjoy the same kinds of status, material, and social advantages over skilled or relatively well-paid manual workers as do their counterparts in capitalist society. Consequently, they cannot really be regarded as forming the tail-end of a professional middle class in quite the same way.' (Parkin, 1971 : 147.)

If this argument is sound, it follows that mobility across the manual/non-manual division means rather different things in the two types of society, at least from the perspective of *vertical* mobility. In practice, however, as I have suggested earlier, it may not be very sensible to think of manual/non-manual movement as necessarily involving vertical mobility, even in the West. Such movement entails a shift of class position, but it is by no means clear that a dichotomous class model is nowadays an appropriate way of characterizing Western capitalist society. In this respect, capitalist and socialist societies may be more similar than Parkin allows.

Nevertheless, the problem in principle remains, and it is, I suspect, even more serious when we consider the 'elite'. When writers such as Miller (1960) talk of elites, they are thinking of the occupations with the highest social standing or general desirability – the kind of occupation that comes into the Class I that we have been using throughout this book. They are not thinking of the very small *governing* elite, for members of this elite so seldom appear even in the largest mobility enquiries that no safe conclusions can be drawn about them from such sources. This does not matter, provided we make clear what we are talking about. The more serious problem, however, is where we draw the line between the elite and the mass. By virtue of its size, a big elite is likely to be relatively open, and it could be claimed that when Blau and Duncan found 'outstanding opportunities for long-distance upward mobility' in the United States, they had merely created a statistical artefact: the categories they used gave the USA an enormous elite, and the statistical techniques they deployed did not control for this satisfactorily.

The size of the categories raises the major statistical problem of comparative mobility research; indeed, until it is solved no real progress can be made. If we wish to discriminate between technological functionalism and the cultural variation thesis, for example, we must be able to sort out how much mobility there is, while *controlling for differences in the occupational structures* (that is, in the size of the categories). Industrialization, it is suggested, shapes the occupational structure, expanding the elite and the non-manual strata and thus leading to greater mobility. If societies are at slightly different levels of industrialization they will have different occupational structures, and to sustain a cultural variation thesis we need to know whether there are differences in mobility rates over and above the ones that the changing structure has induced. True, it can be argued (as we have already done in the Eastern European context) that culture may itself shape occupational structure; the pace of industrialization and the particular direction it takes may well be determined by political forces. They cannot really be treated as exogenous economic changes brought about by some autonomous 'logic of industrialism'. But at the least the technological functionalist needs to show that there are no cultural variations beyond these structurally induced ones, and his opponent is accordingly on stronger ground if he can demonstrate such variation.

Controlling for differences in the occupational structures is no easy matter. There are two sources of trouble, the *size* of the categories distinguished and their *rate of change*. Thus if the elite has been static over time and contains 10 per cent of the employed population, a maximum of 20 per cent of the population and a minimum of zero can be mobile across the elite/non-elite border; if it has doubled in size, over what could loosely be termed a generation, from 5 to 10 per cent, the maximum is 15 and the minimum 5 per cent; if it has doubled in size from 10 to 20 per cent of the population, the maximum is 30 and the minimum 10 per cent; and if it has remained static at 20 per cent of the population, the maximum becomes 40 per cent and the minimum returns to zero.

All kinds of statistical techniques have been used to try to deal with these problems – the distinction between net and exchange mobility, the use of the index of association, the disparity ratio or the odds ratio, log-linear modelling and proportional marginal adjustment.[3] None of them is entirely satisfactory, and it would be silly to maintain that there is at present a 'correct' statistical technique for analysing mobility tables. Given that there is no right way, there is a lot to be said for using simple techniques which can be readily interpreted, and this is what we shall do. We must remember, too, that no amount of statistical sophistication can make up for the questionable quality of the data. As ever, the chain is as strong as its weakest link.

Mass mobility

We shall start with mobility across the manual/non-manual line. For all its defects this has one great advantage – it is a division that nearly all mobility enquiries report in some form or other and so it maximizes our sample of countries. There are in fact nineteen industrialized societies on which I have been able to obtain usable data: Australia, Belgium, Bulgaria, Canada, Denmark, England and Wales, Finland, France, Hungary, Italy, Japan, Norway, Poland, Spain, Sweden, USA, USSR, West Germany and Yugoslavia.[4] In selecting countries three rules were employed: (1) the sample had to be a representative national one; (2) the sample had to be relatively recent, that is, post-1960; (3) the report had to distinguish between manual, non-manual and farm categories.

The first of these three rules leads to the exclusion of studies of cities in developing countries such as Malaysia, the Philippines and Latin America.[5] A comparison with these societies would be extremely interesting, particularly as the technological functionalist thesis makes an implicit comparison with pre-industrial societies which are alleged to have lower rates of social mobility. But what is distinctive about pre-industrial society is the size of the rural and agricultural sector, and it is here, one suspects, that the lower rates of mobility are to be found. Reliance on urban studies might thus be very misleading as a basis for comparison with the industrialized world. However, I must confess that I have allowed myself to break this rule in the case of the USSR – the data used here coming from three towns in the Tatar Republic. Earlier work such as that of Miller had used data collected from Russian emigrés and had reported unusually high rates of upward mobility. Emigrés must be one of the worst possible sources of information, but the intrinsic interest of stratification processes in the Soviet Union is such that one is prepared to stoop to almost any source. I sympathize with Miller but hope that Soviet data such as those on the Tatar Republic may help to put his figures in perspective.

The second rule ensures that there is no overlap between our material and that of Lipset and Bendix or Miller. By starting with new sets of data, all collected since they wrote, we give ourselves a fresh start and the best chance of an independent test of their theses.

The third rule did not prove to be a very restrictive one (removing only Scotland from the list of countries included).[6] The point is again that the mobility chances of landless agricultural workers are often extremely poor, while inheritance among farmers themselves is particularly high. This is not crucial in England and Wales, where the agricultural sector is very small, but to combine agricultural labourers with the industrial working class would have a marked effect on the results in any East European country – it is considerably more important than where we draw the line between the manual and non-manual categories.[7]

Now for some results. We shall begin with the simplest kind of analysis, that carried out by Lipset and Bendix. They looked at the mobility of the non-farm population across the manual/non-manual line, finding, it will be recalled, high and similar rates of mobility of around 30 per cent. Column 2 of Table 7.1 gives the proportions for our nineteen societies. The new sample suggests high and similar rates around 30 per cent just as did Lipset and Bendix's. In other words the grounds for saying that all industrial societies end up with comparable high rates of mobility as a result of the inherent features of industrialism are at least as good now as they were when Lipset and Bendix wrote. But they are not very good. Judgements like 'height' and 'similarity', as we have remarked before, lie very much in the eye of the beholder. With a little statistical sleight of hand we could easily make them look low or dissimilar.

One simple step, for example, would be to include the farm population in our calculations of mobility. Lipset and Bendix wholly excluded farmers and farm workers from their analysis, but it is easy enough to construct a three-class model consisting of non-manual, manual, and farm workers respectively and to calculate the percentage moving between these three categories. This is done in column 3 of Table 7.1. The resulting percentages are much higher than Lipset and Bendix's, reflecting the common-place fact that the more categories we employ, the more mobility we detect.

A more interesting point is that it is by no means the same societies which exhibit the highest rates of mobility

Table 7.1 International comparisons: mass mobility

Country (column 1)	Manual/ non-manual mobility (%) (column 2)	Total mobility (column 3)	Size of non- manual class (%) (column 4)
Australia (1965)	33·2 (7)	41·4 (11)	40·5 (13)
Belgium (1968)	30·1 (13)	37·0 (16)	58·6 (11)
Bulgaria (1967)	28·5 (14)	51·2 (2)	23·0 (19)
Canada (1974)	37·5 (1)	50·1 (3)	53·9 (3)
Denmark (1972)	31·0 (9)	37·9 (14)	44·2 (6)
England & Wales (1972)	33·7 (6)	37·6 (15)	43·6 (7)
Finland (1972)	25·6 (18)	42·3 (9)	32·9 (17)
France (1970)	34·0 (5)	43·7 (8)	48·5 (1)
Hungary (1973)	30·2 (11)	50·0 (4)	28·6 (18)
Italy (1963)	25·5 (19)	37·0 (16)	41·4 (11)
Japan (1965)	28·0 (15)	46·4 (7)	57·0 (9)
Norway (1972)	36·1 (4)	47·6 (6)	55·2 (4)
Poland (1972)	30·7 (10)	40·7 (12)	35·1 (15)
Spain (1974)	27·2 (16)	40·3 (13)	52·2 (2)
Sweden (1974)	37·0 (2)	51·5 (1)	43·4 (8)
USA (1973)	36·5 (3)	48·2 (5)	44·8 (4)
USSR (1967–8)	31·5 (8)	– –	34·0 (16)
West Germany (1969)	27·0 (17)	41·7 (10)	58·0 (10)
Yugoslavia (1960)	30·2 (11)	37·0 (16)	37·3 (14)

Source: see Note 4 to Chapter 7.
Figures in columns 2 and 4 are calculated for non-farm populations.
Figures in column 3 give the total mobility between manual,
non-manual and farm categories.
Figures in brackets in column 1 give the dates of the surveys, those
in columns 2–4 give the rank orderings.

as calculated by the two different measures used for columns 2 and 3. Thus Bulgaria and Hungary come well down the ranking in column 2 but are at the top of the ranking in column 3. The reason for this reversal is clear enough: Bulgaria and Hungary are two societies which have experienced particularly rapid contractions in the size of their agricultural sectors, and on that account have had high levels of 'forced' mobility out of farm work into manual work.

The pattern of mobility in a given country cannot, then, sensibly be summarized by a single index. But let us for the moment concentrate on the manual/non-manual mobility discussed by Lipset and Bendix. Providing we remember to accept this measure for what it is, we can derive considerable illumination. But unlike Lipset and Bendix let us pay attention to the variation in the figures rather than the 'similarity'.

The first point of interest is that Canada, Sweden and the USA head the ranking in column 2 – they are the countries which exhibit the highest rates of manual/ non-manual mobility – while Italy, Spain and West Germany are the most closed (on this criterion). Even from these relatively crude data, then, there is a clear pattern, with 'new' or left-wing democratic countries towards the top and the 'old' conservative societies of Western Europe towards the bottom.

This is certainly a good start for any cultural variation thesis, but how far can these results be explained by occupational structure? Column 4 in Table 7.1 provides the beginning of an answer, ranking societies according to the size of their non-manual classes. As we have seen, the closer the manual/non-manual division gets to 50:50, the higher is the maximum amount of mobility that the society could exhibit. Conversely, the more skewed is the distribution between the two classes, the lower is the amount of mobility that could take place across the border. Accordingly we rank France first with its 48·5 : 51·5 division between the two classes; next comes Spain at 52·2 : 47·8; third comes Canada at 53·9 : 46·1 and so on. We would expect to find, simply as a consequence of the arithmetic of mobility tables, a clear similarity in the rankings of columns 2 and 4, and so we do on the whole. The correlation between the two rankings is actually ·454, quite high by sociologists' standards.

Much more interesting, however, are the *differences* between the two rankings. These are what really begin to tell us whether there are any cultural variations not explained by occupational structure. To begin with, we find a group of countries whose rank is very similar in the two columns. They are Belgium, Canada, Denmark, England and Wales, Finland, Norway, the USA and Yugoslavia. Next there is a group which exhibits markedly *more* mobility than the relative sizes of their classes would predict: Australia, Bulgaria, Hungary, Poland, Sweden and USSR. And thirdly there are the societies with markedly *less* mobility than expected: France, Italy, Japan, Spain and West Germany. It is a distinctly different picture from our first one, and also rather remarkable. The countries have fallen into three groups that are surprisingly homogeneous culturally and about whom it is really quite easy to tell plausible explanatory stories. Consider our first group, those with the 'predictable' mobility rates. These are the middle-of-the-road Western European countries like Britain, which has had an alternation of right- and left-wing governments. It also includes Yugoslavia, the communist society which comes closest to the Western European model with its practice of 'market socialism'. The surprising inclusions are those of the USA and

Canada, 'new' societies which the theory had anticipated would prove relatively open, but here there is a technical problem. These are two of the societies which come closest to the 50:50 division between manual and non-manual employment; they come towards the top of the rank ordering of column 4, and so they can hardly get a much higher ranking in columns 2 or 3. There *may* be a cultural variation here which we have failed to pick up.

Our next group is more clear-cut. It contains all our Eastern European socialist societies, with the exception of Yugoslavia; and from the West it has Sweden, a country with a long history of socialist government, and Australia, another of our 'new' societies (although not a particularly socialist one). Finally, the countries with less mobility than expected are another clear-cut group of traditional, right-wing societies from Western Europe joined by a traditional society from the orient, Japan, a country with a strong feudal heritage and whose people show as strong (or stronger) a deference for social status as any in the 'old' societies of Europe. Indeed, we observe that, with the exception of France, all the countries in this last group have had fascist governments at some stage in the present century. Overall, the results seem to lend strong support to the view that the political regime and ideology of a country are associated with its level of mobility. The left-right political continuum seems to predict quite well whether a society is more or less mobile than its occupational structure would have suggested. The old-new dichotomy receives less support on the other hand, but is not entirely without evidence in its favour. In short, technology, industrialization and occupational structure may be powerfully related to societies' levels of mobility (although they cannot entirely be separated from the decisions of sociologists where to draw the lines between social classes), but they still leave room for cultural variation.

Unfortunately, no argument in sociology can ever be settled quite this easily. So far we have taken account only of the current size of the two classes, not their rate of change. But we know that the faster the rate of change, the more mobility is forced upon a country, and Table 7.2 shows very clearly that the societies of Eastern Europe which came in our 'mobile' group have also had the fastest rates of change, while the 'old' societies of Western Europe which belong to the 'immobile' or 'closed' group have had more static occupational structures.[8] The technological functionalist could certainly argue that these 'immobile' societies are the mature industrial ones which have achieved large white-collar sectors, the growth of which has necessarily levelled off, while the apparent openness of the Eastern bloc is more a function of their earlier stage of industrialization, and their consequent more rapid change, than of their political and ideological complexion. They are, it might be claimed, societies in transition. We have caught them at an earlier stage in the move to full industrial development. But once they have achieved occupational structures of similar sizes and rates of change to Western ones, their mobility patterns will tend to converge too.

There is undoubtedly some merit in this argument, and it is difficult to refute, although we should also remember the theoretical point which we have already made: rates of change may themselves be influenced by political action and might indeed be one of the main mechanisms whereby left-wing regimes secure higher rates of mobility. We cannot test this particular hypothesis, but there are some other relevant pieces of evidence to which we can turn.

First of all, Table 7.2 looks at levels of inflow into the non-manual classes. These are of great interest in their own

Table 7.2 International comparisons: inflow into the non-manual class

Country	% of non-manual class recruited from manual and farm backgrounds	% increase in size of non-manual class
(column 1)	(column 2)	(column 3)
Australia	55·4 (11)	34·6 (16)
Belgium	44·7 (16)	47·6 (11)
Bulgaria	77·7 (2)	144·6 (3)
Canada	56·3 (9)	70·5 (5)
Denmark	50·3 (14)	38·3 (15)
England & Wales	53·4 (12)	40·4 (14)
Finland	62·1 (5)	47·1 (13)
France	44·4 (17)	19·9 (19)
Hungary	77·8 (1)	220·7 (1)
Italy	42·9 (18)	28·3 (17)
Japan	48·8 (15)	49·5 (10)
Norway	55·7 (10)	63·7 (7)
Poland	72·5 (3)	153·3 (2)
Spain	52·8 (13)	63·9 (6)
Sweden	60·4 (6)	58·5 (9)
USA	58·2 (7)	59·8 (8)
USSR	56·4 (8)	47·6 (11)
West Germany	36·5 (19)	20·4 (18)
Yugoslavia	70·0 (4)	123·9 (4)

Sources: see Note 4 to Chapter 7.
Figures in brackets give the rank orderings.

right, since they tell us about the social homogeneity of the white-collar world. They might also be expected to show a close relationship with rates of expansion and differences in the rank orderings may therefore be a particularly illuminating source of evidence on cultural variation.

There are in fact fewer deviations in the two sets of rank orderings in Table 7.2 than there were in 7.1. As expected, we see that the Eastern European countries have had extremely rapid change and enormous inflows. They head both lists, and so there is no scope for any cultural variation to show itself. Conversely, France, Italy and West Germany come at the bottom of both lists. There are, however, three distinctive exceptions to this general pattern – Australia, Spain and Sweden. At the very least these three societies reveal the influence of social and cultural forces that cannot be attributed to occupational change.

Consider, first, Australia, our remaining representative of a 'new' society, and Sweden, our representative 'left-wing' democracy. They prove to be more mobile than expected in *both* tables and do markedly better than other societies at comparable levels of industrialization. Sweden, for example, has a more skewed occupational structure and a slower rate of change than the USA, Spain, Canada or Norway, and yet on almost every index is more open than they are. Again, Australia has a more skewed occupational structure and lower rate of growth than Denmark, England and Wales, Japan, Spain and Belgium, but on most criteria is more open than they are. In the other direction we find that Spain's division between the classes comes closer to 50 : 50, its rate of growth is faster, and yet its mobility lower than that of Australia, England and Wales, Norway and the USA.

In these three cases, then, we can make clear and unambiguous comparisons and show that between comparable societies there are still definite differences in mobility rates. These comparisons give us the strongest basis for asserting that cultural variations have an impact on patterns of mobility. They confirm our picture of Canada, Denmark, England, Norway and USA as middle-of-the-road societies, of Australia and Sweden as relatively open, and Spain as relatively closed, given their levels and rates of industrialization. It becomes progressively harder to know where to place the other societies where direct and unambiguous comparisons of this kind cannot be made, but I would have little hesitation in placing Japan in the 'closed' category; and, by extension from the cases of Sweden, of the middle-of-the-road countries, and of Spain, I would suggest that the weight of evidence supports a left/right interpretation which could also apply to Germany, France and Italy.

The only countries on which I do not think we can express a clear view are those in the Eastern bloc. Their stage of development is still perhaps too different for us to venture soundly based conclusions. There is, however, one unambiguous comparison which we can make between East and West Europe. The USSR has a more skewed occupational structure than Belgium, has had the same rate of growth of the white-collar class, but is clearly more open on all our indices.

By thus using the simple statistical technique of paired comparisons we can provide the clearest evidence that has yet been achieved for cultural variations. All of our main groups – 'old' and 'new' societies, democratic and communist, right- and left-wing – have at least one member involved in these comparisons, and the upshot is that, even when we control for *both* size *and* rate of change (the two bugbears of international comparisons) our initial hypotheses about political and cultural variation are sustained.

Elite mobility

International comparisons of elite mobility have usually been thought to give more scope for cultural variation, but in fact we shall find that they are rather disappointing. Earlier writers such as Miller (1960) did not control adequately for the size of the elites they distinguished, and a lot of the variation they detected is actually a statistical artefact.

There are two main problems with elite comparisons (in addition to all the usual ones, of course). First, only a limited number of studies distinguish a separate elite at all, and so our sample is immediately reduced from nineteen to eleven countries. Secondly, and more importantly, the definitions of the elite vary far more than do those of white and blue collar, and the consequences of this variation are far more drastic. It is indeed rather strange that sociologists have traditionally worried over the manual/non-manual borderline and its meaning but have paid little attention to the elite and the occupations which should be included.

The problem with the nature of the elite can be seen from Table 7.3. We see that the spread in elite size, leaving England and Wales aside, is enormous and extremely consequential for our indices of openness. They range from the USA, where the 'upper middle class', as Featherman and Hauser (1978) termed it, includes almost a third of the adult male population, to Italy where the ruling class (Lopreato's term) covers less than 3 per cent. There is clearly no sense in which these are comparable. America's upper middle class includes all professionals and managers as well as some salesmen whereas Italy's ruling class is restricted to 'national political leaders; large-scale proprietors and entrepreneurs; high executives and govern-

Table 7.3 International comparisons: access to the 'elite'

Country (column 1)	Elite/non-manual odds ratio (column 2)	Elite/manual odds ratio (column 3)	Size of elite (%) (column 4)
Australia	1·3 (1)	5.9 (2)	17·4 (3)
England & Wales 1	7·5 (11)	239·9 (11)	1·5 (13)
England & Wales 2	2·5 (4)	20·9 (5)	13·7 (6)
England & Wales 3	2·7 (5)	9·8 (3)	25·1 (2)
France	4·3 (10)	46·8 (10)	7·6 (8)
Hungary	3·0 (6)	33·3 (9)	6·4 (10)
Italy	9·6 (13)	582·0 (12)	2·8 (12)
Japan	3·7 (7)	21·2 (6)	14·9 (4)
Spain	8·3 (12)	1181·0 (13)	7·6 (8)
Sweden	3·8 (8)	23·7 (7)	10·5 (7)
USA	1·9 (2)	4·9 (1)	31·2 (1)
West Germany	4·2 (9)	19·8 (4)	14·5 (5)
Yugoslavia	2·4 (3)	29·7 (8)	4·1 (11)

Sources: see Note 4 to Chapter 7.
Figures in brackets give the rank orderings.

ment officials; professionals with a university degree' (Lopreato, 1965 : 314). We are certainly not comparing like with like here; nor can the differences in size be attributed to America's higher level of industrialization – they are differences rather of the sociologists' classification. Indeed, it would be quite wrong to suppose that Table 7.3 gives any support whatever for a technological functionalist theory and for the thesis that the elite expands and becomes more open as a society industrializes. It simply tells us that if the sociologist includes a larger and less select group in his topmost category he will find that it is more accessible to the lower strata. He is simply rediscovering the elementary truth we described in Chapter 2: the higher we climb the more exclusive is the company.

The most satisfactory solution would be to reanalyse all our surveys including only a standard set of occupations, preferably those which Lopreato uses, in our topmost category. Unfortunately very few studies permit us to do this. They distinguish between salaried and self-employed professionals, for example, and between professionals and managers, but they do not distinguish within these categories the higher and lower grades, and this is what we really need. Fortunately, however, the British survey does give us more detail, and from this we can calculate three different 'elites'. Elite 1 includes only the self-employed professionals and large entrepreneurs which, as we saw in Chapter 2, were the two most exclusive groups in Class 1. To make it really comparable with Lopreato's ruling class we would need to add some top executives, civil servants and politicians, but we do at least know that their inclusion would serve to increase the openness of this category. Elite 2 is simply the Class I that we have used throughout, containing the higher grades of manager, official and professional. And elite 3 is composed of Classes I and II, thus adding the lower grades and coming into line with Featherman and Hauser's (very generous) definition of the upper middle class.

Now for the results. We have not computed the rates of mobility across the elite/non-elite borderline since this will be so influenced by the size of the elite as to be meaningless. Instead we present two sets of odds ratios: the first compares the chances of men from elite and non-manual backgrounds of achieving and avoiding occupations in these two categories; the second compares the chances of men from elite and manual backgrounds.

The odds ratio is a measure of *relative* mobility chances rather than the *absolute* rates which we have used before. Thus the odds ratios computed in column 2 compare the relative chances of people from elite and non-manual backgrounds of entering these two classes. Or, as Goldthorpe puts it, odds ratios may 'be most usefully interpreted sociologically as showing the outcome of a series of "competitions" between men of different class origins to achieve – or avoid – occupationally one rather than another location within the class structure. The closer the value of an odds ratio to unity, the more "equal", or the more "perfect", is the particular competition to which it refers; that is, the lower within this competition is the association between class of origin and class of destination.' (Goldthorpe *et al.*, 1978: 452.)

The odds ratio also has some convenient statistical properties. It is not affected by the marginal totals in the way that the Index of Association and the disparity ratio are (see Appendix II). Nevertheless, as we can see from Table 7.3, it is still quite closely related to the size of the elite which has been distinguished.[9] This is because (as we have seen for Britain) rather different social processes occur at the apex of the class structure from those which prevail lower down. As before, then, we must compare countries' positions on the different rank-orderings.

Following this procedure, the same pattern emerges as before. Australia has a more open elite than its size alone would predict. So do the two communist countries that remain in our sample. England and the USA remain middle-of-the-road, while Italy, Japan, Spain and West Germany are again the most closed. The only significant changes are that Sweden's relatively high rate of mass

Table 7.4 International comparisons: inflow into the elite

Country (column 1)	% of elite recruited from non-elite origins (column 2)	% of elite recruited from manual and farm origins (column 3)	% increase in size of elite (column 4)
Australia	75·4 (6)	53·9 (4)	40·2 (9)
England & Wales 1	78·6 (3)	30·2 (10)	0 (12)
England & Wales 2	76·1 (5)	44·5 (6)	87·4 (5)
England & Wales 3	69·2 (9)	48·6 (5)	90·5 (4)
France	71·0 (7)	23·2 (12)	44·2 (8)
Hungary	83·2 (1)	65·8 (1)	224·3 (1)
Italy	56·7 (12)	13·5 (13)	7·5 (13)
Japan	68·7 (10)	42·2 (8)	47·0 (7)
Spain	53·9 (13)	29·1 (11)	40·1 (10)
Sweden	76·4 (4)	43·2 (7)	113·6 (2)
USA	70·7 (8)	54·0 (3)	102·8 (3)
West Germany	61·3 (11)	33·7 (9)	6·5 (11)
Yugoslavia	80·4 (2)	56·0 (2)	84·2 (6)

Sources: see Note 4 to Chapter 7.
Figures in brackets give the rank orderings.

mobility does not seem to apply to its elite, while France appears to have a somewhat less closed elite than the other traditional, right-wing societies. These two countries' elites seem to be about as open as their size would predict, and they shift from the 'open' and 'closed' categories which they joined after Table 7.1 to the middle-of-the-road category instead. This again provides some slight evidence that elites are less influenced by social and cultural variation than had been supposed.

Finally, let us turn to an inflow analysis. Table 7.4 gives the picture. It shows extraordinarily high levels of inflow into the elite. The flow of 'new men' into Class I, which was such a striking feature of mobility in Britain, now proves to be a commonplace by international standards. Even Italy and Spain, the most closed of our societies, still have over half their elites drawn from new men, while in the communist world the proportion is more than four-fifths. Heterogeneity of the elite would seem to characterize all our industrialized societies.

But this initial picture is almost certainly a misleading one. Dissimilarity re-emerges if we look at the origins of the inflows. At one extreme comes Italy with only an eighth of its elite drawn from manual or farm backgrounds. At the other comes Hungary with nearly two-thirds drawn from these origins. This is perhaps the most dramatic contrast we shall find between capitalist and socialist society, and even if the difference can be explained by their rates of growth, the implications for the cultural and social cohesion of the elites in these two countries must be substantial. Italy conforms most closely to our stereotype of an entrenched and exclusive ruling class. The 'new men' who are allowed in, one imagines, are fairly 'safe', being largely drawn from lower-middle-class backgrounds. Here, less than anywhere else that we have surveyed, do we find a circulation of elites, and here above all would we expect to find that 'accumulation of superior elements in the lower classes and, conversely, of inferior elements in the upper classes' that Pareto held would be a 'potent cause of disturbance in the social equilibrium'. In contrast, it is in Hungary and Yugoslavia that the working class has the strongest representation in the elite and here, in

Sorokin's phrase, we might expect that 'instead of becoming leaders of a revolution they are turned into protectors of social order'.

The attainment process

The differences which we claim to have detected between our traditional right-wing societies, the 'middle-of-the-road', and the socialist ones ought to be reflected in the process of occupational attainment which prevails in each type. Here we can draw on some recent applications of path analysis to different countries. We now have path models for two 'middle-of-the-road' societies – the USA and Britain; and these can be supplemented by another 'new' society – Australia (see Jones, 1971), a socialist society which we have not touched before – Czechoslovakia (Šafář, 1971), and a traditional right-wing society – Spain (Nicolás et al., 1975). International comparisons between path models, as might be expected, raise some difficult technical problems,[10] so the results have to be treated with caution. Nonetheless, they may be a useful check on the conclusions which we have reached so far.

First of all, the process of occupational attainment in Britain and the USA proves to be very similar. Treiman and Terrell (1975), using different sources of data from those we have employed, found that the relative importance of social origins and schooling was much the same in the two countries.[11] This is a rather reassuring start and encourages our belief that, at least in respect of social mobility and attainment, the two societies are much alike. Next, Jones (1971) found no great difference between the USA and Australia except in the determinants of educational attainment: here, however, father's occupation was

Diagram 7.1 The attainment process in Czechoslovakia

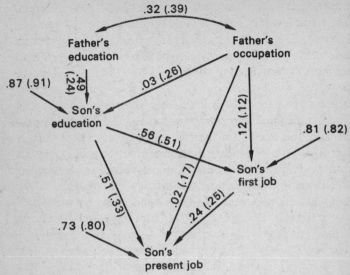

Source: Šafář (1971).
Figures in brackets give the coefficients for England and Wales (computed from Appendix I, Table 9).

quite unimportant and its place was taken by father's *education*. This, if soundly based, is a rather interesting finding. It suggests that the cultural distinctiveness of the social classes may not be so great in Australia as elsewhere in the Anglo-American world – hence the relative openness which we find when we look at class mobility. But it also suggests that there may be other bases of social differentiation which a purely class analysis overlooks.

The most interesting contrasts, however, are with Spain and Czechoslovakia. Diagram 7.1 gives the Czechoslovak path model (figures in brackets being the corresponding British coefficients calculated from Appendix I, Table 9).

In Czechoslovakia education (both father's and son's) proves to be far more important than it does in Britain, while father's occupation seems almost inconsequential. In Blau and Duncan's terms it looks as though the move from ascription to achievement has progressed much further in socialist society than it has in the West. But as in the case of Australia, the lesser importance of social class (narrowly defined in occupational terms) does not mean that social background (more broadly conceived) is unimportant – witness the powerful effect of father's education on his son's and thence on his occupational career. Cultural capital becomes far more important in the attainment

Diagram 7.2 The attainment process in Spain

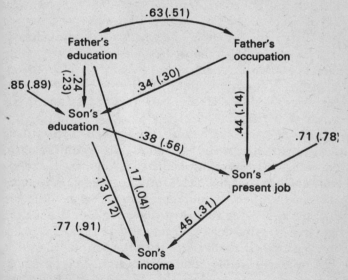

Source: Nicolás *et al.* (1975).
Figures in brackets give the coefficients for the USA (computed from Jencks, 1972: Table B-1).

process and new bases of social differentiation replace the old. The socialist societies, therefore, may be 'open' when we are thinking in conventional occupational mobility terms. But they may be as 'closed' as the Anglo-American West when we are thinking of the overall influence of social background on occupational achievement. Path analysis therefore provides an important corrective to that based on mobility tables alone.

But if Czechoslovakia shows us what happens in an achievement-oriented society, Spain demonstrates what ascription looks like. Nicolás et al. (1975) use a slightly different path model from the one we have employed so far, but we can construct a comparable one for America.[12] Diagram 7.2 gives the results.

In Spain, father's occupation comes into its own. Its direct effect on son's occupation is far higher than we see elsewhere, while the role of education in the attainment process is accordingly reduced. Schooling plays a relatively minor part in the transmission of status from father to son. Inheritance, discrimination, nepotism or whatever else generates the direct effect of father's occupation takes the centre of the stage.

Spain and Czechoslovakia, then, present two extreme cases, with Britain and the USA once again falling in between. Our earlier distinctions are confirmed, and we can conclude that the *process* of occupational attainment is distinctly different in our three types of society. But there is also one striking similarity which we should note: the known factors included in the models have roughly similar *combined* effects on attainment in the various countries. The residuals are of very similar orders of magnitude in Spain, Czechoslovakia and the USA. The predictability, although not the mechanisms, of the attainment process is therefore surprisingly comparable.

Conclusions

That countries differ in their rates of social mobility both into the elite and across the manual/non-manual line cannot be doubted. That these differences are connected to the shapes and rates of change of their occupational structures is highly probable. But even when we have taken account of these structural factors differences still remain and, as far as we can tell, these differences are reflected in the processes of attainment as well.

Among so-called Western societies we find that the USA, Canada and Sweden have the highest *de facto* rates of social mobility, but once we take account of the shape and rate of change of the occupational structure it is Australia and Sweden which come to the fore while the USA and Canada are consigned to the intermediate category, along with Britain, where mobility is of the expected level. West Germany, Japan, Italy, Spain and France, on the other hand, countries which have all had long periods of right-wing or fascist rule, turn out to be more closed than expected on the basis of their occupational structures.

The distinctive features of mobility patterns in the communist bloc are the very high rates of inflow into elite and white-collar occupations. These *may* be due more to their rapid industrialization than to any permanent features of their societies, but their consequences could be real enough for all that. The broad social mix within their elites, with large numbers drawn from manual and farm backgrounds, may well have important implications for the character and culture of these societies. Parkin has suggested that 'European socialist societies appear to display less normative differentiation along class lines than do Western societies' (Parkin, 1971 : 157), and the results of the Czechoslovakian path analysis would seem to be in line with this.

Whether the socialist societies will converge to a Western pattern – or rather, to a North American pattern, for that is what most commentators have in mind – at some future date as their rates of industrialization slow down, we cannot be sure. Rates of industrialization themselves may reflect cultural and political forces, and in any event, if we can generalize from the Czech example, it may be that the socialist societies have already progressed beyond the Western ones in their move from ascription to achievement.

But perhaps the main lesson of these international comparisons is that we should not talk about 'Western capitalist society' as though it constituted a single un-differentiated type. The main conclusion of our analysis is that there are distinct differences even between capitalist societies such as the USA, West Germany, Japan and Sweden which are at roughly similar levels of economic development. Whether or not these differences are becom-ing less we cannot say. Technological functionalism can always postpone its nemesis by extending the predicted convergence of the industrialized societies into the distant future. But in the meantime we live in a world where social and cultural variation persists.

To what, then, are we to ascribe the variations which we have detected? Answers to this kind of question are inevitably tentative as there is an almost infinite variety of ways in which Japan differs from the USA or Sweden from West Germany, any one of which might account for the variations in mobility. Consider, for example, our two main findings. The weaker one is that 'new' societies are more open than the 'old'; the stronger is that countries with longer periods of socialist government are more open than those which have had more conservative, and sometimes fascist, regimes. These two findings illustrate our problem. There is considerable overlap between these categories with Italy, France, Spain, West Germany and Japan appearing both as 'old' societies and as predominantly conservative ones. This brings out a fundamental point about international comparisons: national characteristics do not vary at random. They come as more or less firmly tied bundles whose individual components cannot easily be pulled apart or altered at will (even a government's will). It is hardly surprising that the 'old' societies of Europe, with a heritage of an hereditary aristocracy or long-established bourgeoisie, have had strong conservative or fascist parties. It is hardly sensible to ask whether it is their inherited class structure or their right-wing governments which 'cause' their closure. They are not separable causes.

8 Class Formation and Social Stability

'The more a ruling class is able to assimilate the foremost minds of a ruled class, the more stable and dangerous becomes its rule,' wrote Marx (1894 : 587). The same basic idea appears in Pareto's work: 'The accumulation of superior elements in the lower classes and conversely of inferior elements in the upper classes is a potent cause of disturbance in the social equilibrium.' (Pareto, 1916 : 2055.) And we see it again in Sorokin: '. . . the open doors of a mobile society offer a great chance for the majority of leaders and ambitious persons to rise. Instead of becoming leaders of a revolution they are turned into protectors of social order.' (Sorokin, 1927 : 533.)

All three quotations are concerned essentially with the opportunities for potential leaders – the 'foremost minds' or 'superior elements' – to rise from the subordinate to the ruling class, depriving the former of its most talented leaders and reinvigorating the latter's stock. In this way, it can be argued, the 'circulation of elites' preserves the existing social order and maintains the stability of the social system. But this mechanism must be distinguished from a second one which is implicit in Marx's writings and explicit in Sorokin's. This is the process whereby social mobility increases the social contacts between the different classes, reducing their internal solidarity and diminishing their antagonism. As Sorokin argues: 'In an immobile society the social solidarity of its members is concentrated within the social box to which they belong. It rarely surpasses its limits because the social contact of an individual with the members of other different "boxes" is very weak and rare. . . . Within each box the ties of solidarity of its members are most intensive; for the same reason that the solidarity of the members of an old-fashioned family is strong. They have a complete understanding and a complete community of interests. . . . In a mobile social body a "delocalization", and "atomization", and diffusion tend to take place. Since an individual belongs to different social groups and shifts from one box to another, his "area" of solidarity is not limited within one box. . . . At the same time the phenomena of solidarity and antagonism are likely to lose their intensiveness. They become colder and more moderate.' (Sorokin, 1927 : 539.) This is the same as the argument about cross-pressures and cross-class affiliations which we sketched in Chapter 4. On this view social mobility is inimical to class formation, reducing the size of the permanent and stable cores of the two main classes and leaving a larger and more fluid 'middle mass' with no clear class identity or class loyalty.

But, as ever, counter-arguments can be adduced. The upwardly mobile individuals may not be fully assimilated into the ruling class. They may lose their ties with their social origins but still fail to gain full acceptance from their new associates. Rather than turning into protectors of social order, their radicalism may instead increase. Lipset and Bendix gave the example of the French bourgeoisie in the eighteenth century which 'developed its revolutionary zeal when it was denied recognition and social prestige by the old French aristocracy; wealth had not proved to be a gateway to high status and power, and the mounting resentment over this fed the fires of political radicalism.' (Lipset and Bendix, 1959:23.) Occupational mobility, then, if it is not accompanied by social acceptance and recognition in the class of destination, may generate a new group of radicals who turn against the established social order as their hopes for *social*, as opposed to *occupational* mobility are frustrated.

Again, mobility may not necessarily undermine class formation. While it is clear that mobility entails cross-class affiliations, a large surplus of upward over downward mobility (such as we have seen recently in Britain) may have the effect of reducing the solidarity of the upper or dominant class but at the same time leave a working class that is increasingly composed of 'hereditary proletarians' (in Sorokin's phrase). This leads Goldthorpe to advance an alternative hypothesis, that of the 'maturation' of the working class in contemporary Britain in which it remains a powerful force for collective action and social change. To summarize his arguments drastically: he contends that in countries at an earlier stage of industrialization a large proportion of the industrial labour force is drawn from the land; they are 'green' recruits who are new to the traditions and values of the urban working-class community. But this is no longer true in Britain and, coupled with the low rates of downward mobility into manual work, means that the working class is tending to be 'increasingly second-generation in its composition' (Goldthorpe, 1980:262). In addition, Goldthorpe argues, while there may be a substantial amount of career mobility out of the working class as those who started their working lives as apprentices move up to become engineers and managers, much of this intra-generational mobility is achieved at a relatively early age. It follows that 'the bulk of the working class, as it exists at any one point in time, is made up of men whose mobility opportunities are in fact relatively few and limited.' (Goldthorpe, 1980 : 262.)

For Goldthorpe, then, there is an important contrast between the cultural and social heterogeneity of the 'service class' as he calls it (Classes I and II in the seven-fold schema) and the homogeneity of the working class. He concludes: 'In direct contrast with the recruitment pattern of the present-day service class, which means that in spite of the stability of its membership it is almost inevitably a class "of low classness",[1] the recruitment pattern of the working class may be regarded as a key factor in its formation as a relatively well-defined socio-cultural as well as demographic entity. Thus collectivist orientations have become backed by the potential for solidarity that is essential to their successful expression in action. The nature of mobility flows in the post-war period, we have suggested, has played a major part in the maturation of the working class as a socio-political force.' (Goldthorpe, 1980 : 272.)

It is quite possible, therefore, to produce cogent arguments on the one hand in favour of the view that the recent high rates of mobility in Britain will have increased social stability and strengthened the hold of the dominant class, and on the other that mobility flows have helped in the maturation of the working class as a socio-political force while weakening the cohesion of the white-collar classes. On which side does the weight of the evidence fall?

It is perhaps one of the most difficult of all sociological tasks to determine *empirically* the sources of social stability and conflict. It is possible to spin endless strands of *a priori* argument, but the empirical data which would enable us to produce any very decisive judgements for or against the various assertions are extremely hard to come by. This arises in large part from the nature of concepts such as stability and equilibrium. They are what are called 'dispositional' concepts, as, for example, is the concept 'inflammable'. Thus we know that paper is inflammable, but if no one puts a match to it, a sheet of paper could lie around for centuries without being burnt. Similarly, a society may in a real sense be unstable, but if no one puts a match to the fuse and actually tries to organize a revolution, it may remain for a long time with an unchanging political system. This means that when we deal with dispositional concepts, we really need real-life experiments. It is not very convincing, as evidence for Britain's stability, to point out that the political institutions of Parliament have remained unchanged for many years; it is much more relevant to see what happens when there is an actual threat to those institutions. As Marx made clear, the truth of his theory can only be established by action, not by academic argument.

Fortunately, concepts like class formation are more amenable to academic research. Here it is useful to employ Lockwood and Goldthorpe's distinction between the *economic*, *normative* and *relational* aspects of class.[2] In looking at intergenerational mobility between our seven classes we are concerned essentially with the economic aspects of class; we are comparing the class positions of fathers and sons in the sense of their respective positions in the occupational division of labour. But when we turn to questions of class formation we are asking whether people who share similar economic positions are also involved in a common web of social relationships, sharing common attitudes and values. In other words, do we merely have a set of people carrying out similar jobs, or is there a definite social group with a recognizable identity of its own?

In looking at the *relational* aspect of class we can make use of the extensive material on friendship patterns and contact with kin. On the *normative* side we shall take voting behaviour as our main index, assuming that Conservative voting is congruent with the norms and values (and indeed economic interests) of the dominant class, while the Labour Party is to be taken, as usual, as the party of the working class. Clearly, this is to oversimplify. High levels of Conservative voting from the upwardly mobile, for example, need not necessarily imply strong normative commitment to the present social order and its governing elite. It may be, for some people at least, a more instrumental act – a vote cast for the party expected to do most at controlling inflation or promoting economic growth and one that would be quickly switched if those goals were not achieved. Again, working-class disenchantment with the Labour Party need not necessarily indicate a rejection of collective action in pursuit of working-class aims. We must remember (as sociologists sometimes forget) that voting is not merely a reflection of one's economic position and social affiliations but is also, and crucially, a response to the actions and ideologies of the political parties themselves. Working-class support for the Labour Party may decline not only because there has been an increase in cross-class affiliations or a change in economic fortunes (as was believed to have happened in the 1950s) but also because the party itself may have moved to the right, making it less easily distinguishable from the Conservatives and making support for it a less socialist act. In short, we must look at the 'meaning' of Labour or Conservative voting. We have to interpret our findings, for the data will not speak for themselves. With these caveats in mind, let us turn to the evidence.

Class, friendship and politics

In the Oxford Social Mobility Group's enquiry in 1972, respondents were asked about the way they voted at the last general election, that of 1970 when the Conservatives were returned to office with a narrow majority after six years of Labour government. They were also asked to give some details (notably occupational ones) 'about the people you most often spend your spare time with' (excluding wife and children). For the sake of convenience we shall simply call these people 'friends'. In the follow-up enquiry in 1974 when a sub-sample of 'stable' and 'mobile' individuals were re-interviewed, Goldthorpe also obtained some more detailed information about kinship and friendship contacts.

Table 8.1 Class patterns of friendship

Friend's class	Respondent's class (%)						
	I	II	III	IV	V	VI	VII
I	43·9	22·1	16·1	15·9	11·7	4·8	3·4
II	17·1	31·6	11·9	10·3	9·1	6·5	6·6
III	10·5	12·5	22·5	6·3	10·4	7·2	9·0
IV	10·7	10·6	11·9	32·5	10·2	10·0	9·7
V	7·4	8·7	9·8	8·3	21·9	10·1	10·4
VI	6·9	6·9	14·6	14·6	17·9	37·7	24·1
VII	3·5	7·6	13·2	12·1	18·9	23·8	36·7
Total	100·0	100·0	100·0	100·0	100·1	100·1	99·9
N	665	538	378	446	549	961	995

Source: Oxford Social Mobility Group.
Sample: men aged 25–64 in 1972.
The sample size is reduced to 4532 as a result of missing data (respondents who failed to name any 'friends').

Before turning to the relation with mobility, we need to establish our baseline. Table 8.1 gives the friendship patterns of the respondents according to their current social class.[3] In its general outline the table is very like the mobility tables which we saw earlier in Chapters 2 and 4. The percentages are largest in the diagonal cells, showing a tendency for people to choose friends from their own social class. This tendency is highest at the two extremes, in Class I on the one hand and Classes VI and VII on the other, just as self-recruitment was highest in these two places. But there is also substantial friendship choice across class lines. The picture is certainly not one of rigid class boundaries with socially exclusive groups rejecting outsiders. In relational terms, at least, there is no distinct cleavage between the classes. The boundaries are blurred and fuzzy with, for example, one in six men from Class I naming a friend from the three blue-collar classes. From the point of view of class formation a dichotomous model is hardly appropriate. What we see are two 'cores' at top and bottom which gradually shade into each other through an amorphous middle area.

There is, however, a slightly different way in which we can view the table. If we compare it with an inflow mobility table (Table 2.2, for example) we see that friendship connections have a markedly different pattern from kinship connections. Compared with the one in six men from Class I naming a blue-collar friend, one in three has a father who was in a blue-collar job and nearly one in two has a father-in-law from these classes. The friendships of men in Class I are more narrowly circumscribed than their kinship. But exactly the reverse holds for working-class men. They are far more likely to have a white-collar friend than a white-collar father or father-in-law. The picture to which we have become accustomed from mobility tables of a heterogeneous dominant class and a homogeneous subordinate class no longer, therefore, looks quite so clear cut.

Table 8.2 Class and voting

	Respondent's class						
	I	II	III	IV	V	VI	VII
Conservative	54·4	44·7	42·9	53·9	30·6	19·3	20·4
Labour	16·7	25·4	30·3	17·9	44·2	53·2	50·9
Liberal	5·1	5·6	4·0	5·3	2·8	3·1	2·3
Other	0·6	0·6	0·5	0·1	0·5	0·7	0·2
Refused etc.	3·1	3·0	1·8	1·6	2·4	1·5	1·3
Did not vote	20·1	20·6	20·4	21·2	19·5	22·1	24·9
Total	100·0	99·9	99·9	100·0	100·0	99·9	100·0
N	1248	999	769	885	1032	1876	2106

Source: Oxford Social Mobility Group.
Sample: men aged 25–64 in 1972.
The category 'refused etc.' contains respondents who would not divulge, or could not remember, how they had voted in 1970.

If we now move on to voting behaviour the pattern becomes more complicated still. Table 8.2 gives the basic data. The broad outlines of the table are much as we might expect. There is a large lead for the Conservatives among men currently in Class I while the figures are almost, but not quite, reversed in Class VII. If we divide the vote into the socialist and non-socialist respectively (combining the Conservative and Liberal shares), we find that Class I divides 17:60 whereas for Class VII the ratio is 51:23. On this first crude view of the material, Class I turns out to have greater political as well as relational homogeneity than Class VII.

The complications emerge when we turn to the other five classes. Class VI, the skilled manual workers, is actually rather more solidly Labour than Class VII, whereas the Conservative lead falls off quite sharply, from 28 points to 19, as we move from Class I to Class II, and thence even lower to 13 points in Class III. Class IV, the petty bourgeoisie, on the other hand, returns a Conservative lead of massive proportions, but in Class V, the foremen and technicians, we switch to a Labour lead of 14 points. While there is the usual blurring, then, as we move from Class I downwards, there is a marked cleavage between the white- and blue-collar classes which we do not observe in mobility or friendship patterns. A dichotomous model of society has far more plausibility in political terms than it has had before.

What we think of class formation, then, depends very much on where we choose to look. If we look at Class I, we are struck by the predominance of Conservative voters and we can make out quite a good case that it constitutes a relatively cohesive social formation. If we compare Classes III and V (or IV and V), we are struck by the extent of the cleavage between the white- and blue-collar groupings: in political if in no other terms we can discern a definite discontinuity instead of our usual blurring. And if we focus on Classes VI and VII, we are struck by the uniformity throughout the manual groups. No simple characterization of the British class structure, therefore, will do.

Mobility, friendship and politics

Perhaps the most common view is that mobility favours the Conservative Party: the upwardly mobile are believed to switch from Labour to Conservative while the downwardly mobile fail to make the reverse move in the same numbers.[4] It is a view which would see the former as identifying with their class of destination while the latter retain their identification with their class of origin. And, if true, it would support the thesis that mobility strengthens the hold of the dominant class and weakens the cohesion of the subordinate. To be sure, it does not require that the upwardly mobile are fully assimilated in relational as well as normative terms. They might remain rather marginal members of their new classes, aspiring to full membership but failing to gain full acceptance from the stable, second-generation members. Lipset and Bendix's example of a radical bourgeoisie could well be countered with examples of 'social climbers', denied recognition but nonetheless determined to distance themselves from their erstwhile peers. Cobbett's merchants, great manufacturers and great farmers who had risen suddenly from the dunghill to the chariot might well fit the bill.

In practice, the truth seems rather more prosaic. Tables 8.3 and 8.4 tell the first part of the story. The white-collar/blue-collar divide proves to be the critical one. There is a Conservative lead in all the white-collar groups, irrespective of their class of origin. But there is also a Labour lead among blue-collar workers, even among those who have been downwardly mobile from Class I. It is certainly not a one-way traffic to the benefit of the Conservatives. The direction of one's vote is clearly influenced both by one's present class and one's origins, the mobile thus being more divided than the stable, adopting, in aggregate, an intermediate position between the second-generation members of the white- and blue-collar classes. There is, however, one interesting asymmetry between the upwardly and downwardly mobile. The Labour lead among the blue-collar sons of Class I fathers is much smaller than the Conservative lead among Class I sons of blue-collar

Table 8.3 Mobility and voting

Percentage voting Conservative at the 1970 election

Father's class	Respondent's class		
	I	II, III, IV	V, VI, VII
I	56·7	59·0	29·5
II, III, IV	59·3	55·2	31·2
V, VI, VII	49·6	40·7	20·2

Percentage voting Labour at the 1970 election

Father's class	Respondent's class		
	I	II, III, IV	V, VI, VII
I	12·4	10·4	33·0
II, III, IV	13·0	16·7	39·6
V, VI, VII	21·5	31·8	53·3

Source: Oxford Social Mobility Group.
Sample: men aged 25–64 in 1972.

fathers. It is an asymmetry which is much more marked
in the lower panel of Table 8.3 than in the upper. In other
words the downwardly mobile represent a distinct loss to
the Conservatives but they do not yield an equivalent gain
to the Labour Party. It is almost as though they are willing
to reject the Conservative loyalties of their class of origin
but find the ideological jump to socialism more difficult.

But in general the results fit the cross-pressure thesis
better than any other. People appear to be influenced both
by their social origins and by their current class position.

Where these influences work in opposite directions the outcomes are less clear-cut than when they are congruent. Indeed, even the asymmetry between the upwardly and downwardly mobile fits the thesis, since Butler and Stokes (1974) have shown that the upwardly mobile are more likely to come from Conservative backgrounds than are the stable members of the working class. There is little sign, from these voting data at any rate, that the mobile as a whole either reject or are rejected by their class destinations. True, their intermediate pattern of voting might suggest that they remain rather marginal members of both their old and new classes, but this would be an unsound inference if extended to the mobile as a group. The downwardly mobile, for example, may divide in roughly equal numbers between the Labour and Conservative Parties, but this does not mean that each *individual* feels divided in his loyalties. The downwardly mobile who vote Labour, for all we know may feel thoroughly identified with the new class. It is important to remember that we are dealing with proportions, not individual propensities.

This point becomes clearer if we consider friendship patterns. Goldthorpe shows that the mobile differ, in aggregate, from the stable in the class distribution of their friends, the pattern being an intermediate one as it is in voting. But this means that there is wider variation among the mobile. Some of the upwardly mobile, for example, draw all their friends from their current social class; in other words, they appear to be fully assimilated. Others draw all their friends from their origin class; in relational, although not economic terms, they seem not really to have experienced mobility at all. And yet others report few or no friends from any class at all. These are the truly marginal men, and yet they are hardly more common among the mobile than among the stable. In other words, mobility itself can hardly be the cause of social isolation and marginality.

None of the simple hypotheses about the effects of mobility, then, will suffice. The mobile are not, in general, a rootless and marginal group denied social acceptance and recognition. Whatever may have been true in pre-revolutionary France, the newcomer to Class I in contemporary Britain is not a resentful radical smouldering over his social rejection by the established members. Nor does he appear to be a marginal social climber, eager to gain an entrée to a select world of insiders. Both these views live too much in the past. Britain may once have had a rigid and exclusive social hierarchy, although probably never as rigid as in France. Hollingsworth's evidence on peers' marriages which we reviewed in Chapter 3 shows that even in the seventeenth century a few commoners could marry into the peerage. Lipset and Bendix took an extreme case of social rejection in support of their thesis, an example that has little relevance for modern Britain (or in their case America) where social groups are ill-defined and permeable.

Today, then, there is little doubt that the majority of the upwardly mobile assimilate, both in normative and relational terms, into their new class. While retaining kinship links with their social origins, they draw most of their friends from their current class (many of whom, of course, may have been upwardly mobile contemporaries); and they tend to follow the voting patterns of their fellow class-members too. As a result, Class I, for example, may be quite heterogeneous in its members' origins – 40 per cent coming from blue-collar homes; but it is much more homogeneous in its friendship and voting patterns – only 20 per cent voting Labour. On this score it is hard to dissent

from the view that upward mobility replenishes the talent
in the dominant class but without unduly undermining its
cohesion and potential for communal action to further its
interests. We cannot tell, from our evidence, whether
Sorokin was correct to argue that the upwardly mobile
'having climbed through their personal efforts' will be
'sure of their rights ... if it is necessary they will not
hesitate to apply force and compulsion to suppress any riot
... in this way they facilitate the preservation of social
order.' (Sorokin, 1927 : 534.) But he could be right.

We must, however, remember that by no means all the
upwardly mobile assimilate. A substantial minority retains
working-class friends and, in opposition to their new class
interests, votes Labour. It is not obvious, therefore, that
upward mobility necessarily deprives the working-class
movement of its potential leaders. As we have already
suggested, many of the upwardly mobile came from Conservative homes in any event and so were hardly potential
Labour leaders in the first place. Those from solidly Labour
backgrounds may well retain their allegiance despite the
change in their objective class situation. The embourge-
oisement of the Labour Party – the growing number of
its MPs and Cabinet members drawn from white-collar
occupations – has often been noted (and criticized).[5] But
what has been less often suggested is that these 'bourgeois'
Labour leaders may in fact be upwardly mobile men from
working-class backgrounds who have retained the loyalties
and ideals they learned at home. It is not so much, as Lipset
and Bendix might have argued, that occupational mobility
without the hoped-for social recognition has 'radicalized'
them; rather mobility has failed to destroy their radicalism.

Class affiliations and class formation

In looking at father/son mobility and its relation with friendship and voting patterns, we are again ignoring the role of women in the contemporary class structure. And while it may be true that for most families the husband has historically been the major bread-winner and his occupation has largely determined the family's objective class position, it is by no means obvious that the role of women for the normative and relational aspects of class is insignificant. Quite aside from their own votes and union activities, they may have important influence on the political loyalties and class consciousness of their families. Or, to put the argument at its weakest, the Class I man married to an upwardly mobile woman from working-class origins has by that fact some cross-class affiliations and may on that account be subject to cross-pressures. If class affiliations are important for class formation, as we argued in Chapter 4 they were, then we cannot ignore those affiliations which are mediated by women.

To examine this issue we have drawn a 'map' of the class structure grouping the male respondents of the 1972 Oxford enquiry according to their own current class and their own and their wife's class origins. To simplify the contours of the map, we have reduced the classes to three (and we shall use Arabic rather than Roman numerals in order to avoid confusion): we keep the old Class I as it is; we group Classes II, III and IV together to form the new class 2; and we group Classes V, VI and VII into the new class 3. If we wish to give them labels we could call them the elite, the white-collar class and the blue-collar class respectively. Each of the areas of our map now receives a three-digit code, the first giving the respondent's class, the second his father's and the third his father-in-

Diagram 8.1 Class affiliations and voting

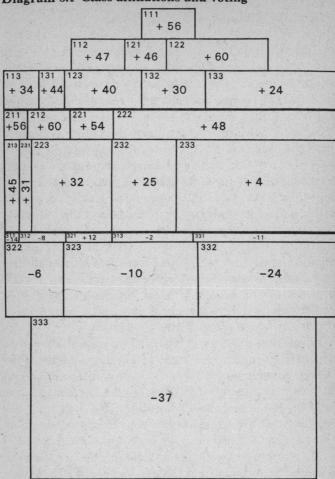

Source: Oxford Social Mobility Group.
Sample: married men aged 25–64 in 1972.
For details see text.
The numbers in each cell are as follows: 111–86; 112–85; 121–65; 122–159; 113–67; 131–46; 123–150; 132–122; 133–261; 211–34; 212–67; 221–67; 222–345; 213–74; 231–55; 223–384; 232–304; 233–755; 311–7; 312–24; 321–24; 313–42; 331–75; 322–218; 323–502; 332–533; 333–2371.

law's. The size of each area is drawn in proportion to the number of its occupants, and Diagram 8.1 is what results.

In each area of the map we have entered the Conservative lead over Labour of its inhabitants. Thus at the top of the map we have the small stable and permanent core of men currently holding elite occupations with similarly privileged fathers and fathers-in-law. They show a massive Conservative lead of 56 points (70 per cent voting Conservative and only 14 per cent Labour). At the bottom, in contrast, we have a huge area of people from solidly working-class backgrounds among whom there is a strong, although not quite so overwhelming, Labour lead. The relative sizes and political solidarity of these two extreme groups are central to an understanding of contemporary British society. They are the groups whose families share a common social experience and history and which might be expected to embody most fully the attitudes and values of their separate classes.

As we move away from these two extreme areas we come to groups which have experienced some degree of cross-class affiliations. This is our impermanent and fluid middle mass of cross-pressured voters. It is not, however, a wholly amorphous area for some clear contours emerge. First we see that there is, without exception, a Conservative lead among all groups where the respondents currently hold either an elite or white-collar occupation. Secondly, we see that blue-collar affiliations, whether through husband or wife, substantially depress the size of that lead; wives' class origins are clearly associated with the patterns of their husbands' vote. To be sure, the diagram does not tell us what causal mechanism underlies this finding – we can never know from this kind of data whether left-wing men choose working-class wives or working-class wives encourage their husbands to be left-wing. But the pattern is clear enough.

The other striking feature of the top half of the map is the size and voting characteristics of the upwardly-mobile groups from solidly blue-collar origins (the groups coded 133 and 233). These are the ones which are most 'out of line' in their voting. The more interesting of the two is the enormous group of white-collar workers with blue-collar affiliations on both sides of the family (coded 233). It contains over 10 per cent of the sample and is by far the biggest of all the 'mobile' groups. And it shows only the barest of Conservative leads. To put the matter a little differently, this group is divided in its political preferences; it contains a large block of people voting against their notional class interest – indeed it includes more than half the total of Labour white-collar workers; and it is probably responsible for a lot of the fragmentation and normative diversity of the so-called middle class. Its sheer weight of numbers makes it potentially a major political force.

Let us now move on to the bottom half of the map. With one, numerically small, exception all the groups show a Labour lead – even those with elite affiliations do so. As might be expected, the latter are on the whole rather small and do not produce in total all that many blue-collar Conservatives. The three groups with white-collar but not elite affiliations (those labelled 322, 323, and 332) are more important. Their size is perhaps the first surprise. We see that about a third of the blue-collar workers fall into one of these three groups and thus have some kind of white-collar affiliation. This may at first seem to contradict the general picture which we established earlier in this book that downward mobility was relatively uncommon, but we must remember two things. First, there was greater mobility of women through marriage than of men through the labour market, and one of the largest areas of the map (namely that coded 332) consists precisely of such mobile women. Secondly, mobility across the white/blue-collar borderline, while it may be important politically, cannot always be regarded as 'upward' or 'downward' in the sense in which we have been using those terms. In short, normative divisions need not coincide with occupational ones. For our present purposes, however, the important finding is that there is a substantial group of blue-collar workers who have, via their wives, affiliations with the white-collar world and who are in their voting preferences less solidly Labour than those with blue-collar origins on both sides of the family.

Cross-class affiliations, then, whether mediated by husband or wife, are associated with cross-class voting. Just how important this is for the political parties can be seen if we turn to the equivalent of an inflow table giving the sources of their support. This is provided by Table 8.4.

It is often said that the Labour Party is the party of the working class while the Conservative Party has a wider appeal which cuts across class divisions. Table 8.4 is in line with this view. It shows that 96 per cent of the Labour votes come from blue-collar workers or those with blue-collar affiliations. The Labour Party has made very little inroads into the groups which are solidly white-collar in their current positions and backgrounds. It is, so to speak, the expatriate who provides them with their support from across the class boundary.

The Conservative Party, on the other hand, is not quite so dependent on its expatriates. Rather surprisingly the majority of its cross-class supporters are those from solidly blue-collar positions and backgrounds. The theory of

Table 8.4 The social bases of Labour and Conservative support

Respondent's occupation and affiliations[6]	Conservative (%)	Labour (%)	All (%)
Uniformly elite	2·3	0·3	1·2
Elite or white-collar occupation and affiliations	20·5	3·3	11·9
Elite occupation and blue-collar affiliations	13·2	4·9	9·3
White-collar occupation and blue-collar affiliations	28·7	16·7	22·7
Blue-collar occupation and white-collar or elite affiliations	16·6	23·4	20·6
Uniformly blue-collar	18·7	51·4	34·3
Total	100.0	100.0	100.0
N	2492	2612	6922

Source: Oxford Social Mobility Group.
Sample: men aged 25–64 in 1972.

'white-collar affiliations' is not nearly as good at accounting for the 'working-class Conservative' as that of 'blue-collar affiliations' for explaining 'middle-class socialists'. Partly, of course, there are so many middle-class socialists with blue-collar affiliations because these affiliations are so common anyway, but this is not the whole of the story. Returning to Diagram 8.1 we see that there is a Conservative lead of 56 points among the solidly established members of the elite (the group coded 111); there is a Conservative lead of 48 points among the solidly established white-collar workers (coded 222); but a Labour lead of only 37 points among the core members of the blue-collar class (coded 333). There is an important asymmetry here.[7]

Conclusion

What we find, then, is a core to the elite which is highly homogeneous in political terms. It is greatly outnumbered by newcomers, but the majority of these seem to assimilate in both normative and relational terms. The diverse social origins of the elite do not, as far as we can tell, greatly undermine its cohesion. At the other extreme is a much larger core to the working class, although one that is not quite so homogeneous in its political preference. And in between we have our many cross-pressured groups with their different political leanings. It is these groups which are perhaps crucial for the evolution of the British class structure. We have noted that there has been a recent weakening of the class alignment in British politics. Electors have become less likely to vote in accordance with their notional class interest, and this increase in cross-class voting has been particularly marked among white-collar workers.[8] It is a fair guess that the increasing numbers of upwardly mobile families from solidly blue-collar origins have been largely responsible for this. But what are the longer-term consequences of this likely to be?

At heart, what we want to know about is the *normative* development of our various groups. The newcomers into the elite have tended to be assimilated, but will the same happen to the new recruits to white-collar work? Or will they gradually change the class identity and political loyalties of the white-collar world as a whole? We saw from Table 8.2 that there is a political cleavage between the white- and blue-collar classes that was not evident from friendship or mobility tables. Will it persist, or is it an example of cultural lag which will gradually disappear under the weight of numbers of the new arrivals?

No easy answer can be given. Political loyalty and class identity are not a straightforward consequence of mobility flows and kinship affiliations. They depend, too, on political forces and deliberate political action. The working class, for example, derives much of its identity and consciousness from the actions of the organized Labour movement. The social forces produce a *potential* for communal class action and class solidarity, but that potential needs to be harnessed. The large numbers of white-collar workers with blue-collar affiliations and, we suspect, sympathies are potential recruits to a Labour movement that shows itself willing and able to act in defence of their interests. The growth of white-collar unions is a case in point. But there is nothing inevitable about their recruitment. If they see their interests as taking second place to those of the industrial working class on the one hand or the corporate rich on the other, they could equally well become alienated from the two main political parties, or indeed from the political system more generally.

How the normative map of the British class structure is to be drawn in future, then, depends partly on the actions of the organized political and Labour groups. Loyalty and allegiance have to be earned, and if the interests of white-collar workers, or for that matter women or blacks, are neglected by the established parties, they will not be able to count on their support. The mobility-flows, the discrimination and inequality, and the social affiliations which we have documented in this book tell us about the *potential* of the different groups for collective action to support, or subvert, the existing order. But political will is needed to realize that potential.

Appendix I
Supplementary Tables

Table 1 The destinations of 'educationally unsuccessful men'

Father's class	Respondent's class in 1972							
	I	II	III	IV	V	VI	VII	Total
I – III (N = 512)	7·8	7·4	8·8	9·8	14·5	23·6	28·3	100·2
V – VII (N = 3925)	3·4	5·4	6·6	7·4	13·0	30·4	33·8	100·0

Source: Oxford Social Mobility Group.

'Educationally unsuccessful men' are defined as those who attended elementary or secondary modern schools and left at the minimum school-leaving age without obtaining 'O' levels or School Certificate.

Table 2 Average annual income of 'educationally unsuccessful men'

Father's class	Respondent's class in 1972						
	I	II	III	IV	V	VI	VII
I – III (N = 389)	2213 (29)	1770 (29)	1539 (38)	2481 (36)	1946 (59)	1720 (87)	1505 (111)
V – VII (N = 3047)	2506 (115)	1938 (175)	1507 (211)	1841 (218)	1734 (431)	1667 (910)	1447 (987)

Source: Oxford Social Mobility Group.
'Educationally unsuccessful men' are defined as for Table 1.
The figures in brackets give the number in each cell. The totals are different from those in Table 1 because of missing data on income.

Table 3 The proportion of 'educationally unsuccessful men' obtaining apprenticeships

Father's class	Respondent's class in 1972						
	I	II	III	IV	V	VI	VII
I – III (N = 454)	23·1 (39)	45·5 (33)	31·1 (45)	31·1 (45)	50·0 (66)	44·6 (101)	17·6 (125)
V – VII (N = 3618)	30·4 (135)	34·3 (198)	17·6 (250)	36·7 (275)	37·3 (475)	35·2 (1070)	10·4 (1214)

Source: Oxford Social Mobility Group.
Figures in brackets give the numbers in each cell.

Table 4 Channels of mobility into elite occupations

	Respondent's occupation in 1972 (%)				
Respondent's education	Self-employed professionals	Salaried professionals	Senior administrators	Industrial managers	Large proprietors
Private	31·9	14·5	19·3	14·6	26·5
Grammar	46·8	44·7	36·5	33·7	8·8
Technical	3·2	15·0	13·6	13·6	11·8
Non-selective	18·1	25·7	30·6	38·2	52·9
Obtained degree	26·6	28·2	10·6	9·0	5·9
Obtained apprenticeship	10·6	25·1	14·0	38·7	26·5
First job in Class I	61·7	40·9	9·9	15·5	14·6
in Classes II–IV	22·3	28·2	55·5	27·6	32·4
in Classes V–VII	16·0	30·9	34·6	56·8	52·9
N	94	447	472	199	34

Source: Oxford Social Mobility Group.

Table 5 The inheritance of wealth

Size of father's estate (1956 prices)	Size of son's estate in 1973 (1956 prices)			
	Over £100,000	£100,000–£50,000	£50,000–£25,000	£25,000–£10,000
Over £100,000	36	11	8	1
£100,000–£50,000	11	10	12	5
£50,000–£25,000	11	12	11	9
£25,000–£10,000	13	18	16	21
Under £10,000	29	49	53	64
Total	100	100	100	100
N	108	57	74	78

Source: adapted from Harbury and Hitchens (1979: Tables 3.3, 3.4 and 3.5).

Table 6 Career types of steel manufacturers (%)

Type of career	Period in office				
	1865	1875–95	1905–25	1935–47	1953
Independent	56	35	15	5	3
Heir	30	37	51	41	40
Salaried administrator	11	24	30	41	49
Professional	3	4	4	13	8
Total	100	100	100	100	100
N	70	160	184	130	73

Source: Erickson (1959: Table 19).

Table 7 Men's occupational mobility

Father's class	Respondent's class (%)								
	I	II	III	IV	V	VI	VII	Total	N
I & II	31·8	19·9	15·8	1·0	3·9	18·0	9·6	100·0	768
III	21·1	19·0	16·6	0·3	5·6	22·8	14·5	99·9	337
IV	14·0	10·8	12·2	1·1	8·6	32·7	20·5	99·9	278
V	11·9	11·9	11·3	0·5	12·4	32·5	19·6	100·1	194
VI	11·0	9·7	10·9	0·7	8·2	39·2	20·3	100·0	1787
VII	6·7	9·0	9·0	0·5	7·6	36·5	30·6	99·9	1205
%	14·3	12·1	11·7	0·7	7·3	33·0	20·8	99·9	(4569)

Source: GHS, 1975; a special tabulation prepared by George Psacharopoulos.
Sample: men aged 25–64 in 1975 who reported income.
For details of the social class classification see Note 5 to Chapter 4.

Table 8 Social origins of male employees

Father's class	Respondent's present occupation (%)			
	Classes I & II	Class IIIa	Class IIIb	Classes IV–VII
I & II	32·9	22·6	22·2	8·8
III	11·2	9·8	22·2	5·2
IV	5·7	6·1	11·1	6·2
V	3·8	4·3	0·0	4·5
VI	30·7	36·7	25·9	43·2
VII	15·7	20·4	18·5	32·1
Total	100·0	99·9	99·9	100·0
N	1207	509	27	2826

Source: GHS, 1975; a special tabulation prepared by George Psacharopoulos.
Sample: men aged 25–64 in 1975 who reported income.
For details of the social class classification see Note 5 to Chapter 4.

Table 9 Correlations for fathers and sons in the 1972 survey

	FO	FE	SE	SFO
FE	·385			
SE	·358	·345		
SFO	·303	·251	·555	
SPO	·363	·224	·530	·487

FO – father's occupation
FE – father's education
SE – son's education
SFO – son's first occupation
SPO – son's present occupation

Source: Halsey (1977).
Sample: men aged 25–59 who were resident in England and Wales at age 14.
For details of the construction of the variables see Note 3 to Chapter 5.

Table 10 Correlations for the expanded model

	FO	FE	SE	SIQ
FE	·385*			
SE	·358*	·345*		
SIQ	·310†	·223‡	·473‡	
SPO	·363*	·224*	·530*	·480†

Sources: correlations marked * are those from Table 9. Correlations marked ‡ are from Kerckhoff's reanalysis of Douglas's data (Kerckhoff, 1974). Correlations marked † are from Mascie-Taylor and Gibson (1978) deflated by 25%. The reason for the deflation is that Mascie-Taylor and Gibson's correlations are all uniformly higher than those obtained elsewhere for Britain. For example, Douglas's data yield $r_{FO.SIQ} = ·265$ compared with their ·41; the Oxford Social Mobility Group's data yield $r_{FO.SPO} = ·363$ compared with their ·46. Deflation thus brings Mascie-Taylor's and Gibson's correlations into line with those known from other sources and thus enables us to use their correlation between SIQ and SPO, which we cannot obtain elsewhere.
Variables are the same as in Table 9, except that SIQ = son's IQ.

Table 11 Correlations for fathers and sons over time: the 1972 survey

	FO	FE	SE	SFO
FE	·341/·422			
SE	·327/·379	·298/·368		
SFO	·300/·297	·214/·264	·521/·567	
S10O	·368/·345	·246/·243	·557/·566	·603/·568

Source: Oxford Social Mobility Group.

Variables are the same as in Table 9, except that S10O = son's occupation after ten years in the labour market.

In each pair of correlation the first relates to men aged 40–59 in 1972 and educated in England and Wales; the second relates to men aged 25–39 in 1972 and educated in England and Wales.

Table 12 Correlations for 'fathers' and 'sons' in the 1949 survey

	FO	SS	SE	SFE
SS	·358/·407			
SE	·208/·239	·398/·598		
SFE	·231/·231	·257/·367	·245/·337	
SO	·431/·444	·392/·463	·259/·432	·354/·438

SS – son's type of secondary school
SE – son's examination success (Ordinary School Certificate)
SFE – son's type of further education
SO – son's occupational status
FO – father's occupational status

Source: Ridge (1974: Table 2.1).

In each pair of correlations the first relates to the respondent and his father, the second to the respondent and his son. Whether the respondent counts as a 'father' or a 'son' therefore depends on the relation under consideration.

Appendix II
A Reader's Guide to
Statistical Terms

Social mobility is inevitably one of the more statistical and technical areas of sociology, and it is no longer possible to understand the current literature without a fair knowledge of statistical concepts. This Appendix is intended to give the reader a guide to the most commonly used concepts. I shall not present formal or mathematical definitions and proofs but simply some worked examples to show non-mathematical readers how to calculate the various measures and indices for themselves. Readers may find it helpful to experiment with alternative figures to check the logic of the arguments.

Structural and circulation mobility

Many of the statistical problems involved in the analysis of social mobility arise from the fact that mobility tables are rarely symmetrical. Consider, for example, the following table:

Table 1 The basic numbers

Father's class	Son's class			
	I	II	III	Total
I	34	25	11	70
II	51	113	111	275
III	59	161	435	655
Total	144	299	557	1000

This table shows the distribution of 1000 notional respondents (based on real data from the 1972 Oxford enquiry).[1] The 582 respondents in the three cells lying on the main diagonal (running from top left to bottom right) are 'intergenerationally stable', leaving 418 mobile respondents in the off-diagonal cells. Of these, 271 are upwardly mobile and 147 downwardly mobile.

This net upward mobility is explained by the fact that the distributions of fathers and sons are different from each other. The row and column 'marginal totals', as they are called, are not the same with, for example, 144 sons but only 70 fathers in Class I. This asymmetry in the marginal totals has led some sociologists to distinguish between 'structural' and 'circulation' mobility (sometimes also called 'net' and 'exchange' mobility). If we regard the marginal totals as fixed, it follows that some respondents must inevitably fall into off-diagonal cells. We clearly cannot have more than 70 people in the top-left cell, 275 in the middle cell and 557 in the bottom-right cell. In other words, given the marginal distributions, the maximum number of respondents who could be stable comes to 902, and 98 must therefore be mobile, lying in the two off-diagonal cells in the bottom row. Table 2 shows the distribution of respondents that maximum stability thus entails.

Table 2 Maximum stability

Father's class	Son's class			
	I	II	III	Total
I	70	0	0	70
II	0	275	0	275
III	74	24	557	655
Total	144	299	557	1000

The very structure of the table, then, requires that at least 9·8 per cent of the respondents be mobile, and this represents the amount of structural mobility. We can also see that one simple way to calculate the amount of structural mobility is to look at the differences between the row and column totals. Thus there are 74 more sons than fathers in Class I and an extra 24 in Class II, giving our overall 98. There are correspondingly 98 fewer sons than fathers in Class III.

Circulation mobility is simply the difference between total and structural mobility. This comes to 418 minus 98, i.e. 320, or 32 per cent. It is important to be careful in interpreting this figure. It does *not* represent the amount of mobility that would have taken place if the structure had been symmetrical. Structural mobility is an artificial concept – no real mobility table would ever actually look like Table 2 – and the concept of circulation mobility is therefore equally artificial.

The Index of Association

As well as the asymmetry in the structure of the table a major problem with mobility tables is that the sizes of the classes themselves will be unequal. As in Table 1, for example, Class I is very small while Class III includes more than half the sample. This means that some people from Class III origins must inevitably end up in that class themselves – there is not enough room for them all to be upwardly mobile. In contrast, everyone from Class I origins could at least in theory be downwardly mobile. They are only few in number and there is plenty of room for them elsewhere. This needs to be taken into account if we wish to interpret the proportions in each cell as evidence of rigidity in the class structure. Thus from Table 1 we can calculate that 66·4 per cent of respondents from Class III origins but only 48·6 per cent from Class I origins are intergenerationally stable. But this is hardly good evidence of greater rigidity at the bottom than top.

The Index of Association is an attempt to deal with this problem. It compares the actual numbers in each cell of the table with those that would have occurred if there were 'perfect mobility', that is if fathers' and sons' class positions were unrelated to each other. It is easy enough to calculate perfect mobility. Thus we see from Table 1 that 14·4 per cent of the sons as a whole had Class I positions. If fathers' and sons' class positions were unrelated, it would follow that only 14·4 per cent of the 70 sons from Class I origins would themselves end up in Class I. Equally, 14·4 per cent of the 275 from Class II origins and 14·4 per cent of the 655 from Class III would also end up there. (Another way to do the calculation is to multiply the relevant row and column totals and divide by the sample size. For example,

144 times 70, divided by 1000, equals 10 – the 'expected' figure for the top-left cell.) Continuing these calculations we obtain the following picture:

Table 3 Perfect mobility

| Father's class | Son's class | | | |
	I	II	III	Total
I	10	21	39	70
II	40	82	153	275
III	94	196	365	655
Total	144	299	557	1000

To compute the values for the Index of Association we now compare the entries in the corresponding cells of Tables 1 and 3. Thus in the top-left cell of Table 1 we find 34 and in Table 3 the corresponding figure is 10. The ratio is thus 3·4 to 1 – there are over three times as many respondents intergenerationally stable in Class I as would be expected if fathers' and sons' positions were unrelated. We continue with these calculations to obtain the complete set of Indices as shown in Table 4.[2]

Table 4 Indices of Association

| Father's class | Son's class | | |
	I	II	III
I	3·4	1·2	0·3
II	1·3	1·4	0·7
III	0·6	0·8	1·2

The more the index diverges from unity, the greater is the departure from perfect mobility. Table 4 therefore suggests that by far the greater rigidity is to be found in Class I.

Unfortunately there is a serious difficulty with the Index of Association. Consider the case of maximum stability (as shown in Table 2). There are 70 respondents in the top-left cell, and dividing this by the 'expected' 10 from the corresponding cell of Table 3 we obtain a value of 7 for the Index. In the bottom-right cell, on the other hand, we find 557 respondents, and dividing by the 'expected' number (365) we obtain a value of 1·5. These represent the maximum possible values which the Indices could take for these two cells, and it means that we could never actually get an Index of, say, 3·4 for the bottom-right cell, given the observed marginal distributions. In other words, however much stability there is in Class III, it could never appear as rigid as Class I actually does. It is important to remember this in using the Index.

Disparity and odds ratios

Another set of tools for analysing mobility tables are disparity and odds ratios. In essence these are concerned with *relative* mobility rates. Consider Table 5, a standard outflow table derived from Table 1.

Table 5 Outflow

Father's class	Son's class			
	I	II	III	Total
I	48·6	35·7	15·7	100·0
II	18·5	41·1	40·4	100·0
III	9·0	24·6	66·4	100·0

We see that 48·6 per cent of sons from Class I origins themselves reached Class I whereas only 9·0 per cent of sons from Class III origins did so. The ratio of these two percentages – the disparity ratio as it is called – comes to 5·4 : 1. This tells us the relative chances of men from Class I and Class III backgrounds respectively of getting to Class I. We can compute ratios for other pairs of origin class and for other destinations. For example, 40·4 per cent of men from Class II origins ended up in Class III compared with 66·4 per cent from Class III origins, giving a ratio of 0·6 : 1. Table 6 gives the set of disparity ratios which results when we take the chances of men from Class III origins as our base-line. (The choice of base-line is purely a matter of convention; we could, for example, set the chances of Class I at 1 instead.)

Table 6 Disparity ratios

Father's class	Son's class		
	Relative chances of being found in Class I	Relative chances of being found in Class II	Relative chances of being found in Class III
I	5·4	1·5	0·2
II	2·1	1·7	0·6
III	set at 1	set at 1	set at 1

The values which the disparity ratio can take are not so stringently limited by the marginal distributions of the table as was the case with the Index of Association. Thus, given the marginal totals, the disparity ratios in the first column of Table 6 could in theory vary from zero to infinity. However, there are upper limits in the case of the third column (as the reader can verify by considering the case when mobility is at a maximum).

The odds ratio is an extension of the basic idea lying behind the disparity ratio. But whereas the disparity ratio looks at the relative chances of getting to a *single* specified destination, the odds ratio compares the chances of getting to *alternative* destinations. An odds ratio may be thought of as the outcome of a competition between men of different class origins to achieve (or avoid) one rather than another destination in the class structure.

Consider Table 5 again. Of men from Class I origins 48·6 per cent remained in Class I while 15·7 per cent were downwardly mobile to Class III. The 'odds' of their achieving these two alternative destinations were thus roughly 49 : 16 or 3 : 1. For men from Class III origins the corresponding percentages were 9·0 and 66·4, and so their 'odds' were 0·14 : 1. We now take the ratio of these two 'odds', and we can see that it comes to 23 : 1. This represents the advantage which respondents from Class I origins have over those from Class III origins in the competition to reach Class I rather than Class III destinations. Table 7 gives the full set of odds ratios.

Although it is perhaps the most complicated of the measures which we have seen so far, the odds ratio is probably the most useful. It is not affected by the marginal totals in the way that the Index of Association and the disparity ratio are, and for this reason it is preferable when comparing different mobility tables (as in cohort analysis

Table 7 Odds ratios

Pairs of origin classes 'in competition'	Pairs of destination classes competed for		
	I/II	II/III	I/III
I v. II	3·0	2·2	6·7
II v. III	1·2	2·7	3·4
I v. III	3·7	6·1	22·8

or with international comparisons). If we had two tables with differing marginal distributions we could never obtain two identical patterns using Indices of Association; we might be able to with disparity ratios; but we could definitely do so with odds ratios.

Adjustment to uniform marginals

Another approach to the problem is to take the bold step of changing the table itself so as to secure uniform marginal totals. This is a surprisingly straightforward procedure and means that we no longer need to worry about asymmetry or the differing sizes of the classes.

Suppose we wish to change Table 1 so that all the marginal totals contain a standard 333 people each. This means, for example, that the marginal total of the first column must be increased from 144 to 333, and so we simply multiply it by $\frac{333}{144}$. We do the same to the three cells in the column to ensure that they add up to the right total. In the case of the second column we multiply all the entries by $\frac{333}{209}$ and in the case of the third by $\frac{333}{557}$. This yields the following table:

**Table 8 Marginal adjustment
– the first stage**

Father's class	Son's class			
	I	II	III	Total
I	79	28	7	113
II	118	126	66	310
III	136	179	260	576
Total	333	333	333	999

Because of rounding errors the figures
in the top row do not appear to sum.

This is only the first stage. We now have to turn our
attention to the row totals. We multiply all the entries in
the top row by $\frac{333}{113}$ to secure the desired total, and so on
with the other rows. Unfortunately this throws our column
totals out, and so we have to repeat the process all over
again. Eventually, if we continue the process long enough,
we will get both the row and column totals which we want.
The table will now look like this:

**Table 9 Marginal adjustment
– the final stage**

Father's class	Son's class			
	I	II	III	Total
I	196	102	35	333
II	89	139	105	333
III	48	92	193	333
Total	333	333	333	999

Since the marginal totals are now all the same, we can straightforwardly compare the frequencies in the various cells. We make the interesting discovery that the degree of rigidity in Classes I and III now appears to be about equal.

Multiple regression

Multiple regression, path analysis and log-linear analysis are all ways of handling more complicated analyses than those with which we have dealt so far. Multiple regression and path analysis are more appropriate when we have 'continuous' variables, such as income; log-linear models are more appropriate for 'binary' variables, which take the value 0 or 1, such as membership of a discrete social class. It is for this reason that Blau and Duncan (1967) make greater use of the former technique while Goldthorpe (1980) uses the latter.

These techniques involve mathematics more sophisticated than we have met earlier in this Appendix, and I will not therefore show rigorously how they are to be calculated. However, the general character of multiple regression can be illustrated from the following table.[3]

Table 10 Education, occupation and income

Occupation	Years of education				
	10	11	12	13	14+
Managerial	£3022 (50)	£4045 (50)	£3699 (20)	£5006 (22)	£5328 (37)
Professional	£3890 (10)	£4069 (26)	£7169 (6)	£4089 (9)	£4511 (69)
Manual	£2769 (712)	£3078 (124)	£2867 (11)	£2362 (12)	£3163 (10)
Non-manual	£2206 (127)	£2944 (82)	£2481 (24)	£2924 (38)	£3021 (60)

The figures in each cell give the average annual income of men with that particular occupation and educational level. The bracketed figures give the number of respondents occupying the cell in question.

There are many interesting features of this table, but take two straightforward ones to start with. First, as we move along the rows average income tends by and large to increase; on average it goes up by about £200 for each extra year of education. Second, we see that income also increases in general as we move up the columns; on average it goes up by something like £400 for each step up the ladder. We could present these two findings in the form of an equation:

$$\text{Income} = 2200 + 200\text{Ed} + 400\text{Job}$$

where the figure of 2200 represents, so to speak, the starting point. This equation tells us that, controlling for job level, each extra year of education typically brings an additional £200 of income and that, controlling for years of education, each step up the occupational ladder typically brings an extra £400. This is really all that a regression equation does. It is a way of summarizing the results of an ordinary table. It comes into its own when we want to control for several variables at once and presentation through conventional tables would be very cumbersome.

The summary presented by our equation is a rather drastic one. It involves a great deal of averaging and omits all kinds of interesting features of the table. For example, extra years of education tend to bring bigger gains to managers than to other groups. Again, it is the first year of education beyond the minimum leaving age (the step from 10 to 11 years of schooling) that brings the biggest gains. Subsequent years do not bring such large increments. Neither of these points is recorded by our summary. We have 'fitted' a very simple equation or 'model' which ignores them, but it would be possible to fit a more complicated equation which would capture these additional findings. There is nothing in regression analysis itself which limits us to simple summaries.

Path analysis

Path analysis in principle is very simple. It is really nothing more than a visual representation of a set of regression equations where the different variables are assumed to have some temporal ordering – social origins, for example, are placed before education which in turn is placed before the respondent's occupation. However, there is one additional feature of most path analyses which deserves a mention. Observe that in Table 10 four categories of occupation are distinguished whereas there are five in the case of education. And in principle, of course, we could have much more dramatic differences. We could, for example, use the 124-category Hope-Goldthorpe scale for ranking occupations or we could distinguish further years of education instead of grouping them all in the '14 plus' category. It is clear, then, that we cannot directly compare the 'coefficients' which we obtained from our inspection of Table 10. The fact that one step up our occupation scale brings a bigger increment than one step up the education scale is partly an artefact of our particular method of categorization. If we switched from a 4-point to a 124-point scale of occupations the relative sizes of the coefficients would immediately be reversed.

In path analysis we often wish to compare the 'effects' of different variables, and so it is customary to standardize the scales so that comparison becomes legitimate. This is done by changing the units. Instead of years of education we take as our unit the 'standard deviation' (a measure of dispersion) of the scores on the original scale. Similarly, instead of the 124-point Hope-Goldthorpe scale we would use as our unit the standard deviation of the scores. Path coefficients are thus merely standardized regression coefficients.

Log-linear analysis

Log-linear analysis in many ways does the same job for binary variables as multiple regression does for continuous variables. It does not lend itself to simple tabular presentation, but it is in essence an extension of the idea lying behind the concept of 'perfect mobility' described earlier. Thus in a model of perfect mobility we calculate the expected number of respondents in a given cell by multiplying the relevant row and column totals together and dividing by the overall sample size. Thus we could say that

$$\text{Cell}(1,1) = \frac{\text{Row}(1) \times \text{Column}(1)}{\text{Sample size}}$$

If we take logarithms this can be reformulated as:

Log cell $(1,1)$ = Log row(1) + Log column(1)
$\qquad\qquad$ − Log sample size

This reformulation, where we add and subtract logarithms instead of multiplying and dividing frequencies, is much more convenient mathematically when complex tables are to be handled. But the general idea is simple enough: we formulate a model and compare the expected results of the model with the observed ones in the real world, just as we did with the model of perfect mobility.

Notes

1 Landmarks

1. The phrase 'sponsored mode of ascent through education' is from Turner (1960). Burt's actual influence on British educational thinking and practice is arguable. See Hearnshaw (1979).

2. The best example of such a Marxist critique (although one primarily addressed to the American situation) is Bowles and Gintis' (1976).

3. For a more detailed treatment of Marx and social mobility see Goldthorpe (1980, Ch. 1).

4. For a more detailed account see Finer (1966).

5. Functionalism means different things to different people, but the central concern is with the *needs* which a society must fulfil if it is to survive or to maintain equilibrium. Some writers adopt the 'teleological' position that society will evolve so as to ensure that these needs are met. Others, like Sorokin, hold that needs will often not be met, with resulting disorder or collapse. The best discussions of functionalism are still those of Merton (1949) and Hempel (1959).

6. See, for example, the work of Jencks (1972).

7. Sorokin himself had studied saints and millionaires and refers to this work in *Social Mobility*. Men of genius were a popular topic, see Galton (1869), Havelock Ellis (1904) and Schneider (1937). Early studies of businessmen were those of Taussig and Joslyn (1932) in America, and the defective work of Chapman and Marquis (1912) in Britain. A good British study of the wealthy was that of Wedgwood (1929). Other early studies are those of Perrin (1904), Chapman and Abbott (1913) and Ashby and Jones (1926).

8. We must not exaggerate Glass's radicalism, however. Questions of the efficient use of manpower concerned him too, and he was also worried about the disadvantages of mobility. See Glass (1954:25).

9. One of the crucial chapters of the book, Chapter 2 on 'social mobility in industrial societies' was in fact written by Lipset and Zetterberg. See also Lipset and Zetterberg (1956).

10. These are the percentages of the total non-farm population who were mobile across the manual/non-manual line. Thus according to the American study which Lipset used 70 per cent of the sample were in the same class as their fathers, 10 per cent were downwardly mobile (that is were manual workers whose fathers were non-manual), and 20 per cent were upwardly mobile (that is, were non-manual workers whose fathers were manual). The British figures, unlike the others, include the farm population.

2 Mobility in Britain Today

1. For useful overviews of British mobility studies see Macdonald and Ridge (1972) and Stacey (1968).

2. The main critiques have been by Ridge (1974b), Hope (1975) and Payne, Ford and Robertson (1977).

3. Glass's results do not in fact show an 'arithmetical impossibility' but at worst a 'sociological improbability'. His tables are internally consistent and show the *contraction* of opportunities that is required for there to be net downward mobility (assuming that differential fertility, mobility or migration has not occurred). The problem is to reconcile this picture of contracting opportunities with the census material. It can in fact be done (see Chapter 3) as there was some contraction during the depression years. The other relevant consideration is that Glass's respondents were reporting on their fathers' present or last main occupation; this means that the fathers' jobs will on average relate to a later stage in their working careers than will the sons', thus giving them more opportunity to take advantage of any expansion in opportunities that occurred after the depression.

4. The Oxford Social Mobility Group has had a fluctuating membership. It has contained, among others, P. Duncan-Jones, Jean Floud, John Goldthorpe, Sara Graham, A. H. Halsey, A. F. Heath, K. Hope, C. Llewellyn, K. I. Macdonald, R. Martin, J. M. Ridge and P. Thorburn.

5. The General Household Survey (GHS) is an inter-departmental survey sponsored by the Central Statistical Office and conducted by

the Social Survey Division of the Office of Population Censuses and Surveys.

6. The distinction between market and work situations is taken from Lockwood, who wrote: 'Under "class position" will be included the following factors. First, "market situation", that is to say the economic position narrowly conceived, consisting of source and size of income, degree of job-security, and opportunity for upward occupational mobility. Secondly, "work situation", the set of social relationships in which the individual is involved at work by virtue of his position in the division of labour.' (Lockwood, 1958:15.)

7. The distinction between 'real' and 'nominal' definitions is relevant here. We can say that an ordinary-language definition is right or wrong in that it correctly or incorrectly describes how members of the language community use the term. This is what is meant by a 'real' definition. But most technical and scientific definitions are 'nominal' ones where the scientist simply stipulates that he proposes to use a term (often a neologism) in a specific way. We can then ask whether this new term is useful in that it groups together phenomena that have interesting properties in common. See Bierstedt (1959).

8. Two of the best discussions of the meaning of occupational prestige are those of Gusfield and Schwartz (1963) and Goldthorpe and Hope (1972). On the Hall-Jones scale see Hall and Jones (1950) and Macdonald (1974).

9. I have placed 'top', 'middle' and 'bottom' in inverted commas as these are terms which strictly belong to an hierarchical view of society and not to a class schema such as Goldthorpe's. He writes: 'Our class schema should not then be regarded as having – nor should it be expected to have – a consistently hierarchical form. As Giddens has aptly observed, divisions between classes do not always "lend themselves to easy visualization in terms of any ordinal scale of 'higher' and 'lower', as [statistically defined] strata do – although ... this sort of imagery cannot be escaped altogether".' (Goldthorpe, 1980:42, quoting Giddens, 1973:106.)

10. This is not exactly the same position that Goldthorpe takes. He talks of upward and downward mobility only in the cases of movement into and out of Classes I and II. However, if we look at the rank (on the Hope-Goldthorpe scale) of the occupations which make up the seven classes, we see that Class VII, as well as Classes I and II, overlaps little with the other four. Thus if we take the collapsed, 36-category version of the scale we see that Class I is composed of categories 1, 2, 3, 4 and 7; Class II of categories 5, 6, 8, 9, 10, 12, 14 and 16; Class III of categories 21, 25, 28 and 34; Class IV of categories 11, 13, 19, 24, 29 and 36; Class V of categories 15, 17 and 20; Class VI of categories 18, 22, 23, 27 and 30; and Class VII of categories 26, 31, 32, 33 and 35. There is thus very substantial overlap between Classes III, IV, V and VI in the general desirability of the occupations which make them up, and they can in this sense be regarded as being 'at the same level'. If our only concern had been with questions of upward and downward mobility, it would have been preferable to construct an alternative classification to Goldthorpe's, grouping occupations into 'strata' solely on the basis of their Hope-Goldthorpe ranking. But since we share Goldthorpe's interest in class formation, his class schema will be used. We should make it clear, however, that it is being made to serve a dual purpose for which it was not designed. On the Hope-Goldthorpe scale, see Goldthorpe and Hope (1974).

11. For fuller details see Goldthorpe, 1980 : 39–42.

12. It differs from the tables reported by Goldthorpe (1980) in that it is restricted to men aged 25–64, not 20–64. Some of the younger men aged 20–24 will still be in full-time education and can be expected to go straight into Class I jobs. Since many of these men will come from Class I origins, the 20–64 table which necessarily omits them will tend to underestimate the degree of occupational inheritance. As Goldthorpe points out, however, the phenomenon of 'counter-mobility' will have a similar effect (Goldthorpe, 1980: 53).

13. We must note, however, that while the respondents constitute a representative sample of the male labour force in 1972, their fathers do *not* constitute a representative sample of the male labour force at any earlier point in time. This is because the dates when the respondents were aged fourteen (the age for which their fathers' occupations were given) will vary widely. Also, fathers with several sons will be over-represented, those without sons under-represented. This means that we cannot strictly infer changes in the distribution of the male labour force from the distribution of fathers and sons in the sample although to do so is often a convenient short-cut which will not involve us in any great error (see Duncan, 1966b).

14. This is a slightly higher figure than that used in Chapter 7, which has been calculated from Erikson, Goldthorpe and Portocarero (1979) in order to obtain greater comparability with the other studies used in Chapter 7.

15 See Raffe (1979) and Halsey, Heath and Ridge (1980).

16 The 'top' group that we can distinguish from the 1972 survey is that of self-employed professionals. These came to 1·1 per cent of the sample and the index of association comes to 16·5. The next group we can add (ranking them by their scores on the Hope-Goldthorpe scale) are the salaried professionals, higher grade. These bring the size of the group up to 6·3 per cent and bring the index of association down to 5·4. If we could distinguish a 'top 3 per cent', the index would certainly lie somewhere in between.

17. The fact that change in the occupational structure will necessitate some mobility has led sociologists to distinguish between 'structural' (or 'net') and 'circulation' (or 'exchange') mobility. See Rogoff Ramsøy (1966), Featherman and Hauser (1978 : 70–1).

18. See Goldthorpe (1978 and 1980 : 262).

19. I do not particularly like the term 'middle class', although it is occasionally a convenient shorthand. It was probably a much more useful concept in the nineteenth century when white-collar workers more clearly came in the 'middle' between the industrial working class and the upper class of the aristocracy and landed gentry. Nowadays, if used to include both junior clerical workers and senior administrators and managers, it covers too disparate a group that does not obviously fall in between other classes.

20. The controversies over C. Wright Mills's *The Power Elite* (1956) bring out the major issues. See Dahl (1958), Bell (1960), Parsons (1960), Kornhauser (1961) and Domhoff and Ballard (1968).

21. This is based on the fact that there are about 24,000 names in *Who's Who* whereas the adult male population is about 16,000,000. Since *Who's Who* includes women, the 'expected' figure of 0·15 per cent will be an over-estimate.

22. The figures given are all in 1956 prices. An estate of over £10,000 in 1956 would have placed its holder well within the top 10 per cent of wealth-holders.

23. The best treatments of the relation between education and mobility are those of Anderson (1961) and Boudon (1974).

24. On access to the boardroom of the industrial corporation see Clements (1958) and Stanworth and Giddens (1974).

25. These estimates are based on very rough-and-ready calculations. Assume that 0·15 per cent of men have fathers in *Who's Who*, 7 per cent have fathers in Class I, 39 per cent in Classes II–V, and 54 per cent in Classes VI and VII (see Table 2.2) out of a total adult male population of 15·5 million. The estimates in the text would then imply that around 20 per cent of the elite came from elite backgrounds, a further 20 per cent from Class I, 40 per cent from

Classes II–V, and 20 per cent from Classes VI and VII. These figures do not look at all implausible in the light of Halsey and Crewe's findings on the origins of top civil servants – 22 per cent from the Registrar General's Class I, 61 per cent from Classes II and III (N) and 19 per cent from Classes III (M), IV and V.

3 Trends

1. Noel Annan (1955) quoted in Musgrove (1979).

2. The objectives behind the reforms were probably not quite so simple as the *Quarterly Review* makes out. Compton has argued: 'Central to the competitive scheme was the idea of hierarchy. The Northcote-Trevelyan Report had delineated a hierarchy within the civil service parallel to the social and educational hierarchy in the country at large. Competitive examination was to be the agency that linked the two. There was thus little that was egalitarian in the schemes of the most convinced advocates of competition. Gladstone believed that, given the essential principle of a division between mechanical and intellectual work, the aristocracy would surely prove their 'immense superiority'. One of the great recommendations of the change would, be that it would 'strengthen and multiply the ties between the higher classes and the possession of administrative power' (Compton, 1968 : 266, quoting Gladstone to Russell, 20 January 1854).

3. Sanderson (1972) looks at 'mass' mobility at the beginning of the nineteenth century using the Lancaster Charity School Register 1770–1816 and marriage certificates from 1837–9. Unfortunately trends cannot really be estimated as the two sources are so different. See Laqueur (1974).

4. In the case of those men in the youngest cohort who had not completed ten years in the labour market by 1972, their present (i.e. 1972) job was used instead.

5. We should point out that, while this conclusion is the same as that reached by Goldthorpe in his more detailed study of absolute or *de facto* mobility rates, he went on to find a rather different picture when he turned to relative mobility rates, using disparity and odds ratios. He concluded: 'Overall, therefore, the picture obtained, once the perspective of relative mobility is adopted, is no longer one of significant change in the direction of greater opportunity for social ascent but rather, of stability or indeed of increasing *in*equality in class mobility chances.' (Goldthorpe, 1980 : 76.)

Goldthorpe's conclusion rests largely on the lack of change over time in relative chances of being found in given class destinations at the time of the enquiry rather than ten years after entry into the labour force. (If job ten years after entry is taken as the criterion, relative and absolute mobility rates show much the same picture.) Goldthorpe's case for using 1972 job depends on the concept of 'occupational maturity'. He rightly points out that after the age of thirty-five there is 'a marked falling-off in the probability of job changes which involve major shifts of occupational level' (Goldthorpe, 1980:52).

There is one interesting piece of evidence here. The Oxford enquiry asked respondents what job they had been doing three years before – that is, in 1969. We find that of the 1908–17 cohort, 91·4 per cent were in the same class (using the seven-class schema) then as in 1972. For the 1918–27 cohort it was 88·0 per cent; for the 1928–37 cohort it was 84·6 per cent; and for the 1938–47 cohort it was 77·3 per cent.

6. Glass's results are certainly not as worthless as Musgrove (1979) suggests, but there are still some problems with them. The most thorough analysis has been carried out by Hope (1975). He compared the results for younger men from the 1949 survey with those for men of the same age who appeared in the 1972 survey. The overlapping age-groups are quite considerable (covering twenty years) and can be divided into a series of birth cohorts. Hope found that the two surveys gave systematically different results, Glass's showing less mobility, but that the difference remained constant over time. 'Clearly, the two enquiries are not in perfect concert, but can the Oxford enquiry be regarded as singing the tune of the earlier enquiry at a lower pitch?' Hope asks (1975:17), and he concludes that it can: 'the upshot of this analysis is that there is a difference between the mobility processes of the two enquiries ... but the difference appears to be constant from cohort to cohort.' (1975:18.)

7. For his own trend analysis Glass reduces his original seven-fold classification to a five-fold one, grouping categories 1 and 2 together, and treating 6 and 7 as a single unit. In addition I have grouped together categories 4 and 5. This gives us four new categories:
(i) professional and high administrative; managerial and executive;
(ii) inspectional, supervisory and other non-manual, higher grade;
(iii) inspectional, supervisory and other non-manual, lower grade; skilled manual, and routine grades of non-manual; (iv) semi- and unskilled manual. Movement between these four categories was treated as upward and downward accordingly. The actual trend we obtain is very similar to Glass's; the main benefit of the change is really only

cosmetic – the proportions in Tables 3.1 and 3.2 are brought roughly into line.

8. Glass in fact finds that, taking all categories together, there is no statistically significant difference in the proportions mobile in the five cohorts, although for subjects who differed in status from their fathers there were 'significant differences between those with a higher and those with a lower status, explained primarily by the behaviour of two cohorts, the earliest and the most recent' (Glass, 1954:186). He found a few other significant differences in self-recruitment for men whose fathers were in status categories 1 and 5, 'But in general the picture of rather high stability over time is confirmed' (Glass, 1954:188).

9. The upper curve in Diagram 3.1 relates to men whose fathers held jobs in Classes I and II (Goldthorpe's 'service' class) when the respondents were aged fourteen. It shows, as we move from left to right, the average rank on the Hope-Goldthorpe scale of their fathers' jobs, their own first jobs, and so on. The lower curve gives the corresponding ranks for men from Classes VI and VII.

10. Boyd himself concludes that there has been no change. He writes: 'Only one chi-square value is significant at three degrees of freedom; this is the Civil Service, and the significance is marginal (·655 over the base value of 7·815). Moreover, there is no evidence of a trend at one degree of freedom. No group shows a significant value for linear regression. The findings indicate a stable relationship where proportionality has not changed through time.' (Boyd, 1973:93.)

11. See also Cressy (1970) and Aston (1977).

12. On the changing occupational structure see Gregory King's estimates for 1688 and Colquhoun's for 1801–3 (both given in Soltow, 1968).

13. On the connections by marriage between the City and the aristocracy see Lupton and Wilson (1959).

4 The Mobility of Women

1. For an alternative view, however, see Garnsey (1978).

2. See, for example, Glenn, Ross and Tully (1974) and Tyree and Treas (1974).

3. By this I mean that a married woman who works as a secretary but whose husband is a senior official would be regarded as belonging to a family with a privileged not a subordinate position in the class structure.

4. The pattern of women's mobility shown by the 1972 GHS data has been analysed by Hope and Keeling (forthcoming) and the 1975 GHS data by Psacharopoulos. I am very grateful to them for giving me access to their results and I wish to acknowledge the assistance I have received from them. They are not, of course, in any way responsible for the interpretations which I have placed upon their material.

5. Occupational data from the General Household Survey are coded according to socio-economic groups (see Office of Population Censuses and Surveys, *Classification of Occupations 1970*, Appendix B.2). In Class I I have placed SEG 1.1 (Employers in industry, commerce, etc., large establishments), SEG 1.2 (Managers in central and local government, industry, commerce etc., large establishments), SEG 3 (Professional workers – self-employed) and SEG 4 (Professional workers – employees). In Class II are SEG 2.1 (Employers in industry, commerce, etc., small establishments), SEG 2.2 (Managers in industry, commerce, etc., small establishments), SEG 5.1 (Ancillary workers and artists) and SEG 5.2 (Foremen and supervisors – non-manual). In Class III are SEG 6 (Junior non-manual workers) and SEG 7 (Personal service workers). In Class IV are SEG 12 (Own account workers other than professional), SEG 13 (Farmers – employers and managers) and SEG 14 (Farmers – own account). In Class V is SEG 8 (Foremen and supervisors – manual). In Class VI is SEG 9 (Skilled manual workers). And in Class VII are SEG 10 (Semi-skilled manual workers), SEG 11 (Unskilled manual workers) and SEG 15 (Agricultural workers). In the case of respondents' fathers the GHS did not in most cases distinguish between SEGs 1.1, 1.2, 2.1, and 2.2. Accordingly we have to combine Classes I and II for fathers. We should also note that the GHS questioning related to father's *usual* occupation.

6. We cannot, of course, compare Table 4.2 directly with Table 2.1 since the methods of coding differ. To make male/female comparisons, therefore, we have to compute tables for both men and women from the General Household Survey.

7. In using phrases like 'women's work' or 'white-blouse work' the only connotation I intend is that these are jobs in which women are heavily concentrated – largely, one imagines, as a result of discrimination which prevents them entering other types of work. The large literature on dual labour markets is relevant here; see for an overview Barron and Norris (1976).

8. The instructions given to Goldthorpe and Hope's interviewers for administering the grading task do not actually mention that the task is grading men's occupations, but in many cases the occupational titles given to the respondents for grading make this clear. See Goldthorpe and Hope (1974:182). It can be argued that a different grading exercise is required for women's jobs. See Havens and Tully (1972).

9. This argument is taken from Greenhalgh (1977).

10. We cannot place much reliance on the one case in Table 4.6 where the figures for men and women are not parallel – that of Class IIIb. The number of men in this class is so small that no useful conclusions can be drawn from them. See Appendix I, Table 8.

11. The phrase 'white-collar affiliations' comes from Goldthorpe *et al.* (1968).

12. The precise figure we get will depend on whether we wish to count personal service workers (Class IIIb) as strictly white-collar or not.

13. See *Social Trends* (1975:12), reproduced in Garnsey (1978).

14. The comments on 'cumulation' and 'redundancy' in Chapter 5 would also tend to apply here, however. The daughters of blue-collar workers who have not experienced mobility through marriage into the white-collar classes are the ones most likely to have blue-collar jobs themselves.

15. Kelsall and Mitchell (1959) show that women who have both husbands and fathers in non-manual work are the least likely to work themselves.

5 Who Gets Ahead (or Stays Behind)?

1. For a detailed account of Duncan's socio-economic index see Blau and Duncan (1967:Ch. 5).

2. For other critiques see Crowder (1974), Horan (1978) and Pawson (1978).

3. The variables are scaled as follows: father's occupation, son's first job and son's present job are all scaled on the 124-category Hope-Goldthorpe scale (see Goldthorpe and Hope, 1974); father's education and son's education are scaled on a five-category scale:

    0 – Respondent had (in 1972) none of the qualifications below
    1 – School examinations except CSE, clerical and commercial, and foreign
    2 – Level C qualifications
    3 – Level B qualifications
    4 – Degree or Dip. Tech.

Level B and C qualifications are defined in the Qualified Manpower

Tables, *Sample Census 1966*, HMSO 1970. See Appendix 1, Table 9 for the correlation matrix.

4. This does not apply to the double-headed arrow running between father's education and father's occupation. This does not represent an 'effect' but a correlation.

5. Duncan does however insist that variables be entered in the path model in an appropriate temporal sequence so that causation is at least feasible.

6. See also Duncan (1968a).

7. See Blau and Duncan (1967 : 316–28).

8. We have to assume that brother's attainment has no causal effect on the respondent's and that the residuals are uncorrelated with one another and with prior variables in the model. For further discussion see Halsey, Heath and Ridge (1980 : Chs. 6 and 9).

9. The correlations are drawn from the results of the 1972 survey, Kerckhoff (1974) and Mascie-Taylor and Gibson (1978). For further details and the actual correlation matrix used see Appendix I, Table 10.

10. Keith Hope has been re-analysing the data reported by Maxwell (1969), and this will give us a much better basis for assessing the role of IQ without resorting to dubious practices such as combining data from different sources. Maxwell's material, however, refers to Scotland and so we still may not be able to draw conclusions more generally about Britain.

11. For a short and clear account of the concomitants of deprivation see Wedge and Prosser (1973), and for a fuller study see Townsend (1979).

12. Strictly speaking, of course, Class VII does not represent a score on the Hope-Goldthorpe scale, being composed of occupational groups which are spread over the bottom end of the scale and are interspersed with a few occupational groups belonging to other social classes.

13. That is, respondents who scored zero on the two scales used in the path model. See Note 3 above.

14. For further details see Halsey, Heath and Ridge (1980).

15. That is, respondents who scored 2, 3, and 4 on the scale used in the path model. See Note 3 above.

16. 13 per cent of the sample in fact fell into this category of 'low pay' in 1972.

17. We find that two-thirds of the respondents from Class VII origins had two or less siblings.

18. High pay is defined as an income greater than £3000 per annum. It includes 8·7 per cent of the respondents.
19. Valentine (1968) provides an excellent critique of the concept of the culture of poverty.

6 Ascription and Achievement

1. The correlation matrix from which the path coefficients are calculated is given in Appendix I, Table 11.
2. We have to be careful when comparing path (standardized) coefficients between models. The path coefficient may change because the relative variances (the patterns of distribution) of the variables have changed or because the 'slope' (the unstandardized regression coefficient) has changed. It is the latter in which we are really interested, and in the present case it is fortunate that they have all changed in the same direction as the path coefficients.
3. This is not true, of course, if we look at the overall relation between father's occupation and son's job after ten years. The expanding opportunities which particularly benefited the younger cohort in this first stage of their careers means that the correlation between first job and job ten years later has been declining, and the overall father-son correlation has similarly declined too.
4. For the correlation matrix from which the path coefficients can be derived see Appendix I, Table 12.
5. If we exclude respondents who were in Class IV ten years after entry into the labour market, then we find that (for the 25–39-year-old cohort) the direct effect of father's occupation on son's jobs after ten years falls from ·124 to ·117. For this calculation a model was used in which education was scaled according to number of years of full-time education rather than according to examinations and qualifications, hence the slight discrepancy with Diagram 6.1.
6. Unfortunately, however, McNabb and Psacharopoulos do not control for father's occupation in their analysis. To the extent that this has a direct effect on earnings (controlling for all the other variables in the equation), and to the extent that non-whites' fathers have lower occupational levels than whites', then the 'cost' of being non-white (as opposed to the cost of being lower class) will be reduced. I think it is

in fact very doubtful that the inclusion of father's occupation would make much difference to the results.

7. For men aged twenty-five to sixty-four in 1972 the average annual income from Class I origins was £2950 and of those from Class VII origins £1729.

8. For men aged twenty-five to sixty-four in 1972 the average annual income of those currently in Class I was £3250·7 and of those currently in Class VII was £1475·7.

9. Of men aged twenty-five to sixty-four in 1972 8·7 per cent earned £3000 or more and 13 per cent earned less than £1200. Because respondents assigned themselves to an income range rather than giving a more precise estimate of their earnings, we cannot compute the top and bottom tenths more accurately. The average annual incomes of these two groups will of course be considerably further apart than the two figures presented.

10. This estimate has been derived from Psacharopoulos (1977).

7 International Comparisons

1. Garnsey (1975) shows how occupational structures may vary in societies at comparable levels of industrial development. In addition to Lipset and Bendix (1959) and Miller (1960), there is a long line of articles arguing about the variability of mobility rates in industrial society. See Matras (1961), Marsh (1963), Yasuda (1964), Svalastoga (1965), Fox and Miller (1965), Cutright (1968), Miller (1975), Hazelrigg and Garnier (1976) and Tyree, Semyonov and Hodge (1979).

2. In addition to problems of nomenclature and meaning, surveys in different countries vary in the age-range of the population which they cover, their treatment of women, and of social origins. Thus respondents may be asked about the job their fathers held when they (the respondents) were born, were growing up, or entered their first job; or, as with Glass's survey, respondents may be asked about their fathers' last main or present job.

3. On the index of association, see Glass (1954), Billewicz (1955) and Tyree (1973); on net and exchange mobility, see Rogoff Ramsøy (1966) and Duncan (1966b); on the disparity ratio and odds ratio, see Goldthorpe et al. (1978) and Noble (1979); on log-linear models, see Hauser et al. (1975) and Everitt (1977); and on proportional marginal

adjustment, see Hazelrigg (1974) and Tyree (1973). For an introduction to these techniques, see Appendix II.

4. The sources were as follows: Australia – Broom and Jones (1969); Belgium – Delruelle (1970); Bulgaria – Atanasov and Mashiakh (1971); Canada – Goyder and Curtis (1977); England and Wales – Erikson *et al.* (1979); France – Pohl *et al.* (1974); Hungary – Andorka (1976); Italy – Lopreato (1965); Japan – Tominaga (1970); Poland – Zagorski (1976); Spain – Fundacion FOESSA (1976); Sweden – Norlén (forthcoming); USA – Featherman and Hauser (1978); USSR – Shkaratan (1973); West Germany – Kleining (1971); Yugoslavia – Milić (1965). The figures for France and Sweden are also cited in Erikson *et al.* (1979) and were calculated from the latter source. I was unable to obtain Delruelle (1970) and Atanasov and Mashiakh (1971), but the figures were given to me by Hazelrigg, who also very kindly supplied me with unpublished figures for Denmark, Finland and Norway. I am very grateful to him for his assistance. For details of these studies, see Hazelrigg and Garnier (1976).

5. See Hazelrigg and Garnier (1976) and Tyree *et al.* (1979) for details of studies on these countries.

6. For Scotland, see Payne *et al.* (1976).

7. On the nature and importance of this distinction, see Bertaux (1976).

8. In making these assertions I am, of course, assuming that the rate of change of an occupational structure can be inferred from the marginals of a mobility table. This is an unwarranted assumption, as the classic article by Duncan (1966b) makes clear, but I doubt if Census material would yield a picture very different from that given here.

9. The rank-order correlation between columns 2 and 4 in Table 7.3 is ·587; and between columns 3 and 4 is ·859.

10. In addition to the usual problems of comparability of data and measures, there is the problem (which also arises with comparisons over time – see Chapter 6, Note 2) that the size of a path coefficient is affected by the relative variance of the variables. For example, if in one society education has a highly skewed variance whereas the distribution of occupation approximates more closely to the normal distribution, the 'effect' of education is likely to be relatively small. On the other hand, one could reasonably argue that in such a society education really did not differentiate much between people since they all received much the same levels anyway. In short, the low path coefficient reflects a 'real' feature of the society.

11. Treiman and Terrell (1975) used the data from the Current Population Survey of the US Bureau of the Census (the same material which had been used by Blau and Duncan) and those collected by Butler and Stokes (1969) from a representative sample of the adult population of England, Wales and Scotland in 1963.

12. The coefficients for the USA were calculated from the correlation matrix presented in Jencks (1972: Table B–1). Nicolás *et al.* follow the convention of dropping from the model all paths where the coefficient is less than ·1 and then recalculating the values of the coefficients. For the USA we have not done this, but calculated the coefficients for the same final model that Nicolás *et al.* use. This increases comparability. For example, if Nicolás *et al.* had found a positive coefficient but one less than ·1 for the path from father's occupation to son's income, its omission would tend to increase slightly the coefficients for the indirect path via son's present occupation. To retain the path in the model for America, therefore, would have the effect of exaggerating the difference between the two societies in the importance of father's occupation for son's.

8 Class Formation and Social Stability

1. In referring to the 'stability' of the service class's membership, Goldthorpe has in mind *intra*- not inter-generational stability. While many members of the service class are newcomers in intergenerational terms, they have considerable security of tenure once they are there. Few men move out once they have arrived. And in referring to 'low classness' Goldthorpe is, I imagine, intending to say that it exhibits a low degree of class formation. He points out that the phrase was coined by Teodor Shanin in reference to the peasantry.

2. See Goldthorpe *et al.* (1969: 24) and the references cited there.

3. Table 8.1 cross-tabulates respondents' class by the class of the *first* of the friends they named on their list.

4. This is the view of Butler and Stokes (1974: 95–102). For other discussions of social mobility and politics see Abramson (1972) and Thorburn (1977).

5. See Guttsman (1974) and the references cited there.

6. By the 'uniformly elite' I refer to the group coded 111 in Diagram 8.1.

By 'elite or white-collar occupation and affiliations' I refer to groups 112, 121, 122, 211, 212, 221, 222.

By 'elite occupation and blue-collar affiliations' I refer to groups 113, 131, 123, 132, 133.

By 'white-collar occupation and blue-collar affiliations' I refer to groups 213, 231, 223, 232, 233.

By 'blue-collar occupation and white-collar or elite affiliations' I refer to groups 311, 312, 321, 313, 331, 322, 323, 332.

By 'uniformly blue-collar' I refer to group 333.

7. The reader may wonder whether this result is an artefact of my social class classification. If I had used Goldthorpe's distinction between 'service', 'intermediate' and 'working' classes, for example, would I have obtained the same result? I have in fact carried out the alternative analysis, and the general outline of the results is much the same. The Conservative lead (52 points) in the 'uniformly service class' category is still larger than the Labour lead (42 points) in the 'uniformly working class' category.

8. See Crewe et al. (1977).

Appendix II: A Reader's Guide to Statistical Terms

1. The table covers respondents aged twenty-five to sixty-four in 1972, the original number of 8343 being scaled down to 1000 for ease of presentation. Class I consists of Goldthorpe's Class I (described on pages 52–3 above); Class II of Goldthorpe's Classes II, III, and IV; and Class III of Goldthorpe's Classes V, VI and VII.

2. In their original presentation of the Index, Glass and his co-workers (1954) restricted the term Index of Association to the values on the top-left/bottom-right diagonal and used the term Index of Dissociation in the case of the off-diagonal cells.

3. The table covers white men aged twenty-five to thirty-four in 1972 and the source is the General Household Survey 1972.

Bibliography

ABRAMSON, ᴰ R. (1972). 'Intergenerational social mobility and partisan choice', *American Political Science Review* 66: 1291–4.

ANDERSON, C. A. (1961). 'A skeptical note on the relation of vertical mobility to education', *American Journal of Sociology* 66: 560–570.

ANDORKA, R. (1976). 'Social mobility and education in Hungary', *Social Science Information* 15: 47–70.

ANNAN, N. (1955). 'The intellectual aristocracy', in Plumb, J. H. (ed.), *Studies in Social History*, London: Longmans.

ASHBY, A. W. and JONES, J. M. (1926). 'The social origins of farmers in Wales', *Sociological Review* 18: 131–8.

ASTON, T. H. (1977). 'Oxford's medieval alumni', *Past and Present* 74: 3–40.

ATANASOV, A. and MASHIAKH, A. (1971). *Promeni v sotsialnata prinadlezhnost na zaetite litsa v Bulgaria*, Sofia: Nauchnoizsledovatelski institut po statistika.

BARRON, R. D. and NORRIS, G. M. (1976). 'Sexual divisions and the dual labour market', in Allen, S. and Barker, D. (eds), *Dependence and Exploitation in Work and Marriage*, London: Longmans.

BELL, D. (1960). 'Is there a ruling class in America?' in *The End of Ideology*, New York: The Free Press.

BENDIX, R. (1956). *Work and Authority in Industry: Ideologies of Management in the Course of Industrialization*, New York: Wiley.

BENJAMIN, B. (1958). 'Inter-generation differences in occupation', *Population Studies* 11: 262–8.

BERTAUX, D. (1976). 'An assessment of Garnier and Hazelrigg's paper on intergenerational mobility in France', *American Journal of Sociology* 82: 388–98.

BIERSTEDT, R. (1959). 'Nominal and real definitions in sociological theory', in Gross, L. (ed.), *Symposium on Sociological Theory*, Evanston, Illinois: Row, Peterson.

BILLEWICZ, W. Z. (1955). 'Some remarks on the measurement of social mobility'. *Population Studies 9:* 96–100.

BLAU, P. M. and DUNCAN, O. D. (1967). *The American Occupational Structure*, New York: Wiley.

BOUDON, R. (1974). *Education, Opportunity and Social Inequality: Changing Prospects in Western Societies*. New York: Wiley.

BOURDIEU, P. (1973). 'Cultural reproduction and social reproduction' in Brown, R. (ed.), *Knowledge, Education, and Cultural Change*, London: Tavistock.

BOWLES, S. and GINTIS, H. (1976). *Schooling in Capitalist America*, New York: Basic Books.

BOYD, D. (1973). *Elites and their Education*, Slough: NFER Publishing Company.

BROOM, L. and JONES, F. L. (1969). 'Father-to-son mobility: Australia in comparative perspective', *American Journal of Sociology 74:* 333–42.

BUSCH, G. (1975). 'Inequality of educational opportunity by social origin in higher education', in *Education, Inequality and Life Chances* Vol. 1, Paris: OECD.

BUTLER, D. E. and KAVANAGH, D. (1975). *The British General Election of October 1974*, London: Macmillan.

BUTLER, D. E. and STOKES, D. (1969). *Political Change in Britain*, London: Macmillan.

BUTLER, D. E. and STOKES, D. (1974). *Political Change in Britain: The Evolution of Electoral Choice*, 2nd ed., London: Macmillan.

CHAPMAN, S. J. and ABBOTT, W. (1913). 'The tendency of children to enter their fathers' trades', *Journal of the Royal Statistical Society 76:* 599–604.

CHAPMAN, S. J. and MARQUIS, F. J. (1912). 'The recruiting of the employing classes from the ranks of the wage earners in the cotton industry', *Journal of the Royal Statistical Society 75:* 293–306.

CLEMENTS, R. V. (1958). *Managers: A Study of their Careers in Industry*, London: Allen and Unwin.

COBBETT, W. (1827). 'An address to the men in Bristol', *The Political Register XXXII*, column 40; page reference is to Cole, G. D. H. and Cole, M. (eds), *The Opinions of William Cobbett*, London: The Cobbett Publishing Co.

COLLINS, R. (1971). 'Functional and conflict theories of educational stratification', *American Sociological Review 36:* 1002–19. Page references are to the reprint in Karabel, J. and Halsey, A. H. (eds), *Power and Ideology in Education*, New York: Oxford University Press, 1977.

COMPTON, J. M. (1968). 'Open competition and the Indian Civil Service, 1854–1876', *English Historical Review 83:* 265–84.

COSER, L. A. (1975). 'Presidential address: two methods in search of a substance', *American Sociological Review 40:* 691–700.

CRESSY, D. (1970). 'The social composition of Caius College, Cambridge 1580–1640', *Past and Present 47:* 113–15.

CREWE, I., SÄRLVIK, B. and ALT, J. (1977). 'Partisan dealignment in Britain 1964–1974', *British Journal of Political Science 7:* 129–90.

CROWDER, N. D. (1974). 'A critique of Duncan's stratification research', *Sociology 8:* 19–45.

CUTRIGHT, P. (1968). 'Occupational inheritance: a cross-national analysis', *American Journal of Sociology 73:* 400–16.

DAHL, R. A. (1958). 'A critique of the ruling elite model', *American Political Science Review 52:* 463–9.

DAHRENDORF, R. (1959). *Class and Class Conflict in Industrial Society*, London: Routledge and Kegan Paul.

DANIEL, W. W. (1968). *Racial Discrimination in England*, Harmondsworth: Penguin.

DAVIS, K. and MOORE, W. E. (1945). 'Some principles of stratification', *American Sociological Review 5:* 242–9.

DELRUELLE, N. (1970). *La Mobilité sociale en Belgique*, Bruxelles: Editions de l'Institute de Sociologie, Université Libre de Bruxelles.

DEPARTMENT OF EMPLOYMENT (1974). *Women and Work: a Statistical Survey*. Manpower Paper No. 9, London: HMSO.

DOMHOFF, G. W. and BALLARD, H. B. (1968). *C. Wright Mills and the Power Elite*, Boston: Beacon Press.

DUNCAN, O. D. (1966a). 'Path analysis: sociological examples', *American Journal of Sociology 72:* 1–16.

DUNCAN, O. D. (1966b). 'Methodological issues in the analysis of social mobility', in Smelser, N. J. and Lipset, S. M. (eds), *Social Structure and Mobility in Economic Development*, London: Routledge and Kegan Paul.

DUNCAN, O. D. (1968a). 'Ability and achievement', *Engenics Quarterly 15:* 1–11.

DUNCAN, O. D. (1968b). 'Inheritance of poverty or inheritance of race?' in Moynihan, D. P. (ed.), *On Understanding Poverty: Perspectives from the Social Sciences*, New York: Basic Books.

ELLIS, H. (1904). *A Study of British Genius*, London: Hurst and Blackett.

ERICKSON, C. (1959). *British Industrialists: Steel and Hosiery 1850–1950*, Cambridge: Cambridge University Press.

ERIKSON, R., GOLDTHORPE, J. H. and PORTOCARERO, L. (1979). 'Intergenerational class mobility in three Western European societies', *British Journal of Sociology 30*: 415–41.

EVERITT, A. (1966). 'Social mobility in early modern England', *Past and Present 33*: 56–73.

EVERITT, B. S. (1977). *The Analysis of Contingency Tables*, London: Chapman and Hall.

FEATHERMAN, D. L. and HAUSER, R. M. (1978). *Opportunity and Change*, New York: Academic Press.

FINER, S. E. (1966). *Vilfredo Pareto: Sociological Writings*, Oxford: Basil Blackwell.

FOX, T. G. and MILLER, S. M. (1965). 'Economic, political and social determinants of mobility', *Acta Sociologica 9:* 76–93.

FUNDACIÓN FOESSA (1976). *Estudios Sociológicos sobre la situación social de España, 1975*, Madrid: Euramerica.

GALTON, F. (1869). *Hereditary Genius, An Inquiry into its Laws and Consequences*. London.

GARNSEY, E. (1975). 'Occupational structure in industrialized societies: some notes on the convergence thesis in the light of Soviet experience', *Sociology 9:* 437–58.

GARNSEY, E. (1978). 'Women's work and theories of class stratification', *Sociology 12:* 223–43.

GASKELL, P. (1833). *The Manufacturing Population of England*, London: Baldwin and Cradock.

GIDDENS, A. (1973). *The Class Structure of the Advanced Societies*, London: Hutchinson.

GINSBERG, M. (1929). 'Interchange between social classes', *Economic Journal 39:* 554–65.

GLASS, D. V. (ed.) (1954). *Social Mobility in Britain*, London: Routledge and Kegan Paul.

GLENN, N. D., ROSS, A. A. and TULLY, J. C. (1974). 'Patterns of intergenerational mobility of females through marriage', *American Sociological Review 39:* 683–99.

GOLDTHORPE, J. H. (1964). 'Social stratification in industrial society', in Halmos, P. (ed.), *The Development of Industrial Society*, Sociological Review Monograph No. 8.

GOLDTHORPE, J. H. (1978). 'The current inflation: towards a sociological account', in Hirsch, F. and Goldthorpe, J. H. (eds), *The Political Economy of Inflation*, London: Martin Robertson.

GOLDTHORPE, J. H. (1980). *Social Mobility and Class Structure in Modern Britain*, Oxford: Clarendon Press.

GOLDTHORPE, J. H. and HOPE, K. (1972). 'Occupational grading and occupational prestige', in Hope, K. (ed.), *The Analysis of Social Mobility: Methods and Approaches*, Oxford: Clarendon Press.

GOLDTHORPE, J. H. and HOPE, K. (1974). *The Social Grading of Occupations: A New Approach and Scale*, Oxford: Clarendon Press.

GOLDTHORPE, J. H., LOCKWOOD, D., BECHHOFER, F. and PLATT, J. (1968). *The Affluent Worker: Political Attitudes and Behaviour*, Cambridge: Cambridge University Press.

GOLDTHORPE, J. H., LOCKWOOD, D., BECHHOFER, F. and PLATT, J. (1969). *The Affluent Worker in the Class Structure*, Cambridge: Cambridge University Press.

GOLDTHORPE, J. H., PAYNE, C. and LLEWELLYN, C. (1978). 'Trends in class mobility', *Sociology 12: 441–68*.

GOULDNER, A. W. (1970). *The Coming Crisis of Western Sociology*, London: Heinemann.

GOYDER, J. and CURTIS, J. E. (1977). 'Occupational mobility in Canada over four generations', *Canadian Review of Sociology and Anthropology 14: 303–19*.

GRASSBY, R. (1978). 'Social mobility and business enterprise in seventeenth-century England', in Pennington, D. and Thomas, K. (eds), *Puritans and Revolutionaries*, Oxford: Oxford University Press.

GREENHALGH, C. (1977). 'Is marriage an equal opportunity?', Centre for Labour Economics, LSE, discussion paper No. 14. A revised version of this paper is to be published in the *Economic Journal*.

GUSFIELD, J. R. and SCHWARTZ, M. (1963). 'The meaning of occupational prestige: reconsideration of the NORC scale', *American Sociological Review 28: 265–71*.

GUTTSMAN, W. L. (1974). 'The British political elite and the class structure', in Stanworth, P. and Giddens, A. (eds), *Elites and Power in British Society*, Cambridge: Cambridge University Press.

HALL, J. and JONES, D. C. (1950). 'Social grading of occupations', *British Journal of Sociology 1: 31–5*.

HALSEY, A. H. (ed.) (1972). *Trends in British Society since 1900: A Guide to the Changing Social Structure of Britain*, London: Macmillan.

HALSEY, A. H. (1977). 'Towards meritocracy? The case of Britain' in Karabel, J. and Halsey, A. H. (eds), *Power and Ideology in Education*, New York: Oxford University Press.

HALSEY, A. H. and CREWE, I. M. (1969). *Social Survey of the Civil Service*. Vol. 3 (1) of *The Civil Service*, London: HMSO.

HALSEY, A. H., HEATH, A. F. and RIDGE, J. M. (1980). *Origins and Destinations: Family, Class and Education in Modern Britain*, Oxford: Clarendon Press.

HARBURY, C. D. and HITCHENS, D. M. W. N. (1979). *Inheritance and Wealth Inequality in Britain*, London: Allen and Unwin.

HAUSER, R. M., DICKINSON, P. J., TRAVIS, H. P. and KOFFEL, J. M. (1975). 'Temporal change in occupational mobility: evidence for men in the United States', *American Sociological Review 40*: 279-97.

HAVENS, E. M. and TULLY, J. C. (1972). 'Female intergenerational occupational mobility: comparison of patterns?' *American Sociological Review 37*: 774-7.

HAZELRIGG, L. E. (1974). 'Partitioning structural effects and endogenous mobility processes in the measurement of vertical occupational status change', *Acta Sociologica 17*: 115-39.

HAZELRIGG, L. E. and GARNIER, M. A. (1976). 'Occupational mobility in industrial societies: a comparative analysis of differential access to occupational ranks in seventeen counties', *American Sociological Review 41*: 498-511.

HEARNSHAW, L. S. (1979). *Cyril Burt: Psychologist*, London: Hodder and Stoughton.

HEATH, A. F. and RIDGE, J. M. (1980). 'Schools, examinations, and occupational attainment', in preparation.

HEMPEL, C. G. (1959). 'The logic of functional analysis', in Gross, L. (ed.), *Symposium on Sociological Theory*, Evanston, Illinois: Row, Peterson.

HOLLINGSWORTH, T. H. (1964). 'The demography of the British peerage', *Population Studies*, supplement to Vol. XVIII, No. 2.

HOPE, K. (ed.) (1972). *The Analysis of Social Mobility: Methods and Approaches*, Oxford: Clarendon Press.

HOPE, K. (1975). 'Trends in the openness of British society in the present century', paper circulated at the SSRC International Seminar on Occupational Mobility, University of Aberdeen, September 1975. To be published in Treiman, D. J. and Robinson, R. (eds), *Research in Social Stratification and Mobility*, Vol. I. (forthcoming).

HORAN, P. M. (1978). 'Is status attainment research atheoretical?' *American Sociological Review* 43: 534–41.

JENCKS, C. (1972). *Inequality: A Reassessment of the Effect of Family and Schooling in America*, New York: Basic Books.

JENKINS, H. and CARADOG JONES, D. (1950). 'Social class of Cambridge University alumni of the eighteenth and nineteenth centuries', *British Journal of Sociology 1:* 93–116.

JONES, F. LANCASTER (1971). 'Occupational achievement in Australia and the United States: a comparative path analysis', *American Journal of Sociology* 77: 527–39.

KARABEL, J. and HALSEY, A. H. (eds) (1977). *Power and Ideology in Education*, New York: Oxford University Press.

KELSALL, R. K. (1955). *Higher Civil Servants in Britain from 1870 to the Present Day*, London: Routledge and Kegan Paul.

KELSALL, R. K. (1974). 'Recruitment to the higher civil service: how has the pattern changed?' in Stanworth, P. and Giddens, A. (eds), *Elites and Power in British Society*, Cambridge: Cambridge University Press.

KELSALL, R. K. and MITCHELL, S. (1959). 'Married women and employment in England and Wales', *Population Studies 13:* 19–33.

KERCKHOFF, A. C. (1974). 'Stratification processes and outcomes in England and the U.S.', *American Sociological Review 39:* 789–801.

KERCKHOFF, A. C. (1978). 'Marriage and occupational attainment in Great Britain and the United States', *Journal of Marriage and the Family 40:* 595–9.

KERR, C., DUNLOP, J. T., HARBISON, F. H. and MYERS, C. A. (1960). *Industrialism and Industrial Man*, Cambridge, Mass.: Harvard University Press.

KLEINING, G. (1971). 'Die Veränderungen der mobilitätschancen in der Bundesrepublik Deutschland', Kölner Zeitschrift für Soziologie und Sozial-Psychologie, 23: 789–807.

KORNHAUSER, W. (1961). 'Power elite or veto groups?' in Lipset, S. M. and Lowenthal, L. (eds), *Culture and Social Character*, New York: The Free Press.

KOTWAL, M. (1975). 'Inequalities in the distribution of education between countries, sexes, generations and individuals', in *Education, Inequality and Life Chances* Vol. 1, Paris: OECD.

LAPOUGE, V. DE (1896). *Les Sélections sociales*, Paris: Thorin et Fils.

LAQUEUR, T. W. (1974). 'Literacy and social mobility in the industrial revolution in England', *Past and Present 64*: 96–107.

LEVASSEUR, E. (1909). 'Discussion de "Les Classes Sociales" par Fahlbeck, P.', *Bulletin de l'Institut International de Statistique, XVIII*: 123–4.

LIJPHART, A. (1979). 'Religious vs. linguistic vs. class voting: the "crucial experiment" of comparing Belgium, Canada, South Africa and Switzerland, *American Political Science Review 73*: 442–58.

LIPSET, S. M. (1960). *Political Man: The Social Bases of Politics*, London: Heinemann.

LIPSET, S. M. and BENDIX, R. (1959). *Social Mobility in Industrial Society*, Berkeley: University of California Press.

LIPSET, S. M. and ZETTERBERG, H. (1956). 'A theory of social mobility', *Transactions of the Third World Congress of Sociology*, V: 155–77, London: International Sociological Association.

LOCKWOOD, D. (1958). *The Blackcoated Worker: A Study in Class Consciousness*, London: Allen and Unwin.

LOPREATO, J. (1965). 'Social mobility in Italy', *American Journal of Sociology 71*: 311–14.

LUPTON, C. and WILSON, C. S. (1959). 'The social background and connections of "top decision makers"', *The Manchester School of Economic and Social Studies 27*: 30–51.

MACDONALD, K. I. (1974). 'The Hall-Jones scale: a note on the interpretation of the main British prestige coding', in Ridge, J. M. (ed.), *Mobility in Britain Reconsidered*, Oxford: Clarendon Press.

MACDONALD, K. I. and RIDGE, J. M. (1972). 'Social mobility', in Halsey, A. H. (ed.), *Trends in British Society since 1900*, London: Macmillan.

MCINTOSH, N. and SMITH, D. J. (1974). *The Extent of Racial Discrimination*. PEP Broadsheet No. 547.

MCNABB, R. and PSACHAROPOULOS, G. (1981). 'Racial earnings differentials in the U.K.', *Oxford Economic Papers*, forthcoming.

MARSH, R. M. (1963). 'Values, demand and social mobility', *American Sociological Review 28*: 565–75.

MARX, K. (1852). *The Eighteenth Brumaire of Louis Bonaparte*. The page references are to the edition of *Selected Works*, Vol. 1, published by the Foreign Language Publishing House, Moscow (1958).

MARX, K. (1894). *Capital, Volume III*. Page references are to the edition published by the Foreign Languages Publishing House, Moscow (1959).

MASCIE-TAYLOR, C. G. N. and GIBSON, J. B. (1978). 'Social mobility and

IQ components', *Journal of Biosocial Science 10:* 263–76.

MATRAS, J. (1961). 'Differential fertility, intergenerational occupational mobility, and change in occupational distribution', *Population Studies 15:* 187–97.

MAXWELL, J. (1969). *Sixteen Years On: A follow-up of the 1947 Scottish Survey*, London: University of London Press.

MERTON, R. K. (1949). 'Manifest and latent functions', in *Social Theory and Social Structure*, New York: The Free Press.

MICHELS, R. (1911). *Zür Soziologie des Parteiwesens in der modernen Demokratie.* Page references are to *Political Parties: A Sociological Study of the Oligarchical Tendencies of Modern Democracy*, translated by E. and C. Paul, New York: The Free Press, 1962.

MILIĆ, V. (1965). 'General trends in social mobility in Yugoslavia', *Acta Sociologica 9:* 116–35.

MILLER, S. M. (1960). 'Comparative and social mobility', *Current Sociology 9:* 1–89.

MILLER, S. M. (1975). 'Social mobility and equality', in *Education, Inequality and Life Chances*, Vol. 1, Paris: OECD.

MILLS, C. W. (1956). *The Power Elite*, New York: Oxford University Press.

MORGAN, D. H. J. (1969). 'The social and educational background of Anglican bishops – continuities and changes', *British Journal of Sociology 20:* 295–310.

MUSGROVE, F. (1979). *School and the Social Order*, New York: Wiley.

NICOLÁS, J. D., LÁZARO, U. M. and MINONDO, M. J. P. (1975). 'Education and social mobility in Spain', in *Education, Inequality and Life Chances*, Vol. 1, Paris: OECD.

NOBLE, T. (1972). 'Social mobility and class relations in Britain', *British Journal of Sociology 23:* 422–36.

NOBLE, T. (1979). 'In pursuit of pure mobility', *Sociology 13:* 483–95.

NORLÉN, U. (forthcoming). *Välfärdsmätning för social rapportering*, Stockholm: Swedish Institute for Social Research.

OTLEY, C. B. (1970). 'The social origins of British army officers', *Sociological Review 18:* 213–39.

OTLEY, C. B. (1978). 'Militarism and militarization in the Public Schools, 1900–1972', *British Journal of Sociology 29:* 321–39.

PARETO, V. (1909). *Manuel d'Economie Politique*, Paris: Giard et Brière.

PARETO, V. (1916). *Trattato di Sociologia Generale*, Florence: Barbera.

PARKIN, F. (1971). *Class Inequality and Political Order*, London: MacGibbon and Kee.

PARSONS, T. (1960). 'The distribution of power in American society', in *Structure and Process in Modern Societies*, Glencoe, Illinois: The Free Press.

PAWSON, R. (1978). 'Empiricist explanatory strategies: the case of causal modelling', *Sociological Review 26*: 613–45.

PAYNE, G., FORD, G. and ROBERTSON, C. (1976). 'Changes in occupational mobility in Scotland', *Scottish Journal of Sociology 1*: 57–79.

PAYNE, G., FORD, G. and ROBERTSON, C. (1977). 'A reappraisal of social mobility in Britain', *Sociology 11*: 289–310.

PEARSON, K. (1914). 'On certain errors with regard to multiple correlation occasionally made by those who have not adequately studied this subject', *Biometrika 10*: 181–7.

PERRIN, E. (1904). 'On the contingency between occupation in the case of fathers and sons', *Biometrika 3*: 467–9.

PILLSBURY, W. B. (1921). 'Selection – an unnoticed function of education', *Scientific Monthly 1921*: 62–75.

PLATO, (c. 380 B.C.). *Politeia*, translated by Lee, H. D. P., as *The Republic*, Harmondsworth: Penguin, 1955.

POHL, R., THÉLOT, C. and JOUSSET, M.-F. (1974). *L'enquête formation – qualification professionelle de 1970*, Paris: Institut National de la Statistique et des Études Économiques.

POLITICAL AND ECONOMIC PLANNING (1971). *Women in Top Jobs: Four Studies in Achievement*, London: Allen and Unwin.

POLLARD, S. (1965). *The Genesis of Modern Management: A Study of the Industrial Revolution in Great Britain*, London: Edward Arnold.

POULANTZAS, N. (1974). *Les Classes sociales dans le capitalisme aujourd' hui*, Paris: Seuil.

PSACHAROPOULOS, G. (1977). 'Family background, education and achievement: a path model of earnings determinants in the UK and some alternatives', *British Journal of Sociology 28*: 321–35.

RAFFE, D. (1979). 'The "Alternative Route" reconsidered: part-time further education and social mobility in England and Wales', *Sociology 13*: 47–73.

RAZZELL, P. E. (1963). 'Social origins of officers in the Indian and British Home Army', *British Journal of Sociology 14*: 248–60.

RICHARDSON, C. J. (1977). *Contemporary Social Mobility*, London: Frances Pinter.

RIDGE, J. M. (1974a). 'Fathers and sons', in *Mobility in Britain Reconsidered*, Oxford: Clarendon Press.

RIDGE, J. M. (1974b). 'Sibling rivalry?' in *Mobility in Britain Reconsidered*, Oxford: Clarendon Press.

ROGOFF RAMSØY, N. (1966). 'Changes in rates and forms of mobility', in Smelser, N. J. and Lipset, S. M. (eds), *Social Structure and Mobility in Economic Development*, London: Routledge and Kegan Paul.

RUNCIMAN, W. G. (1966). *Relative Deprivation and Social Justice*, London: Routledge and Kegan Paul.

RUTTER, M. and MADGE, N. (1976). *Cycles of Disadvantage: a review of research*, London: Heinemann.

ŠAFÁŘ, Z. (1971). 'Different approaches to the measurement of social differentiation and social mobility in the Czecho-Slovak socialist society', *Quality and Quantity 5: 179–208.*

SANDERSON, M. (1972). 'Literacy and social mobility in the industrial revolution in England', *Past and Present 56: 75–104.*

SCHNEIDER, J. (1937). 'Social class, historical circumstances and fame', *American Journal of Sociology 43: 37–56.*

SCHUMPETER, J. A. (1927). 'Die sozialen Klassen im ethnisch homogenen Milieu', *Archiv für Sozialwissenschaft und Sozialpolitik 57: 1–67.* Translated and reprinted in *Imperialism and Social Classes*, Oxford: Basil Blackwell, 1951. (Page references are to the latter version.)

SHKARATAN, O. I. (1973). 'Social ties and social mobility', *International Journal of Sociology 3: 289–319.*

SOLTOW, L. (1968). 'Long run changes in British income inequality', *Economic History Review 21: 17–29.*

SOROKIN, P. A. (1927). *Social Mobility*, New York: Harper and Brothers.

SOROKIN, P. A. (1959). *Social and Cultural Mobility*, New York: The Free Press.

SOROKIN, P. A. (1963). 'Sociology of my mental life', in Allen, P. J. (ed.), *Pitirim A. Sorokin in Review*, Durham, N. C.: Duke University Press.

STACEY, B. G. (1968). 'Inter-generation occupational mobility in Britain', *Occupational Psychology 42: 33–48.*

STANWORTH, P. and GIDDENS, A. (1974). 'An economic elite: a demographic profile of company chairmen', in *Elites and Power in British Society*, Cambridge: Cambridge University Press.

STONE, L. (1966). 'Social mobility in England, 1500–1700', *Past and Present 33*: 16–55.

STONE, L. (1975). 'The size and composition of the Oxford student body 1580–1910', in *The University in Society*, Vol. 1, Princeton: Princeton University Press.

SVALASTOGA, K. (1965). 'Social mobility: the Western European model', *Acta Sociologica 9*: 175–82.

TAUSSIG, F. W. and JOSLYN, C. S. (1932). *American Business Leaders*, New York: Macmillan.

THOMAS, D. (1972). 'The social origins of marriage partners of the British peerage in the eighteenth and nineteenth centuries', *Population Studies 26*: 99–111.

THOMPSON, K. (1974). 'Church of England bishops as an elite', in Stanworth, P. and Giddens, A. (eds), *Elites and Power in British Society*, Cambridge: Cambridge University Press.

THORBURN, P. (1977). 'Political generations: the case of class and party in Britain', *European Journal of Political Research 5*: 135–48.

TOMINAGA, K. (1970). 'Trend analysis of social mobility, 1955–1965', *Shakaigaku Hyoron 21*: 2–24.

TOWNSEND, P. (1979). *Poverty in the United Kingdom*, Harmondsworth: Penguin.

TREIMAN, D. J. and TERRELL, K. (1975). 'The process of status attainment in the United States and Great Britain', *American Journal of Sociology 81*: 563–83.

TURNER, R. H. (1960). 'Sponsored and contest mobility and the school system', *American Sociological Review 25*: 855–67.

TYREE, A. (1973). 'Mobility ratios and association in mobility tables', *Population Studies 27*: 577–88.

TYREE, A. and TREAS, J. (1974). 'The occupational and marital mobility of women', *American Sociological Review 39*: 293–302.

TYREE, A., SEMYONOV, M. and HODGE, R. W. (1979). 'Gaps and glissandos: inequality, economic development, and social mobility in 24 countries', *American Sociological Review 44*: 410–24.

VALENTINE, C. A. (1968). *Culture and Poverty*, Chicago: University of Chicago Press.

VEBLEN, T. (1899). *The Theory of the Leisure Class*, New York: Macmillan.

WATERHOUSE, E. (1665). *The Gentleman's Monitor: or, a sober Inspection into the Vertues, Vices, and ordinary Means, of the Rise and Decay of Men and Families*, London: R. Royston, Bookseller.

WEDGE, P. and PROSSER, N. (1973). *Born to Fail?* London: Arrow Books.

WEDGWOOD, J. (1929). *The Economics of Inheritance*, London: Routledge and Kegan Paul.

WESTERGAARD, J. and RESLER, H. (1975). *Class in a Capitalist Society: A Study of Contemporary Britain*, London: Heinemann.

WRIGHT, S. (1934). 'The method of path coefficients', *Annals of Mathematical Statistics 5:* 161–215.

YASUDA, S. (1964). 'A methodological inquiry into social mobility', *American Sociological Review 29:* 16–23.

ZAGORSKI, K. (1976). 'Changes of socio-occupational mobility in Poland', *Polish Sociological Bulletin 34:* 17–30.

Index